Murder Most Modern

Murder Most Modern

Detective Fiction
and Japanese Culture

Sari Kawana

University of Minnesota Press   Minneapolis / London

The University of Minnesota Press gratefully acknowledges the financial assistance provided to support the publication of this book from the College of Liberal Arts, University of Massachusetts Boston.

Portions of the Introduction were previously published in "Pleasures of Permutation: Detective Fiction and Cultural Globalization," *Proceedings of the Association for Japanese Literary Studies* 5 (Summer 2004); reprinted with permission from the Association for Japanese Literary Studies. A previous version of chapter 3 was published as "Mad Scientists and Their Prey: Bioethics, Murder, and Fiction in Interwar Japan," *Journal of Japanese Studies* 31, no. 1 (Winter 2005): 89–120; reprinted with permission of *Journal of Japanese Studies*.

Copyright 2008 by the Regents of the University of Minnesota

All rights reserved. No part of this publication may be reproduced, stored in a retrieval system, or transmitted, in any form or by any means, electronic, mechanical, photocopying, recording, or otherwise, without the prior written permission of the publisher.

Published by the University of Minnesota Press
111 Third Avenue South, Suite 290
Minneapolis, MN 55401-2520
http://www.upress.umn.edu

Library of Congress Cataloging-in-Publication Data

Kawana, Sari.
    Murder most modern : detective fiction and Japanese culture / Sari Kawana.
       p.   cm.
    Includes bibliographical references and index.
    ISBN 978-0-8166-5025-5 (hc : alk. paper) — ISBN 978-0-8166-5026-2 (pb : alk. paper)
    1. Detective and mystery stories, Japanese—History and criticism. 2. Japanese fiction—20th century—History and criticism. 3. Culture in literature. I. Title.
    PL747.67.D45K38 2008
    895.6'30872—dc22

2008000751

Printed in the United States of America on acid-free paper

The University of Minnesota is an equal-opportunity educator and employer.

15 14 13 12 11 10 09 08   10 9 8 7 6 5 4 3 2 1

Contents

Author's Note **vii**
Acknowledgments **ix**

Introduction: Detective Fiction, Diphtheria, and Modernity **1**

1. Tailing the Tail: How to Turn Paranoia into a Hobby **29**

2. Eyeing the Privates: Sexuality as Motive **69**

3. Mad Scientists and Their Prey: Bioethics and Murder **111**

4. Drafted Detectives and Total War: Three Editors of *Shupio* **147**

5. The Disfigured National Body: Unmasking Modernity in Postwar Mysteries **186**

Epilogue: Beyond the Whodunit **219**

Notes **225**
Bibliography **251**
Index **265**

Author's Note

I follow Japanese convention and give Japanese names in traditional order (e.g., Oguri Mushitarō). I refer to authors by the names by which they are best known. Some authors are referred to by surname (e.g., Satō Haruo) and others by their pen names (e.g., Edogawa Ranpo, Kuroiwa Ruikō). All translations from the Japanese are mine unless otherwise indicated.

In the publication citations in the bibliography, the place of publication for all Japanese-language sources is Tokyo unless otherwise noted.

Acknowledgments

The cover and the copyright page suggest that I am the sole author of this book, but the material herein would not have come together without the patience, kindness, and support of numerous people and institutions.

My sincere thanks and warmest regards go to my mentors, colleagues, and friends from my days as a graduate student at the University of Pennsylvania: Bruce Baird, Linda Chance, Jennifer Chen, Rita Copeland, Edward Drott, Jonathan Eburne, Gregory Flaxman, Stephen Hock, G. Cameron Hurst, Ayako Kano, William LaFleur, Gerald Prince, Deborah Shapple, Matthew Sommer, Sayumi Takahashi, and Liliane Weissberg. Penn's University and SAS Dissertation Fellowships funded the research and writing of my dissertation, on which this book is based.

At various points during my dissertation research, I received invaluable help from archives in Japan, including the Nihon Kindai Bungakukan, the Setagaya Bungakukan, and the Misuterī Shiryōkan, as well as individual libraries at the University of Tokyo. Also, I would like to thank the many scholars and aficionados of detective fiction and *modan* culture that I met along the way: Aizu Shingo, Endō Tomomi, Hayashi Katsurō, Jiichi, Taniguchi Yōko, Uchida Ryūzō, Yohara Takao, Yoshimi Shun'ya, and Yuasa Atsushi. I extend my gratitude to those individuals and institutions that kindly granted permission to reproduce their images: Asahi Shinbun, Hirai Ryūtarō, Mainichi Shinbunsha, Shiozawa Tamae, Tsutsumi Naruki, Yonezawa Yoshihiro, and Yoshida Kanoko.

I would also like to thank the staff of the University of Minnesota Press for their good work in transforming my manuscript into a book. In particular, my appreciation goes to Adam Brunner, Mary Byers, Susan Doerr, Emily Hamilton, Emily Lechner, Rachel Moeller, Richard Morrison, Alicia Sellheim, and Laura Westlund. I am also grateful for the kind consideration of the Press's advisory board and the excellent comments from the manuscript referees, Dennis Washburn and the anonymous reader. I would also like to convey my appreciation to Alan Tansman, who provided crucial feedback on the project in its preliminary stages and has always offered his guidance and encouragement since my days as an undergraduate.

Finally, my heartfelt gratitude goes to my family, who have provided constant support over the years. My three younger brothers have endured my Lucy Van Pelt–style bossiness with quiet patience. My husband, William M. Hammell, has been everything to me for more than a decade, and this project is the product of our mutual respect and affection. And our daughter, Chandra Haruka, made her much-anticipated appearance as this book entered the final stages of production.

The arrival of our child has helped me to realize the importance of good parenting. For this reason, I would like to dedicate this book to the memory of my late parents, Susumu and Haruko Kawana.

Introduction
Detective Fiction, Diphtheria, and Modernity

Detective Fiction and Japanese Diphtheria

"Detective fiction," declared the popular author Yumeno Kyūsaku (1889–1936) in 1935, "is like the serum for diphtheria." Yumeno employed such an unusual metaphor to answer a nebulous question about one of the most popular genres of modern Japanese literature: "What is *tantei shōsetsu* [detective fiction]?" Although works in this genre, with their dazzling plots and shocking secrets, have captivated the Japanese reading public since the late nineteenth century, the genre itself has defied rigid categorization and resisted strict definition. Within the same essay, Yumeno went on to elaborate the comparison:

> Detective fiction is like the serum for diphtheria. Injecting a patient with the antidiphtheria serum works like a miracle. I hear that this remedy kills the disease without fail. Yet, even though we have the treatment, the etiological cause for diphtheria has not yet been found. We have not been able to identify it even with the incredible power of modern medicine. The cure has been found, but the cause has not. It is as if the verdict for a crime has been rendered, but the accused is still on the loose. It is a nonsensical situation. [Although we know that detective fiction is popular], the identity of its charm too remains at large. To decipher the psychology that desires detective fiction is utter nonsense itself: detective fiction is nonsense, humor, adventure, grotesque, mystery . . . it is all of these things and more.[1]

Yumeno's medical metaphor captures the fleeting yet strangely tangible allure of detective fiction in Japan during the early twentieth century, arguably the most fascinating years of modern Japanese history in terms of economic growth, political drama, and cultural diversity. However, it was also a turbulent period plagued by a general melancholy that made its sufferers dizzy and woozy as they tried to acclimate themselves to the new world order—modernity. During the same period, those who were concerned about public moral welfare habitually attacked the genre whenever there was social unrest or a general sense of malaise. Yet the genre enjoyed a steady popularity throughout the ordeal. It was as if the Japanese reading public was suffering from some kind of historical and cultural diphtheria, and the patients sought out detective fiction as treatment.

Yumeno is by no means the only writer who sensed the malaise that hovered over the capital and possibly other areas of Japan. Already in 1909, guidebook author Ishikawa Tengai warned newcomers who arrived in Tokyo with the hope of striking it rich that "Tokyo is a battlefield for a war with no definite end" and "people who live in Tokyo have shorter life spans [than those in the countryside]."[2] The metaphor of Tokyo as a battlefield was also used by cultural critic Hasegawa Tōgai in his *Tōkyō no kaibō* (The Autopsy of Tokyo; 1917): "Tokyo is the city of 'mystery' as well as that of 'destiny.' [Seeing] Tokyo from the front *(omote)* is completely different from [seeing it] from behind *(ura)*."[3] Later observers of the modern capital recorded similar impressions. The contemporary female activist Takamure Itsue (1894–1964) connected the city to illness in the title of her 1925 poetic anthology *Tōkyō wa netsubyō ni kakatteiru* (Tokyo Suffers from Fever). Inhabitants of the city were similarly afflicted: the actor Kamiyama Sōjin (1884–1954), on his return to Tokyo after a sojourn in Hollywood (1924–29), apparently told his friend folklorist Yanagita Kunio (1875–1962) that the gaze of the Tokyoites had become much scarier than he remembered.[4] Such voices of general concern grew especially loud after 1923, when the Great Kantō Earthquake destroyed the capital.

It is likely that Takamure's fever and Kamiyama's antagonistic gazes are symptoms of the "diphtheria" that Yumeno diagnosed. However, pinpointing the exact microbe of this cultural diphtheria is as impossible as locating that of actual diphtheria: we can try to list all of the political, cultural, and economic factors that generated the general sense of unease in early-twentieth-century Japan, but we would soon find the task daunting and ultimately futile. Perhaps, then, it is more fruitful to analyze the historical context in which the "cultural diphtheria" of modern Japan thrived, by treating it not as the decisive cause but rather as the optimal environment in which this sickness flourishes. In the analysis, it becomes clear that it is both an endemic and epidemic: it is endemic in the sense that it required a geographically and culturally specific process—namely, a departure from the blind worship of civilization and progress in the Meiji period (1868–1912) to the self-reflexive culture of decadence in the Taishō period (1912–26)—and epidemic in that the experience of general malaise was felt in other parts of the world.

Japanese "diphtheria" incubated in the Meiji period before it became a full-fledged concern during the subsequent Taishō and early Shōwa (1926–89) periods. As part of the so-called Meiji Enlightenment, Japan imported numerous assumptions about progress and rationality that originated in the West, assumptions similar to those described by the sociologist Anthony Giddens as those "modes of social life or organization which emerged in Europe from about the seventeenth century onwards and which subsequently became more or less worldwide in their influence."[5] When Japan finally fell under the sphere of direct Western influence during the Meiji period, it inherited such assumptions for the brighter future promised by Enlightenment thinking. The tenets of Enlightenment reassured the Japanese of both the possibility and the importance of becoming a subject *(shutaika)*, through which they could help their country survive the fierce competition of colonial dominance. Fukuzawa Yukichi (1834–1901), one of the most important proponents of this ideal, argued that it is to the nation's advantage to create financially and intellectually autonomous citizens capable of rational thinking rather than to direct their business from above: "Independence means to manage one's own personal affairs and not to have a mind to depend upon others."[6] The ideals behind the Meiji slogan *bunmei kaika* (Civilization and Enlightenment) were Japan's keys out of its cultural "immaturity" of feudalism and Confucianism that would put the nation on the fast track to becoming a world power.

The wishes of Fukuzawa and other proponents of the Meiji Enlightenment appeared to be coming true by the early twentieth century, when Japan as a nation seemed to be hitting its stride. From the late Meiji to early Taishō, Japan fought and won three international wars within three decades: the Sino-Japanese War (1894–95), the Russo-Japanese War (1904–5), and World War I (1914–18). Although Japan's victory in World War I was nominal at best, its participation gave the nation an unprecedented economic boost. At the onset of the war, Japan's total exports amounted to 632 million yen and its imports to 648 million yen. Six years later, these figures quadrupled: both rose to more than 25 billion yen.[7]

This exponential growth certainly was short lived. The experience of wealth left a lasting legacy, however, and it was most significantly felt in the form of an altered self-image for Japan: the economic boom, albeit temporary, announced that Japan finally had achieved what it strove so hard to achieve since the early years of Meiji, when it decided to accept Western advances into Asia and colonialism as a way of life. In describing this shift, Elise K. Tipton and John Clark define the Japanese modern culture that flourished from the late 1910s to the 1930s primarily as what it was *not:* that it was not a simple or blind Westernization; that it was not state-led; that it was not fused with a national, political goal.[8] I second Tipton and Clark in saying that there is a significant mental break between the Meiji and Taishō periods. After its three victories, Japan no longer had to sacrifice the present for the sake of a better future, since the ideals proclaimed during the Meiji period had actually arrived. Taishō and early Shōwa culture is often criticized as "decadent": this supposed immorality stems from the shift from the Meiji value system in which the present should be banked for the future.

Japan's military victories and subsequent economic success, Tokyo's emergence as a world-class metropolis, increased participation of women in the workforce, developments in science and technology, acquisition of overseas territories—all of these achievements pointed to the blossoming of Japan as a bona fide world power. However, those who actually lived through these events were quickly realizing that modernization was a double-edged sword. They discovered that rapid urbanization and industrialization came at a steep price: an increase in crime, the disappearance of traditional neighborhoods, unjustified violence against the socially weak, as well as the legitimization of brutality against the human body in the name of science and total war. Things that the Enlightenment precluded—the emergence of the masses as an anonymous and irrational collectivity, the discovery of the unconscious, and the rise of total war—became a reality and started to present a realistic menace to those who once imagined a harmonious society based on one, universal rationality. Such key Enlightenment ideals as *jiyū* (liberty) and *shinpo* (progress) were quickly dissipating. By the late Meiji period, even Fukuzawa reneged on his words when the desires of the enlightened mind started to diverge from the interests of the nation, or, more precisely, of the Meiji government.

The Enlightenment had led Japan astray, and its problems started to pop up everywhere. The early optimism of the Meiji Restoration for a future brought about by modernization, Westernization, and militarization had dissipated by the interwar period.[9] The slogan of *bunmei kaika* served temporarily to inspire Japan to escape feudalism and cultural immaturity, but it also entailed a one-way ticket to modernity, in which modern subjects would constantly be haunted by anxiety for the present as well as the future. Thus, the project of Meiji civilization and enlightenment has run its course and Taishō culture emerged, to reflect on the achievements and values of the preceding culture.

It is with this feeling of anxiety and self-reflexivity that Japanese modernity—a corollary of the Meiji Enlightenment—could be most appropriately defined. The same "backward" concepts—imagination, superstition, and other elements of *fushigi* (strangeness, mystery) described by Gerald Figal—that had been cast aside as part of the Meiji emphasis on reason and progress now resurfaced in Taishō culture to erode the dominance of "modern reason."[10] Taishō is also a historical moment described by Harry D. Harootunian as "an inflection of a larger global process that constituted what might be called co-existing or co-eval modernity, inasmuch as it shared the same historical temporality of modernity (as a form of historical totalizing) found elsewhere in Europe and the United States."[11] Walter Benjamin (1892–1940) and Edogawa Ranpo (1894–1965), born only two years apart, were prompted by the same questions of urban life, modernity, and future in different locales: one was looking at sandwich men in Berlin, and the other one freak shows in Asakusa; other times, it was the remnants of arcades in Paris and show windows in the Ginza.

This kind of murky, uncertain Japanese modernity was the sequel to the Meiji Enlightenment, in which the future is no longer an automatic improvement over the present. Japan's long-desired success in the world political arena also meant more problems for everyone. For the first time in half a century, Japan was left to its own devices: it was no longer enough to emulate the West. Japan had to find its own destiny as a colonial suzerain, a modern nation with both an emperor and a budding democracy, and a cultural power. As sociologist Yoshimi Shun'ya points out, it was during the 1920s—at the height of the Taishō period—that global simultaneity in discourse, media, and imagination was realized as the world started to conceive capitalism, knowledge, and technology on an international scale as imperialism necessitated physical dislocation of its peoples.[12] Japan included itself as part of such a "world" as it became part of the community of industrialized nations. But the admission to such consciousness also gave its participants some new vague concerns and palpable symptoms, and those afflicted were thinking about similar issues in different parts of this continuum.

During this transition, modern subjects learned to acquire self-identity through means other than the state: "The new practices of work, leisure, and home life constituted individuals into new groupings with new identities—'new selves'—which were marked by gender, class, and race."[13] To this list, I would add sexual preference, ideology, and literary interests. The drive to proactively acquire a new identity or identities outside of the state, the urge to envision the future whatever shape it may be: these are the very efforts of modernity. These actions generate the energy that drives modern—and, more important, *modan,* to put the term in its Japanese context—culture and life.[14] This distinction between *modan* and "modern" is significant: the former, as it was often used in Taishō and early Shōwa, is more than a transliteration of the latter. Living "modern" and living *modan* mean different things. As Dennis Washburn explains, living modern in early-twentieth-century Japan is to operate with the awareness that one is living in a world that tries to divorce itself from the past:

> Meiji culture was defined by a heightened awareness of its historical predicament; and it is that awareness, or self-consciousness, that ultimately defines the modern in Japan. The official sanctioning of modernization on the part of the Meiji oligarchy represented a deliberate acceptance of cultural discontinuity, an acceptance that brought with it a simultaneous sense of liberation and loss. The

sanctioning of the modern, even when there was no universally accepted understanding of its meaning, threatened a break in cultural memory that could be compensated for only by reconstituting a cultural self through an act of mythic confabulation that narrated a new understanding of the Japanese tradition into being.[15]

Living modern is thus accompanied by a sense of newness and deracination. On the other hand, living *modan* includes this sense but also envelops the specificities of the Japanese context and burgeons with a pent-up, chaotic energy for which there are few outlets. More specifically, living *modan* meant living with little confidence in the supposedly democratic ideals of government and society; having little money from day to day while being placed in the midst of all kinds of urban capitalist temptations available for sale; and constantly brooding with anxiety for the future. War was certainly one way in which this energy burst manifested itself: "By the early 1930s Japan was widely perceived by the Japanese themselves as 'modern.' The ability to wage war with advanced military technology was to become one indicator of this modernity, and perception of this capability as a positive and justifiable undertaking, a 'modern' thing to do, at both elite and popular levels, has suggestive implications for understanding popular support for war at the end of the decade."[16] The desire to pursue power even if it means self-destruction is the built-in suicide chip of Japanese modernity, in which reason has completely dissipated and is unable to suppress illogical dreams and delusions of grandeur.

Detective Fiction as Treatment

Such were the social conditions under which Yumeno likened detective fiction to antidiphtheria serum. But how could a literary genre help to ease these cultural maladies—especially a genre that in its earlier days had been one of the primary vehicles for the typical Meiji Enlightenment ideals of empirical reasoning and rational thinking? To answer this question, we must examine how detective fiction altered and reconfigured itself to both respond and preempt the devastating effects of these intensifying symptoms of modernity.

As Amanda Seaman argues, "With its emphasis on the minutiae of daily life (clues from which the detective derives his solution) and its attention to 'real-life' social problems (corruption, sexual scandals, financial misdeeds, etc.), detective fiction has reflected more immediately than other literary genres the fears and fantasies of the modern, urban bourgeoisie."[17] Also, in contrast to other contemporary and more "mainstream" literatures such as modernism, detective fiction remained relatively free from the creeping effects of cultural homelessness.[18] Claiming such uniqueness of detective fiction, however, only raises the question: what was it about detective fiction—supposedly an extremely formulaic genre—that continuously fascinated those who lived through these experiences? The elements of detective fiction listed by Yumeno in the aforementioned quote—"nonsense, humor, adventure, grotesque, mystery"—appear too incongruous to constitute either a structured culture or a single literary genre; however, these elements actually coexisted and commingled in the gray mode of confused existence that was the modern condition in Japan. Detective fiction tries to make sense of the world that entered modernity as it both recycles and reshapes the elements of the Enlightenment. In this context, works of both foreign and domestic detective fiction became antidotes to the modern epidemics of angst and anxiety, the roots of which remained obscured in the shadows of everyday life. Several early writers of detective fiction, in the West as well as in Japan, sought through their works to illuminate the dark corners of this modern reality and reveal the true workings of human behavior and social structures; it is not a coincidence, then, that many of these pioneering authors were journalists who aimed to "diagnose" and "treat" the ills of modern life by observing and reporting its symptoms in fictional form. Kuroiwa Ruikō (1862–1920), a one-time student at Fukuzawa's school Keiō Gijuku who became the titan of early Japanese journalism, often turned early in his career to translations of Western detective fiction to criticize the shortcomings of the state's reforms and to point out the underdevelopment of democratic principles in Japan. Ruikō disclosed in an autobiographical essay from 1905 that as a young man he aspired to a career as a politician; his flaming desire to enlighten the masses was only extinguished by the slowness of politics as a vehicle of social change.[19] This early inclination to write and read detective fiction as straightforward social critique solidified the genre's reputation as a faithful mirror that reflects changes in external reality.[20]

This interpretation is most accurate for the detective fiction of the Meiji era as it consisted mostly of translated Western texts and shared this hopeful attitude of spreading intellectual autonomy among the population. Some proponents of the Meiji Enlightenment, especially Ruikō, saw in detective fiction the means to educate the newly literate masses. Though Fukuzawa and Ruikō ultimately may have envisioned different futures for Japan, both deemed their contemporary audiences as intellectually stagnant and sought to educate them through writing. Ruikō's *Hito ka oni ka* (Human or Beast; 1888), a translation of Émile Gaboriau's *L'affaire Lerouge* (1866), is a camouflaged but nonetheless scathing indictment of the Japanese judicial system. In *Muzan* (Merciless; 1889), his first "original" work, Ruikō brings to life a promising future ruled by rationality and science by juxtaposing two types of detectives: one who relies exclusively upon intuition in investigating crimes and one who adheres to "just the facts." In the end, Ruikō lets the scientific and, therefore, "new" and modern detective get the long end of the stick.[21] In the early stages of both Western and Japanese detective fiction, the figure of the detective celebrated the triumph of science and reason, and embodied the certainty of *shinpo* (progress).[22]

As Japan matured as a nation-state, Ruikō's brand of detective fiction, with its emphasis on faith in rationality and progress, faced new challenges and dilemmas. It is no coincidence that he left the genre in the late 1890s at the onset of the three aforementioned international wars, apparently to concentrate on his other passion of political journalism. It is possible that he sensed new challenges were awaiting Japan (and subsequently Japanese detective fiction), and a new medium was needed to deal with them. With Ruikō's departure, the production of detective fiction in Japan, political or otherwise, virtually halted for three decades. It is after the 1910s that the genre revives and solidifies its identity as much more than an amalgam of passive, simplistic responses to contemporary events. Modernity, as a gray mode of existence that cannot rely on reason or humanity for a better future, provided detective fiction an ideal environment in which to flourish, but the genre was not entirely dependent on modernity for inspiration. Although the chronology might suggest it, modernity does not invent detective fiction, Japanese or Western: it would be more accurate to say that detective fiction and modernity create each other through constant repetition of writing, reading, reception, and reconception. Detective fiction shapes and reshapes the world in which it is produced and invites readers to contemplate their logic, surroundings, and existence through tantalizing mysteries of murder and intrigue. Be it a story of murder or of theft, a work of detective fiction lets one explore the dark corners of one's everyday through an imaginary disruption of that everyday.

Less interested in upholding the generic format than their Western counterparts, Japanese detective writers used the framework of the genre to package and disseminate their ideas on such modern phenomena as urbanization, privacy (both its acquisition and its violation), abnormal sexuality, science devoid of ethics, and total war. During the first half of the twentieth century, the central figures of such stories—figures I call "undercover agents of modernity" whose moral status is ever ambiguous—readily immersed themselves in the mayhem of modernity by probing the three sources of modern mystery: city, colony, and body. Their explorations and reconfigurations of these spaces, fueled both by their impulse to uncover the truth, however unpleasant, and their willingness to transgress conventional boundaries, are the primary objects of this study. The activities of these agents of modernity can be likened to those of the "modern painter *par excellence*," to borrow the language of Michel Foucault and Charles Baudelaire: "When the whole world is falling asleep, he begins to work, and transfigures that world. His transfiguration does not entail an annulling of reality, but a difficult interplay between the truth of what is real and the exercise of freedom; 'natural' things become 'more than natural,' 'beautiful' things become 'more than beautiful,' and individual objects appear 'endowed with an impulsive life like the soul of [their] creator.'"[23]

In the context of Japanese detective fiction, these agents amplify negative sensations by making the "ugly" more than ugly, and the "uncanny" more than uncanny. Detective fiction shared much concern and charm with the *ero-guro-nansensu* ("erotic, grotesque, nonsense") phenomenon, the dominant contemporary cultural trend that hid profound philosophical questions underneath the ostentatious displays of flesh, bad taste, and silliness.[24] Even when the agents of modernity attempt to clarify rather than intensify the mystery, they end up pursuing truth into the shadowy depths of modernity's abyss. Criminal and detective alike operate beneath the surface of everyday Japanese reality, and the moral ambiguity of both figures leaves the ultimate decision for ethical action in the hands of the readers. The same sort of inquisitive impulse is seen in other figures—such as the scientist, the fashionable *moga* (abbreviation of the English expression "modern girl"), and the wartime colonizer—who investigate the unknown elements of these three mysterious spaces. Their attitudes resemble that of the conventional detective to the extent that their unrelenting quest for truth often endangers their lives. These figures fight at the front line of battle against Japanese—and more ubiquitous—cultural diphtheria. Rather than simply distracting readers from their everyday problems, dilemmas, and sufferings, interwar Japanese detective fiction pushed seekers of entertainment (and treatment) to look such challenges squarely in the eye.[25] As "painters" of modern life, detective writers have also served as guides to the dark side of modernity, urging readers to examine problems from new angles and devise solutions in and outside the textual space, all the while maintaining the facade that this philosophical quest is nothing more than a frivolous diversion for mass consumption.

Detective fiction is an effective antidote to the uncertainty of modernity, but it is also a very addictive one: while we have yet to completely uncover the identity of what fuels the moderns to read detective fiction, we see that often this desire is insatiable and makes the readers constantly search for newer and stronger antidotes.[26] More than other genres, detective fiction invites readers for repeated reading, often of other texts within the genre but also sometimes of the same text despite the reduced pleasure of uncovering the culprit. Fans of the genre, some of whom would later become authors of detective fiction themselves, unanimously recall being "hooked" on detective fiction, especially in their childhood.

Neither is detective fiction a complete cure for the historical and cultural diphtheria of the modern urban condition: it only brings the temporary semblance of relief while making the patient dependent on the medicine. The function of this ambiguous treatment needs to be examined beneath the critical magnifying glass of close reading. In addition to some stylistic elements, these texts share a commitment to sleuthing the baffling questions of modernity, ranging from the whodunit to the whatdunit, the howdunit, and the whydunit, and grapple with the inconsistencies and irrationalities of the modern world.

Early Detective Fiction and the Everyday in Modan Japan

After Ruikō left the genre in the late 1890s, the production of original as well as translated detective fiction waned during the subsequent decades as if to gauge what would become of Japan in the international political arena. Even during this production stoppage, however, the consumption of detective fiction never completely ended: readers continued to access works of detective fiction despite the slowdown in new publication. The genre survived on the shelves of *kashihon'ya* (rental libraries), secondhand bookstores, and in the closets of faithful fans, who tended to preserve pulp magazines and pass them on to their friends and children. Detective fiction in this period was read en masse, but was not a "disposable" genre by any means. Although printed on cheap paper for the reader's fleeting moment of fun, these books were "pulp" only in appearance. Even when publishers intended their product to be discarded once new issues were published, consumers often accumulated the issues at home.[27] In addition, though the copies at the *kashihon'ya* were less than perfect, readers always returned for more, until they exhausted all the collections.[28]

Some readers who frequented *kashihon'ya* went on to become writers themselves and created undercover agents of modernity that were different from the heroes of Meiji detective fiction. These authors almost uniformly grew up reading Ruikō's translations, suggesting a charm that is beyond the overt political activism of his works. The fictional figures they created—including such popular detectives as Akechi Kogorō, Kindaichi Kōsuke, and Homura Sōroku—hop from one blind spot of modern life to another, letting the reader vicariously experience the problems of modernity in the extreme. Unlike their predecessors, these heroes are not made omnipotent by their scientific and rational power, but exercise agency within the contours of restricted freedom. They represent the multitude of rationalities rather than one universal value, and often overtly admit the limits of their understanding.

Using their fictional characters as guides, detective fiction authors take their readers on a literary journey to explore the shady spaces of modernity. The everyday in early-twentieth-century Japan was neither routine nor monotonous but hid many uncanny spaces and unfamiliar faces. Reflecting this reality, stories from the 1920s often focus upon the previously unexplored spaces within the city and feature characters who turn this anxiety about one's surroundings into a motivation for public spying. As Walter Benjamin points out in his seminal essay on Charles Baudelaire, a modern metropolis allows individuals to fade into anonymity.[29] By taking advantage of the cover of anonymity, urbanization—generally a common cause of anxiety—

could become a source of entertainment. The haphazard growth of Tokyo and the constant influx of people from rural areas made longtime city dwellers feel like strangers in their own town. This rapid and unsystematic urbanization created many "uncanny"—familiar but unfamiliar—places within the parameters of a Tokyoite's daily life. Since the government diverted its resources into the more immediate project of *fukoku kyōhei* ("rich nation, strong army"), the urban reorganization of Tokyo took a backseat during the early years of the twentieth century.[30] As a result, urban development was driven more by desire for commercial growth and fortuitous events such as natural disasters. As a result, it was not unusual to see shady brothels and gambling houses sprouting up next to posh department stores and neighborhood shops with signs almost larger than the stores themselves.[31] Traditional neighborhoods and the sense of familiarity that they nurtured were erased, and a simple stroll around one's house became a trip into the unknown.

More directly than other genres, detective fiction demonstrates the function of public space as source of mystery for urbanites. City streets were particularly important sites of self-expression and self-exploration; as critic Kawamoto Saburō argues, the streets are a space between one's workplace and one's home, where one is temporarily free from the restrictions of capitalism and the traditional *ie* (household) system that dictates family life.[32] The development of railway hub stations such as Shinjuku into entertainment centers during the 1920s and 1930s attests to the desire of commuting workers to prolong otherwise ephemeral moments of transition and use such "down time" for self-expression and exploration.[33] The neon signs and eye-catching advertisements of such urban spaces tempt overworked and dreamy workers to become consumers, while unfamiliar figures and beautiful *moga* inadvertently invite potential thrill seekers and criminals to peek into their lives. Imagination and reality freely crossed in the space of the city streets, and "expanding metropolitan sites like Tokyo and Osaka supplied a vast space for discourse to imagine and figure a new form of life, a place for fantasizing what had not yet become a lived reality for all."[34] When some of the fantasies of these urbanites started to include murder, such trivial spaces of transition became disturbing sites of transgression.

As urban spaces became sources of mystery and intrigue, so too did the people who filled them. The sea of unfamiliar faces turned innocent people watching into a more active and intrusive outlet for learning about others. As spying on others became a legitimate source of not only entertainment but also academic study, some tried to see beyond the skin's surface: they cut people open, physically and figuratively, in order to find answers to the modern mysteries of criminality, deviant sexuality, and the body. Among this group were criminologists, who wrestled with the difficult task of using logic to explain the source of illogical human criminality. Some works from the 1930s capture the moments at which the medical professionals who study the physiognomy of criminals become criminals themselves as they indulge in the desire to chop up fellow human beings. As the boundary between criminals and the medical investigators became blurred, so did the lines between fiction and reality, as well as between legitimate academic study and curiosity-seeking pulp erotica.

This tendency in the medical profession to objectify the human body soon made some medical practitioners completely disregard any other values besides (Western) scientism. Some of the major authors in Japanese detective fiction were men of science by day, and their literary obsession with murderous scientists plays on the popular suspicion toward those who were systematically trained to objectify other human beings. Unfamiliar bodies—female, beautiful, even disfigured—became sources of both anxiety and wonder that attracted popular attention and scholarly investigation.

The body was an uncanny space that inspired fear and curiosity; however, another historical space prompted similar reactions: the colony. The colonial space also worked as a catalyst to let the detective writers see the confluences between fantasy and reality. The critic Ikeda Hiroshi argues that the colony as the source of mystery is as important as the city, since "overseas colonies and battlefields were sites in which these mysteries—often in the form of a crime committed in the metropole—originally hatch."[35] Ikeda illustrates this point by using the example of Sir Arthur Conan Doyle's "A Study in Scarlet," in which Sherlock Holmes makes his first appearance. Not only is the encounter between Holmes and Watson made possible by colonialism (or, more specifically, Watson's participation and injury in the Afghan War), the mysteries they solve together "often have origins in faraway colonies and battlefields."[36]

In the case of Japanese detective fiction, the colonies become most pertinent when they are transformed into battlefields during the war, where normalcy of any kind is completely erased. As Japan became increasingly involved in continental affairs, rumors about the nation's overseas territories and colonists traveled back to the homeland. As some detective fiction writers were drafted as military writers during the war, their stories returned to their home audiences as powerful and frightening sources of information. Through such trips to the colonies, actual and vicarious, detective fiction writers and their readers dealt with the question of cultural relativism. When one realizes that he or she is "an 'other' among others," the previously objectified colonial other begins to assume multiple layers of depth and significance. Like an unfamiliar neighborhood in Tokyo, the tropical jungles of the colonies became places one can visit but never truly penetrate.[37] Any disruption of normalcy in such a setting exposes the distance between natives and outsiders, and forces investigators to deal with the implications of the minutiae of the reality that the colonial power relationship creates.

The experience of war changed soldiers both psychologically and physically, and these effects figured prominently in postwar detective fiction. Most notably, the body of the demobilized soldier became an object of curious gazes and a menace to the postwar Japanese drive for renewal. Postwar detective fiction features disfigured demobilized soldiers as part of the central plot in order to decipher the mystery of the war and colonies—the marks of which they carry on their bodies.

The following chapters will explore how writers of detective fiction depict the ambiguous figures of modernity, such as the tail, *moga*, scientist, spy, and demobilized soldier, in order to express the fast, opaque, and fragmentary condition of modern existence. They most vividly embody the energies of modernity through the undying desire for self-realization and intellectual survival. These figures embody the precariousness of the post-Enlightenment world where rationality has failed and the potential for total mayhem is an ever-present danger: these figures can go in a flash from good to evil, crime fighter to criminal offender, while at times being both concurrently. The writers who tease out fear, excitement, and hope from modernity through these figures are the ultimate undercover agents of modernity who always manage to keep their morality, sincerity, and even identity ambiguous at best.

Chapter 1 deals with the figure of the "tail," the ever-present shadow following a target's every move. Edogawa Ranpo and Kōga Saburō (1893–1945), as well as authors who are now known as proponents of more "mainstream" literature such as Tanizaki Jun'ichirō (1896–1965), experimented with the figure in their works. Japanese detective fiction writers, however, were not the only ones interested in the technique and who practiced it: contemporary criminologists and law enforcement officials, as well as scholars of urban ethnography *(kōgengaku)*, all used the technique in their professional work. Detectives and amateur tails were both reassuring and threatening presences to those around them. For those who had not successfully mastered the art of secretly observing others, the tail was a powerful ally in navigating the complex landscape of the city, where it was no longer possible to fully know one's neighbors. At the same time, the tail might take advantage of his ability to spy on others to expose the dark secrets of people's lives. What emerges through this examination of the discourse of tailing is an image of a society in which one becomes preoccupied with how to retain control over one's own image in both private and public spaces, all the while desiring and exploring ways to spy on others in the anonymity of the city.

Chapter 2 focuses upon instances in which this game of visuality ends in murder—most often the brutal killing of a beautiful young woman. These women go from being objects of viewing to victims of mutilation, hunted down not just as outlets for the homicidal urges of a raving killer but also as vehicles for the "artistic" impulses of such murderers. In both detective fiction and real crimes from this period, the central object of criminal investigation shifted from "whodunit" to "whydunit," and murder became both a medium for creative expression and the object of scientific exploration. Serial killers were not the only ones young women had to watch out for: interwar criminologists cut open murderers as well as victims in order to find the root of human criminality, and when the killer was a woman, the postmortem physical exploration of the bodily space became part of a pseudoscientific discourse that attempted to tie together criminality, physiology, and female sexuality. Two titans of detective fiction, Edogawa Ranpo and Hamao Shirō (1896–1935), used their works to showcase the shortcomings of such a one-dimensional view of female criminality by incorporating and parodying the latest "discoveries" in criminal science. Prewar Japanese criminologists, much like their

Western counterparts, try to hold on to the dream of "rationality"—being able to explain away all curious turns of human emotion—by bending facts to establish a link between abnormal sexuality (especially female sexuality) and criminal tendency. Fundamentally, they aim to serve the community by eradicating crimes from the roots; however, they end up manipulating truth when it does not fit their logic. When Abe Sada, an actual female killer, defies their theorizations and expectations, they in turn reduce her to an innate criminal overflowing with wild, uncontrollable, and irrational emotions.

Chapter 3 reintroduces the contentious relationship between detective fiction and science through an examination of the recurring theme of "mad scientists" as killers. These scientists are "mad" in the sense that they prey on their fellow human beings for their sinister experiments in the name of science. In the worst cases, they also subject themselves to the horror. Under the cover of frivolity, detective writers voice their concerns about unethical science—Western science in particular—by shocking their audiences into anxiety. They invite them to contemplate the gloomy outlook of a future wrought by the potential madness of science without conscience in a manner similar to H. G. Wells, whose works were available to Japanese audiences since the Meiji period. Short stories by Kozakai Fuboku (1890–1929) and Unno Jūza (1897–1949), both men of science, in addition to Yumeno Kyūsaku's magnum opus *Dogura magura,* all deal with the question of what constitutes murder, and gauge the supposed but actually nonexistent distance between killers who prey on innocent victims and mad scientists who drag unsuspecting patients into their strange and harmful experiments. Mad scientists in detective fiction symbolize the fallen status of science, once the driving force of a world guided by rationality, in the apocalyptic madness of a modernity in which lofty ideals have disappeared.

Chapter 4 traces the status of the genre during World War II. According to the currently accepted chronology, detective fiction is supposed to have suffered a great setback at the hands of wartime censors. Considered too frivolous and immoral for times of crisis, detective fiction was monitored closely by the authorities. Many detective writers opted for other less scrutinized genres such as *torimonochō* (tales of investigation set in the Edo period) or science fiction, or gave up writing altogether. The cancellation of *Shupio* in 1938, a small coterie magazine edited by Unno Jūza, Kigi Takatarō (1897–1969), and

Oguri Mushitarō (1901–46), is usually seen as the result of increased pressure from censors. The three authors subsequently pursued other genres, but close examination of their wartime works suggests that they did not "leave" detective fiction overnight. The seeming "demise" of the genre has been exaggerated by recent critics; the actual decline in production took place largely due to the voluntary departure of authors and increasing self-censorship by those who remained active, rather than by bans imposed by censors. Although their works were no longer classified as detective fiction, they used the same elements of intrigue and mystery in their new works to engage their new readers. For example, Unno's first post-*Shupio* work, "Kaitō-ō" (The King of the Mysterious Tower; 1938), in particular suggests that the cancellation of *Shupio* did not automatically mean that the editors left the genre. As the war raged on, the three authors assumed completely different attitudes toward Japanese nationalism, militarism, and colonialism. Their diverse reactions attest that detective fiction is inherently neither liberal nor fascist, and that there were different attitudes within the genre toward the historical and political situation. Kigi originally expressed a reserved attitude toward Japanese nationalism and militarism, but he became an increasingly fervent advocate of these ideologies as Japan found itself in direct conflict with the United States and the world. Oguri, on the other hand, used his fiction to criticize Japan's wartime actions, risking attracting the attention of the censors.

Chapter 5 discusses changes the genre went through during the years immediately following the end of World War II. As the rest of the country emerged from years of suffering, detective fiction writers sought ways to contribute to the project of rebuilding the genre and the nation. In 1946, Yokomizo Seishi (1902–81) called upon his colleagues to promote rational thinking among the population through their writing. In the same year, Sakaguchi Ango (1906–55) published the famous essay "Darakuron" (On Decadence) and encouraged readers to explore ways to make their subjectivity free from the dictates of the state. As Ango preached decadence as new morality, he also tried his hand at writing detective fiction. Although the two authors are not commonly studied together, their works and activities in the late 1940s suggest that they sought to accomplish similar goals through their writing. Both spent the war years reading old copies of Western locked-room mysteries and put this knowledge to use in order to weave a new discourse of rationality in a world that had already witnessed both the defeat of spiritualism and the devastation of the atomic bomb.

Japanese Detective Fiction in the World

The genre's foreign birth, however, poses a few technical difficulties in considering it within the framework of Japanese literature. In the early days of Western scholarship on Japan, many cases of intercultural influence involving Japan and the West were conceived in terms of a unilateral relationship between pupil (invariably Japanese) and master (Western). In this model, the master stands as an insurmountable pinnacle of literary achievement, with the pupil always worried about originality and independence.[38]

This framework, however, fails to account for the self-awareness of Japanese detective fiction authors who did not necessarily see themselves as indebted cultural underlings. They often were proud of being under the influence of a noted figure or renowned work, and willingly disclosed the source of their inspiration. The numerous instances of unintentional overlaps or confluences between Western and Japanese detective fiction suggest that what we may intuitively perceive as results of intercultural influence may be mere coincidences made possible by cultural globalization. Frequent instances of coincidental overlaps, willing and proud imitation, and skillful permutations of generic rules from Japanese detective fiction suggest notions of originality and authenticity that differ from the conventional Romantic ideal of a unique creator and by doing so question models of direct influence that have heretofore dominated the interpretation of this particular genre and possibly others. They encourage us to rethink the idea of originality by suggesting that in detective fiction, the measure of originality is not how "new" the story is but rather how existing tropes and narrative structures are reorganized and reconceived in artful and unexpected ways. Through these examples, I propose a more formal way of looking at how works within a very formulaic prose genre can influence one another, with relative disregard to national boundaries and artificial intellectual hierarchy.

The Fallacy of Direct Influence: Ranpo, Christie, and Hammett

Some examples found within detective fiction, Western and Japanese, question the myth of direct influence in that occasionally what appears to be the result of direct influence is in fact the consequence of the permutation of similar generic rules. One example of this would be Edogawa Ranpo's "Nisen dōka" (Two-Sen Copper Coin; 1923) and Agatha Christie's *The Murder of Roger Ackroyd* (1926). When "Nisen" appeared in *Shinseinen,* the flagship magazine of the publisher Hakubunkan that regularly featured foreign as well as domestic detective fiction, the work was praised by authors such as Morishita Uson (1890–1965) and Kozakai Fuboku for observing some of the signature elements of detective fiction (e.g., the mystery of the missing jewelry, the trick two-sen coin, and the mysterious code found inside) while also overturning some of the central conventions of the genre (e.g., through the deceitful narrator and the absence of resolution). Ranpo completely dismantles the implicit expectation of the narrator as a sidekick to an able detective and a faithful chronicler of his friend's triumphs (as embodied by his Western predecessors such as the anonymous friend of C. Auguste Dupin in Poe's Dupin trilogy and Dr. Watson in Doyle's Sherlock Holmes series). In "Nisen dōka," the nameless *watashi* ("I") gets the last laugh, not only from his friend who took him to be a great detective, but also from the readers who expected his narrative to be sincere and complete.

For today's audience, the presence of the deceitful narrator who is not apologetic for giving the reader an incomplete account of the case and his involvement in the central plot likely suggests Christie's *Ackroyd,* in which the audience accesses the story through the viewpoint of Dr. Shepherd, the sidekick to the retired detective Hercule Poirot. Shepherd is not only the narrator but also the culprit who was in Ackroyd's room at the time of his murder. Shepherd also happens to be the killer, however, and he hides his criminality by omitting the crucial detail in his narrative. In much the same way as in "Nisen dōka," readers are set up to realize the incompleteness and deceptiveness of a (subjective) narrative. The two works share such similar narrative deception that many would assume Ranpo's work to be a "copy" of Christie's.

However, the original publication dates of the two works—"Nisen dōka" predates *Ackroyd* by a few years—exclude the possibility that Ranpo learned the trick from Christie and directly copied it. Instead, the sequence of events suggests that Ranpo and Christie detected the same generic convention and decided to permute it in the same way, making a conscious choice to exploit the naïveté of such an assumption and using it to entertain readers. The speed and quantity of Japanese translations of Western detective fiction in the interwar period were such that it was easy for Ranpo—or any other committed aficionados—to monitor the latest developments in the genre from afar. The facility with which Japanese authors could access translations seems to fuel the fallacy of direct influence and devalue their creative production.

The abundance of translations can also be understood as both proof of the cultural globalization in progress in this era and a means through which detective fiction authors could acquire the common cultural capital of the genre. Ranpo and Christie arrived at the same conclusion via different paths. This is an example of authors coincidentally coming up with the same or similar combinations of elements as they share the same or similar literary heritage. Both Ranpo and Christie are aware of this generic convention of faithful and sincere sidekick narrators that has its origins in Poe's anonymous narrator to Dupin, Doyle's Dr. Watson to Holmes, and Christie's own Captain Hastings to Poirot, and regard it as one of the blind spots the authors can use to outsmart (and entertain) readers.

The example of Edogawa Ranpo's work *Injū* (The Devil in the Shadow; 1928) and Dashiell Hammett's *The Maltese Falcon* (1930) further disproves the fallacy of direct influence. *Injū* is the story of a beautiful woman, Shizuko, who kills her husband while playing three different characters to cover up her crime. In the process, she starts an affair with a young writer named Samukawa, who is also the detective on the case. *The Maltese Falcon* features Brigid O'Shaughnessy, one of Hammett's and the entire hard-boiled genre's most admired femmes fatales. Just like Shizuko with Samukawa, Brigid starts a sexual relationship with Sam Spade, the private eye whose professional partner she has killed. The two characters use very similar—in fact, almost identical—strategies of persuasion toward their lovers as they hide their murders.

In addition to questions of gender and crime, the similar depictions of women in Ranpo and Hammett raise some interesting issues when considered within the framework of authenticity, artistic precedence, and cross-cultural artistic inspiration. During the late 1920s to early 1930s, European dominance in the field of translated detective fiction was slowly being overtaken by its American counterpart. In the midst of this transition, the works of Hammett, with an array of seductive femmes fatales, made their way to Japan through both literary translations and film adaptations.[39] Yet the publication of *Injū* predates that of *The Maltese Falcon* by two years, so there could have been no imitation despite frequent importation of Western works to Japan. Similarly, as Japanese texts were rarely, if ever, translated into Western languages, it is highly unlikely that Hammett emulated a fellow detective writer in the Far East.

If Ranpo's work had been written even a day after Hammett's, the similarity between their works would have been explained away by the usual theory of cross-cultural influence, where Western writers invariably influence the Eastern or Japanese writers. However, as *Injū* predates *The Maltese Falcon*, it preempts this banal (and sometimes misleading) explanation. Rather, the striking similarity between Hammett's and Ranpo's works should be viewed as evidence potentially pointing to at least two theories. From the standpoint of social history, it can serve as another piece of evidence illustrating what critics Yoshimi Shun'ya and Harry D. Harootunian have called *sekai dōjisei* (global simultaneity), the emergence of a global culture to which the United States, Europe, and Japan belonged.[40]

Another more formalist explanation would be that Hammett and Ranpo, both students of the formulas and techniques of detective fiction, arrived at the same conclusion via different paths. In the world of science, such occurrences are more readily acceptable—most famously, Sir Isaac Newton and Gottfried Leibniz developed the same model of differential and integral calculus independently of each other in the same period, and Carl Gauss and János Bolyai came up with identical theories of non-Euclidean geometry without ever consulting each other.[41] In both cases, all parties were given credit for their achievements. Perhaps the case of Ranpo and Christie calls for a new way of looking at various formalist literatures and cross-cultural literary inspiration and encourages the willingness to go beyond the existent hierarchy of influence and de-emphasize originality and priority.

Anti-Romantic Genius: Kuroiwa Ruikō and His Peers

Once we dismantle the notion that absolute value lies in absolute originality, we can begin to appreciate different kinds of creativity that previously went undetected by our critical radar. In many ways, Japanese detective fiction writers' disinterest in originality was already apparent with Kuroiwa Ruikō while he was translating Western works of detective fiction into Japanese during the 1880s and early 1890s. During this period, Ruikō tirelessly undertook projects of translating Western detective fiction—mostly French and English texts by such authors as Edgar Allan Poe (1809–49), Émile Gaboriau (1832–73), and Fortuné de Boisgobey (1821–91). The key players who sustained the genre's boom in the interwar period—such as Edogawa Ranpo and Yokomizo Seishi—all experienced their first thrill of mystery with Ruikō's translations.

However, the fact that Ruikō "translated" other writers' works rather than "created" his own stories from scratch often gives the impression of Japanese detective fiction as derivative of its Western counterpart. To those who value "originality" as the sign of a great writer, to credit Ruikō as the "founding father" of detective fiction in Japan may appear questionable, as he left behind but one "original" work of his own.[42] In addition, Ruikō often emphasized in personal essays and prefaces that his involvement in the text was limited to that of a "translator" *(yakusha)* and his writing a "translation" *(yaku)*.[43] Because of the liberal manner in which he translated, Ruikō's works are now often called *hon'an shōsetsu*, with *hon'an* literally meaning "translating ideas."[44] His seeming disinterest in creativity and originality may have social and commercial roots. In mid-Meiji, the notions of "copyright" and creative licensing were vague at best; for instance, none of the writers whose works sold millions in Japan thanks to Ruikō's translations ever saw any of these profits. Ruikō called his endeavor "translation" partly because of the mask it offered him, partly because of the licensing system of his own time, and partly because of his personal conception of (or indifference to) what we might consider "creativity" and "originality."

Such an utter disinterest in originality and authenticity is a curious phenomenon that needs to be examined in a global context as it may be a historical phenomenon. During the late nineteenth century to the early twentieth century, Anglo-American detective fiction from the tradition of Poe was exported not only to Japan but also to other faraway places such as Italy, Latin America, and China. In China, for instance, the business of translating Western detective fiction took off during the last days of the Qing Dynasty and early days of the Republic;[45] a similar explosion took place in Latin America in the early twentieth century and in Italy in the 1920s.⁴⁶ In studying the work of Chinese translators of detective fiction, Jeffrey Kinkley too points out the existence of a different kind of "originality" in their minds: author-translators such as Cheng Xiaoqing (1893–1976) and Sun Liaohong (1897–1958), who translated works of Conan Doyle and Maurice Leblanc, respectively, "preferred to rationalize their imitativeness rather than cover it up," conceiving the "modern analytical detective story as an international, not just a Western form."⁴⁷ What this suggests is that there is traditionally a willing forfeiting of any claim to originality in detective fiction throughout the regions where it was transplanted. The effects of the development of the notion of copyright on the genre—or the genre's influence on the notion of copyright—certainly merit further investigation.

Genre as Imagined Guild

What enables this referential play—guiding those who have read a substantial body of work in the genre—is the concept of genre as cross-cultural classification tool among both readers and authors. I believe that the best way to describe the awareness of Japanese authors vis-à-vis Western authors and the genre might be the notion of a kind of "guild." The proponents of Japanese detective fiction in this period shared an awareness that they were participating in an international genre, and they often took pride in facilitating the inflow of information from overseas.⁴⁸

This awareness of the global nature of their endeavors allowed Japanese detective fiction writers to operate within an imagined guild of like-minded aficionados. This community is "imagined" in the same sense that Benedict Anderson's idea of "nationhood" is imagined; and it is worthy of the name "guild" as it is a grouping based on professional achievement and skill that stretches across class, race, and gender. The way I conceive of this "imagined guild" is also close to a kind of "synchronic tradition." In discussing the field of English poetry, T. S. Eliot defined "tradition" as the sum of all precedent works, accepted as "great," against which a new work is judged.⁴⁹ Rather than stretching across time, however, detective fiction as synchronic tradition stretches across geographical boundaries and allows individual instances of transnational affinities to emerge. In addition, the guild does not seek active extermination of individual talent as Eliot and his concept of "tradition" do; rather, it recognizes indigenous sensibility as well as the global poetic mind and values the subjective application of taste and judgment involved in the act of permutation. When the participants of this guild import works from faraway places, they learn the mechanisms of the "rules" that make possible the finished product. They take in these rules as "tools" with which to construct their own works. These authors at the receiving end assume that the tools come without the expensive tariffs of intellectual indebtedness. Therefore, when writers wish to use the generic conventions and solutions from other works as part of the plots for their own works, they do not have to shy away from disclosing the underlying texts upon which their current murder mysteries are based; rather, they can actively use them as tools of playful deception.

The feeling of affinity with this imagined community of detective fiction is what allows Japanese detective fiction writers to escape the "pervading feeling of cultural homelessness"—prevalent emotional responses of contemporary modernist writers to various material as well as psychological changes—and reinterpret such sense of loss as freedom and a right to join another community.[50] The genre works as a new "home" and distracts the proponents from "a sense of dislocation for a shared tradition as well as to an uncertainty regarding the boundaries of Japanese culture."[51] In such an imagined guild of detective fiction writers, one is a master among other masters, and one takes and uses the tools others offer as one sees fit. Mentioning names and plots from preexistent works is not an admission of creative piracy but a way to show one's mastery of the genre's conventions.

Generic Conventions and Their Permutations: Yokomizo Seishi

The best example of this willing play on conventions can be found in the works of Yokomizo Seishi from the period immediately after World War II. After spending the war years writing *torimonochō* (Edo-period tales of investigation), Yokomizo wrote mysteries that were inspired by classic texts of Western detective fiction: "Honjin satsujin jiken" (Murders at the Main Manor; 1946) is inspired by a series of locked-room mysteries by John Dickson Carr (1906–77); "Chōchō satsujin jiken" (The Butterfly Murder Case; 1946) is a direct product of *The Casket* (1920) by Freeman Willis Crofts (1879–1958).

Yokomizo shares Ruikō's disinterest in absolute originality and willingly reveals his sources of inspiration. This is reflected in the way in which he describes his first work in the postwar period, "Honjin," through the character of the enigmatic first-person narrator:

> When I heard the truth of what happened in this case, I looked for similar cases among the works of detective fiction I had read. Gaston Leroux's *The Mystery of the Yellow Chamber (Le mystère de la chambre jaune)* immediately came to my mind, and then Maurice Leblanc's *Les dents du tigre*, S. S. Van Dine's *Canary Murder Case* and *Kennel Murder Case*. I even thought of Dickson Carr's *The Plague Court Murders* and Roger Scarlett's *Murder among the Angells*, a perverted locked-room mystery.

The narrator compares the current case with a wide range of existent Western detective fiction and shows his erudition of the genre in the process. He then goes on to make a comment that neither declares nor refutes the case's uniqueness:

> But the current case differed from all of these stories. However, it did occur to me that the killer may have read them, dissembled the elements of tricks in these stories, and constructed the designs for his own crime using only the parts he needed.[52]

This describes not only the actions of the story's killer but also how Yokomizo himself has shaped the story as the author. For instance, Yokomizo reveals in an essay that his other work from the same period, "Gokumontō" (Gokumon Island, 1946), is a montage of stories he read during the war, such as Christie's *And Then There Were None* (1939) and Doyle's "The Problem of Thor Bridge" (1927).

In comparing "Honjin" to other known cases, the narrator discloses that he already knows the entire account of what happened, including "whodunit." After impersonally reporting how Kindaichi (the detective on the case) solves the locked-room mystery of the main manor, the narrator reappears at the end of the story to make a comment about his own storytelling:

> I feel that I have written everything there is to be known about the murders surrounding the main manor. I did not once do anything that would mislead the readers. I specified the location of the waterwheel. Moreover, at the beginning of the record of this incident, I said the following: "In that regard, I have to express great

appreciation for the cruel and violent criminal who *chopped up the man and woman.*" The "man and woman" here, of course, refer to Shimizu Kyōkichi [the man with three fingers] and Katsuko. Katsuko was murdered but Kyōkichi was not [he died a natural death], so I intentionally avoided writing "the criminal who *killed* the man and woman." If you readers thought that the criminal killed both Katsuko and Kenzō, it is a hasty conclusion on your part. In addition, when I described the murder scene, I did write that there were a man and a woman covered in blood and *lying dead,* but not *killed* and covered in blood. It is because Kenzō was not murdered. I learned from Agatha Christie's *The Murder of Roger Ackroyd* that detective fiction writers ought to write like this.[53]

In this passage, Yokomizo's nameless narrator brags about the narrative feats he achieved and willingly discloses his creative master. Yokomizo does not feel threatened or dwarfed by "copying" his predecessors and colleagues in other literary traditions, as he is simply reusing the tools, the means of creation that now exist in the public domain (so to speak), and not duplicating their final product.

Globalization, Locality, and the Pleasures of Permutation

The examples of Japanese detective fiction mentioned in this introduction suggest that the process of literary and cultural globalization (involving Europe, the United States, and Asia) was well under way in the early twentieth century, at least in this genre. This is not to say, however, that everyone everywhere was writing the same kind of detective fiction. As Michael Hardt and Antonio Negri suggest, globalization "should not be understood in terms of cultural, political, or economic *homogenization,*" because the end product and the effects it creates are always different and haphazard. Globalization "should be understood instead as a *regime* of the production of identity and difference, or really of homogenization and heterogenization."[54] The case of detective fiction as a global phenomenon also supports this idea: the same set of "standard" rules, disseminated through translation, end up producing very distinct works, rather than identical ones, because of different processes of permutation and subversion. Just as it is impossible to completely duplicate a text, it is also impossible to completely purge it of its locality, even if such a text comes into being with the consciousness of participating in an international genre such as detective fiction. Creation through permutation has both sociological and aesthetic explanations, and the example of Japanese detective fiction writers attests not only to the realization of the pleasures and values of permutation but also to its active endorsement through practice.

1. Tailing the Tail: How to Turn Paranoia into a Hobby

Tailing in the Capital

In a dark, quiet city street, a detective tails another man. The detective, with his Stetson pulled down over his eyes and the collar of his trench coat turned up, watches the man from the corners of his eyes. The man feels a presence behind him and looks back. The detective darts behind a pole. The man sees no one, thinks that it was his imagination, and walks on. The detective comes out of the shadows and continues to follow.

A scene like this is business as usual for detective fiction. Normally, tailing *(bikō)* is but one technique a detective uses to investigate, one step in solving the mystery of whodunit. In interwar Japanese detective fiction, however, this otherwise auxiliary act appears repeatedly, central to the plots of many stories. In *Higansugi made* (Until After the Equinox; 1912), by Natsume Sōseki (1867–1916), the young protagonist Tagawa Keitarō feels that "he became a character in a dangerous detective fiction," as he follows a man at his employer's request.[1] Many literary detectives from later works echo Keitarō's somewhat funny self-observation, as they decide to tail others to find out their *himitsu*—secrets. With the contours of the genre still vague at best after a few decades of relative nonproduction, tailing was one activity that could be considered typically "detective." The act of tailing allows the characters to assume a detective-like mind-set. In the period when the conventions of the genre are still being worked out, it also works as a cue to the reader that this story should be considered detective fiction.

The interwar Japanese fascination with the act of tailing is also closely linked with changing living conditions in urban areas, particularly Tokyo. In the ever-growing, glittering metropolis, survival entailed mastering secrets of all kinds. One is supposed to uncover as many of the secrets of others while closely guarding one's own, and often the best way to accomplish this is to tail and observe the object of investigation in broad daylight. More than the simple physical act of following, the frequent appearance and practice of tailing in detective fiction symbolize the widespread desire among interwar Japanese urbanites to obtain information about others without being detected. The Freudian concept of the unconscious *(muishiki)*, introduced around this time to Japan through translations and scholarly works, also planted the idea that people reveal their true colors when they unconsciously go about their business, unaware of the gaze of others upon them.[2] Within the psychoanalytic framework, everyone has secrets to hide, whether they know it or not: the unconscious is the unsocial, indefinable, and, most important, uncontrollable part of one's identity. In addition, rapid urbanization during the early twentieth century spread among Tokyoites the vague anxiety that it was impossible to know the other in any meaningful way.[3] The Great Kantō Earthquake of 1923 redistributed the already intermingled population, and the rapid but unsystematic recovery of the city from the disaster further dismantled the notion of a close-knit traditional neighborhood. Rather than encouraging the urbanites to give up the project altogether, such living conditions fueled their desire to know the other, even more than the other might be willing to reveal.

This chapter deals with this obsessive desire to know the other, and takes up the interwar phenomena of physical and visual tailing, both in real life and in literature, as reflections as well as active explorations of that desire. A discussion of what constitutes "secrets"—hidden facts that need to be exposed—elucidates not only the popular fascination with such secrets but also the difficulty in uncovering them when the parties involved are unwilling to share their clandestine affairs. When the increased urbanization of Tokyo put the secret seekers at a disadvantage, tailing, the art of observing others without their knowledge, emerged as a powerful and necessary technique in fulfilling the urge to know.

The desire to spy on others and find out their secrets in interwar Tokyo seems to be fueled by the curiosity for what the critic Uchida

Ryūzō calls the "depth of reality *(sekai no fukasa),*" the opaqueness of daily existence created by the confusions of urbanization and the Great Kantō Earthquake. Building on Carlo Ginzburg's study on Voltaire's *Zadig ou la destinée* (1747), Uchida elaborates the image of a world in which nothing is as it appears to be.[4] Uchida's and Ginzburg's discussions focus on the chapter "The Dog and the Horse," in which Zadig is able to figure out the prominent features of the empress's dog from the marks it left in the sand. Although Zadig sees the traces after the dog is long gone, he is able to ratiocinate the truth as the time elapsed between the two events is virtually negligible: "the traces on the sand and the characteristics of the dog are connected on the surface of the same world, and strictly speaking no historical time has passed between them."[5] Reality starts to spawn multiple layers when certain occurrences interrupt the flow of time within a particular space; after such interventions, the traces in the present, appearing on the surface of things, only maintain a faint relationship to the past. Urban developments, both planned and unplanned, can be considered such "incidents" that drastically change the flow of time at a particular location and disrupt the otherwise preserved traces of the past. Detective fiction exploits this disruption, treating it as something that makes the mystery at hand juicier.

In addition to the fascination with spying on others, various writings attest to the widespread fear among city dwellers of being on the receiving end of this desire and having the skeletons in their closets exposed. Detective fiction transforms such obsession and fear into a consumable entertainment for this paranoid audience: the genre showcases a brand of people who use the seemingly negative aspects of urban life to their advantage. After Michel Foucault put forth the idea of constant surveillance in modern society, seeing has often—if not exclusively—been discussed in terms of a power struggle between the agent of watching and the object of surveillance.[6] Some of the works discussed here will suggest that such a power relationship between the seer and the seen made tailing not a simplistic method of observation but a pleasurable act of domination.

As the increasingly complex conditions of city life often necessitated tailing as the most viable way to gather information on others, we also see some bored, overstimulated urbanites engage in the activity for the sheer pleasure of it. The traces of such "guilty pleasures" are present even in supposedly academically minded writings, as the accounts of tailing by the scholars of modernology *(kōgengaku)*—the study of post-earthquake urban *modan* culture—will show. In the prominent absence of the visually oriented Holmesian detective from Japanese detective fiction, modernologists stand in as experts in reading visual clues. While the modernologists are unwilling to admit the limits of visuality, some stories of detective fiction illustrate the dangers of overreliance on visual data.

More daring and dangerous than his Western counterpart the *flâneur*, the literary tail from the 1910s and early 1920s had the potential to end up both as detective and criminal.[7] In a period when certain kinds of tailing—especially those that we would now consider stalking—were starting to be outlawed in real life, a scene of tailing in literature appears as both a moment at which a regular story becomes detective fiction and a prelude to a narrative of crime in which the tail will find himself entangled in one way or another. These tales of tailing tease out an image of people who actively, and desperately, sought ways to dispel the anxiety created by the actual noncorrespondence between exterior and interior. As we shall see, the tailing gaze in question here is different from the visual exploration that Timon Screech describes developing among Dutch scholars and medical practitioners during the Edo period.[8] The Edo gaze is projected inward: the gazer expects the object to possess interior mechanisms that are not accessible by superficial observation. On the other hand, while the gaze in tailing assumes the same sort of interiority in an object, it assumes that it is possible to know the truth about such interior worlds through their exterior manifestations. Unlike the investigative gaze among Dutch learners during the Edo period that seek access to the object's inner, hidden truth by gaining physical access to interior, the *modan* gaze believes that all manifestations of inner truth can be found on the surface.

As we shall see, chapter 2 will deal with one exception to this rule: the female body, which invited dissection and physical inner explorations in the Taishō and early Shōwa eras. However, even in that case the act of "cutting open" was not done to seek out previously unknown truths about the human body or even female sexuality, but to confirm through *herikutsu* (twisted logic; literally: "fart logic") and pseudoscience various groundless assumptions that most often developed from superstitious beliefs regarding physical attributes.

Secrets on All Levels

In the mind of the interwar tail, the "other" broods on two kinds of information: one that the other volunteers, and another that he or she hides. The latter, the secrets of the other, is what piques the interest of the tail. But what constitutes a "secret" for the interwar Japanese? In 1918, the term figures prominently in the summer supplement of the magazine *Chūō kōron* (Central Review): "Himitsu to kaihō gō" (Secrets and Liberation Issue). The organization of the issue—articles ranging from the harmful effects of covert diplomatic dealings between two nations to the hiding of an extramarital affair within a household—implies a very inclusive definition of the word "secret." On the first page, notable contemporary journalist Miyake Setsurei (1860–1945) writes: "Secret means darkness, and liberation means light. Darkness hides evil, and light does the opposite."[9] His argument in the rest of the article is as straightforward as the two opening sentences: secrets, especially in the realms of politics, international diplomacy, and even individual human relations, are something to be condemned and eradicated. His attitude is also representative of all the articles in the "Opinions" *(kōron)* and "Teachings" *(zeien)* sections as they all recognize fairness and openness as virtues to be upheld in any human relationship.

Some contributors, however, show concern for not being able to control the exposure of one's own secrets in a society that increasingly scrutinizes the lives of private as well as public figures.[10] In the essay "Himitsu naki katei no kōfuku" (The Happiness of a Secret-Free Family), Abe Isoo admonishes: "There is no greater Achilles' heel than having one's secret known to another [against one's will]. The one who knows the secret of another can often command life or death for that person."[11] Abe's statement implies that some risk a great deal to dig up dirt on others precisely because one can possess such a strong grip on their lives. The real-life examples listed in the article "Himitsu wo saguru no kiken to kyōmi" (The Danger and Fascination of the Pursuit of Secrets) by Yamamoto Seikichi, another contributor and a former police investigator, also articulate this idea.[12] His examples, however, are skewed in the sense that they are exclusively about instances in which his own curiosity led to the solving of various murders.

The overall organization and content of this issue of *Chūō kōron* reflect the view that regards favorably the uncovering of anything that is considered a "secret." Full disclosure of all hidden information represents a step toward a more mature democratic society, a more open diplomacy, and a more blissful private life. However, in their enthusiasm for an open, secret-free society, the writers paid little attention to how to accomplish this job of uncovering secrets, especially when the concerned parties refuse to share them with the world. The writers' admonitions and urgings are often directed at the one possessing secrets, encouraging that person or entity to volunteer the information to whatever party is entitled to know. Such appeals seem to have created slight but noticeable ripples in the realm of everyday life. Letters to advice columnists in this period often discuss the senders' dissatisfaction with their dishonest spouses who stubbornly keep silent about their past and/or current affairs.[13] The association of secret with darkness and disclosure with light may have been a powerful enough metaphor, but open discussion as the contributors of *Chūō kōron* recommended did not always prove the most effective way to get to know and understand others. When words become less effective as a tool for two-way communication, seeing is recognized as a viable method of one-way communication.

The City as a Maze

To know others, or more precisely, to identify the person next to oneself and figure out what his or her intentions are, becomes a particularly formidable task, especially in the context of Tokyo in the early twentieth century. The aforementioned cases of Taishō spouses consulting advice columnists about their spouses' past activities indicate that for two relative strangers to get married without really "knowing" each other was a common enough occurrence in this period. In addition to the traditional arranged marriage, in which a go-between introduces two parties with whom he or she is well acquainted, a new kind of "urban" arranged marriage—in which the mediator is not necessarily familiar with either party—was on the rise.

The origin of such a peculiar situation can be traced to the sudden and haphazard growth of the city in the modern period. The history of early-twentieth-century Tokyo offers a striking testimony to the futility of the Tokyo municipal government's efforts in urban "planning," as historical occurrences often superseded the rejuvenation of the capital. Japan's participation in the Sino-Japanese War and Russo-Japanese War, and the Meiji government's emphasis on building a strong national army, turned attention away from various development projects for the capital that were in the blueprint stage.[14] When the problems of overcrowding and soaring land prices commanded the government's immediate attention in the first decade of the twentieth century, the government, on both national and municipal levels, took the initiative to finally implement projects that could alleviate these problems. These improvements were completed in 1917 and included expanding and eliminating roads and rebuilding old buildings as well as constructing new ones. In the process of this redevelopment, the so-called storehouse style *(dozō zukuri)* of architecture competed with the Western style *(seiyō shiki)* to become the dominant architectural style in Tokyo.[15]

Such projects of reorganization and renewal did not, however, simplify everyday life in the capital. The result was a creation of *yōfūnite hinaru kenchiku* (Western-style architecture that is not quite Western), and city landscape that is neither completely rational nor entirely chaotic. The emergence of new and more bustling streets also meant the creation of places that occasioned crime.[16] Instead, such projects of reorganization created uncanny spaces that grew in the shadows of the city's glittering lights and were often treated in contemporary fantasy fiction as "wormholes" in the middle of the city.[17]

Tokyo was once again given a radical facelift seven years later, when the Great Kantō Earthquake struck in 1923. Nearly 150,000 people died and half of the capital burned, resulting in a drastic reshuffling of the remainder of the city's population. The residents of the eastern part of Tokyo, the hardest-hit region, typically sought refuge in the western part of the city. As the post-earthquake confusion dissipated, some of those refugees eventually went back to their native quarters, while others decided to stay in the newer neighborhoods. In addition, as the city bounced back from the destruction of the earthquake rather quickly, more new arrivals flooded in from rural areas in search of a better life. The constant influx and relocation of people further weakened such idealized images as the *edokko* (literally: child of Edo) and the closely knit traditional *shitamachi* (downtown) neighborhood.

These physical as well as social transformations reinforced the mazelike image of Tokyo and necessitated tailing as an effective way to gather information about unfamiliar faces, who do not necessarily readily announce their secrets. The business of private investigation, often called *kōshinjo* (literally: credit agency), flourished in this period.[18] Of all the records from this period, the most interesting are the fictional kind: detective fiction writers quickly worked such changes in the urban landscape into their stories and let tailing assume a central role. Kōga Saburō's "Kohaku no paipu" (The Amber Pipe; 1924) depicts the effects of the earthquake from the point of view of someone who lived through it. The story deals with a crime that was radically impacted by the earthquake. It also showcases three kinds of tailing: one that is designed to prevent a crime from taking place, one that is done out of necessity, and one that is done for sheer pleasure.

The narrator in this story, the nameless and faceless "I," is a young man yet without a wife or children. He survives the earthquake because he lived in the Yamanote area, a posh section of Tokyo that escapes the worst of the calamity. Yet, its residents face some major changes in their daily lives after the disaster. For one, witnessing the general post-earthquake confusion and the inefficacy of the existent police system in time of crisis prompts the residents to organize *jikeidan* (a self-policing unit) in order to maintain safety in their neighborhood. In contrast to the secretive tailing as described in the introduction, the system of community self-policing is a brand of tailing in which the tail lets the object of his scrutiny—namely, a potential criminal—know that he or she is being watched. The organization of such *jikeidan* aimed to prevent potential wrongdoing by imposing upon the target the psychological pressure of surveillance.[19]

In the eyes of the narrator who participates in this program, the formation of the *jikeidan* has one more important advantage:

> The most important benefit of being on night watch is being put together with people one otherwise would never have met. There used to be the so-called educated class from Yamanote who lived in secluded houses called "shells"—some as big as turban shells, some as small as clams, with strictly delineated gardens as crammed as a cat's forehead—who used to pretend not to see what was going on in the yard next door and never talked to neighbors. But they were talking to each other now because of the shared duty of the night watch.[20]

The narrator willingly embraces the unexpected gift of a closely knit community brought together by the disaster. He is also happy that there is an active exchange of information among them: "Since the patrol members in this area included people of various professions coming from various areas of Tokyo, they could now share all sorts of information freely."[21]

However, when he and his patrol mates find a murdered family of three and evidence of arson in a half-burned home, such a false sense of familiarity is brought into question. During a routine patrol, the narrator, along with two other neighbors, finds the victims in the wreckage of the burned house. Initially, a retired soldier who is one of the narrator's patrol mates, Aoki, surfaces as the prime suspect: he had been heard voicing contempt for the family because they did not participate in the *jikeidan* effort. Fukushima, the owner of the burned house, is also questioned as he had insured the property for a sizable amount. As the incident unmasks the real faces of seemingly friendly neighbors, a piece of paper with mysterious scribbles found at the murder scene takes the investigation of this case back to the days before the earthquake. Matsumoto, a young journalist new to the neighborhood, brings the paper to the attention of the police. He was also on the night-watch team with Aoki and the narrator on the night of the murders.

According to Matsumoto, the paper links the current case to an older and more bizarre case of shoplifting, as it bears the same cryptic code as the one found in the room of the accused thief, Iwami, after the incident. Once this connection is brought under consideration, the investigators find themselves confronted with three cases: the theft of a valuable diamond from Oriental Jeweler & Co., during which Iwami, then an employee, was injured; the shoplifting incident in the Ginza for which he was convicted despite never admitting it; and the current bloody murder of the Yamanote family. The first two incidents take place before the earthquake, and ironically the family in question has migrated to the area only because they were burned out of their old home.

The police prove unable to pinpoint the common thread in all three cases and arrest Iwami, although they probably will not be able to convict him. The truth is revealed at the end of the story only when the real culprit, Matsumoto, decides to confide in the narrator that he, the young and able journalist, is in fact the robber who eluded the authorities in the case of the Oriental Jeweler & Co. heist. What the authorities did not know, however, was that he fled the scene without the missing diamond, and Iwami was the one who decided to take advantage of the situation and snatched it. Iwami buried the diamond in a vacant lot, and waited for the attention on the case to die down. Matsumoto, the one the authorities are after, framed Iwami as a shoplifter as he tailed him in the Ginza. While Iwami was in prison, Matsumoto looked for the diamond, and eventually found out that it was hidden in Yamanote, though a house had been built on the lot where Iwami had hidden it. By being in limbo between the pre- and post-earthquake worlds, the former vacant lot thus works as a "wormhole" that allows the two crooks to time-travel to the pre-earthquake world. That what was an open field before the earthquake could be transformed into a residential space so quickly reflects Tokyo's changing landscape; and that a family who fled their earthquake-damaged home could become tenants of that house attests to the equally rapid relocation of the city's residents. As Iwami visited the family on the fateful night, with a box of sweets with which to drug them, the father of the family, for whom the stresses of the earthquake proved to be too much, killed his wife, who just before had killed their child. Iwami, who stumbled upon this tragedy, was caught in a struggle with the father and eventually killed him in self-defense. The house then was set on fire, either by Iwami, the father, or Matsumoto, to make the land as bare as it had been before.

The community that the narrator once recognized as close hides many secrets: an admirable veteran, an innocuous proprietor, and a refugee journalist, all have the potential to become capable of brutal murder and arson. The character of Matsumoto as both a young, pleasant neighbor, and a thief with tremendous patience and the ability to hide behind the facade of a friendly reporter, reflects the city's darkness and depth. At the end of the story, the one-time neighbor and fellow *jikeidan* comrade leaves the astonished narrator for good, with an amber pipe as a memento of their time together and proof of his tailing skill.

The outcome of the story shows how the organization of the *jikeidan*, a nonsecretive surveillance unit, falls short of another secretive kind of tailing. It is also the kind of tailing at which Matsumoto is most adept. In order to exact revenge upon Iwami by framing him as a shoplifter, Matsumoto figures him out by tailing him in the Ginza, the biggest and busiest shopping district in Tokyo. Matsumoto's conduct typifies "physical tailing," the second kind of tailing in this story, in which the tail performs the task having a definite goal in mind, in this case reading Iwami's mind, while taking the utmost care not to be noticed by the target. Matsumoto does not miss that Iwami keenly looks at a pair of cufflinks and then a watch. Matsumoto sneaks into Iwami's pocket the two items and a piece of jewelry he shoplifted in a store. As Iwami is surprised to find them in his possession, Matsumoto steals Iwami's salary envelope. Matsumoto also tails Iwami upon the latter's release from prison, predicting that he would first go to the place where he hid the diamond. As Iwami ponders how to retrieve the diamond from underneath the newly built house, Matsumoto looks for the ideal timing to get back at Iwami. Then the earthquake strikes. The destruction it brings about and the subsequent reurbanization of Tokyo give Iwami the chance to retrieve the coveted diamond and Matsumoto the perfect cover to move into the area. In the end, Matsumoto, the one who better navigated the debris-ridden capital and demonstrated finer tailing skills, wins by running away with the shiny prize.

Matsumoto shows off his skill in tailing once again at the very end of the story, though much of its description is hidden from the readers. The seemingly chance encounter between the narrator and Matsumoto at the busy Shibuya station, one of the newly developed railway hubs that was "crowded like a war zone," is not coincidence but a planned event, as Matsumoto at the end slips the narrator a letter and an amber pipe with the same dexterity he demonstrated with Iwami.[22] Compared to his earlier tailing of Iwami, the one Matsumoto performs on the narrator is far less insidious and more playful, for he follows the narrator neither to take anything away from him nor to entrap him but only to make sure that the narrator is as unsuspecting as he appears to be. The narrator's innocence assures Matsumoto that disclosing his triumphant account will not compromise his victory. Matsumoto boasts two qualities essential for a good tail: a flair for adventure and the determination not to lose sight of his prey even if the earth beneath him trembles.

Tailing for Fun: Artificial Creation of Secrets

Characters such as Matsumoto who derive pleasure from the act of tailing repeatedly appear in other works of interwar detective fiction. While the narrator of "Kohaku no paipu" seems content living an ordinary life as a bureaucrat, his fellow contemporaries are not as satisfied with their lives dominated by routine. Boredom is a common complaint found in writings from before and after the Great Kantō Earthquake, and it is a sentiment that often leads to the artificial creation of secrets and excessive self-tailing. In "Himitsu" (Secret; 1911), Tanizaki Jun'ichirō depicts a native of Tokyo who leaves his familiar surroundings to start a new life in another part of the city for no pressing reason other than sheer curiosity: "Since I love traveling, I have done a walking tour of Kyoto, Sendai, and Kyūshū. But I was convinced that there are streets within Tokyo—the city I've lived in ever since I was born in Ningyōchō [a downtown quarter] some twenty years ago—that I have not yet explored."[23] In elaborating his motivation to delve into the unknown parts of the city, he describes how "tired" he feels: "My nerves are like overused sandpaper, all dull, and only the colorful, vivid, and grotesque *(akudoi)* could excite me."[24] In the story, he rekindles a romantic relationship with an old flame, only to abandon her when the mystery of her current identity wears out once he locates their secret meeting place by revisiting the route they took in a rickshaw in broad daylight—a sort of self-tailing. The story ends with the unnamed protagonist denouncing the comfort of familiarity and safety, and yearning for the adventure of the new and dangerous even if they involve risking his life.

Other characters from other works from shortly after the earthquake repeat similar complaints. In Edogawa Ranpo's "Akai heya" (Red Chamber; 1925), the young narrator without a financial care in the world echoes the narrator of "Himitsu" in describing his boredom: "I think I am sane, and others treat me as such, but deep down I don't know if I really am. Maybe I am mad. Maybe I am not completely mad, but may be a sort of psychotic. In any case, I find this world extremely boring, and life awfully tedious."[25] In the past, he has tried out "various dissipations like a regular person," but none worked for him in the long run.[26] Gōda Saburō, the protagonist from another of Ranpo's works from the same year, "Yaneura no sanposha" (A Wanderer in the Attic; 1925) is also an avatar of the same urban youth who have more time and money than they can handle. Although his boredom ultimately leads him to murder one of his neighbors, he initially tries to dispel the intense feeling of ennui by other, more harmless means. He experiments with everything listed in the *Encyclopedia of Entertainments (Goraku hyakka zenshū),* including dressing as a woman and seducing men, but still feels an emotional void in his heart. In short, he is disappointed at all that the *modan* city has to offer; yet, he finds himself unable to abandon it and retreat to the countryside, where more intense boredom supposedly awaits.

The feeling of ennui from which the nameless narrators in "Himitsu" and "Akai heya," and Gōda Saburō in "Yaneura," suffer appears similar to the symptoms of what Georg Simmel calls "the blasé Metropolitan attitude":

> There is perhaps no psychic phenomenon which is so unconditionally reserved to the city as the blasé outlook. It is at first the consequence of those rapidly shifting stimulations of the nerves which are thrown together in all their contrasts and from which it seems to us the intensification of metropolitan intellectuality seems to be derived. . . . Just as an immoderately sensuous life makes one blasé because it stimulates the nerves to their utmost reactivity until they finally can no longer produce any reaction at all, so, less harmful stimuli, through the rapidity and the contradictoriness of their shifts, force the nerves to make such violent responses, tear them about so brutally that they exhaust their last reserves of strength and, remaining in the same milieu, do not have time for new reserves to form. This incapacity to react to new stimulations with the required amount of energy constitutes in fact that blasé attitude which every child of a large city evinces when compared with the products of the more peaceful and more stable milieu.[27]

While the conditions of urban living desensitize the inhabitants in one way or another, those who are restless and creative always manage to invent new distractions. Sometimes they even create their own secrets in order to entertain themselves. The narrator in "Himitsu" seeks solace in transvestism and frequents the men's section of the cinema, tempting other moviegoers while viewing films. Before starting to peep into his neighbors' private lives through holes in the common ceiling, Gōda Saburō, the protagonist of Ranpo's "Yaneura," takes cross-dressing a step further: he also dresses as a pauper, a laborer, as well as a student. Ultimately, bored urbanites such as those found in detective fiction all try out the same diversion: crime.[28] Peeping itself is a felony, but the best antidote to intense boredom is often murder.

The bored urbanites' prelude to murder often starts with envisioning themselves enacting the crime by projecting their gaze inward.

For instance, the intense feelings of boredom and curiosity prompt Gōda to sleep in the closet and peer in at his room from there, as if he is a robber in hiding. The peculiar setup excites him, as it gives him a false feeling that "he has become a character in detective fiction."[29] With this cue from the author that the story is taking a criminal turn, Gōda's closet becomes a seat in a theater from which he watches the vacant stage, his room, where he imagines shocking events take place before his eyes.[30] Since Gōda does not have any secrets to hide, he creates them and engages in a game of hide-and-seek with himself. It is also while engaged in this that he finds a secret passage to the attic in his closet. He lives in a new building especially designed for young unmarried men, with dozens of individual rooms offering a high degree of privacy that was unavailable in row houses *(nagaya),* a more traditional type of accommodation for young singles such as Gōda.[31] With the passage to the attic, however, Gōda has access to the private lives of his neighbors, who live thinking that they are completely sealed off from the gaze of others. The attic is one big room arching over all of the individual rooms. When he finds that the attic floor has cracks through which he can see what goes on in each room, he becomes a voyeur as well as a wanderer in the attic.

Gōda is captivated by the diverse and multifaceted lives of his neighbors. It seems as though the building structurally nurtures privacy, and its inhabitants develop distinctly different personae between inside and outside. Visually tailing his neighbors from above teaches him that a muscular college athlete behaves as effeminately as a female servant in love, an anticapitalist worker loves money, and only a wall away another man is engaged in shocking acts of sex with someone who appears to be a prostitute.[32] What excites Gōda is not what these people do but the discrepancy between how they act outside and inside their apartments. The building is designed with the protection of the tenants' privacy in mind; yet, one oddity in the very structure of the building allows Gōda to enjoy an omnipresent, godlike view of their activities.

Gōda's thrills are largely fueled by the belief that people reveal their true identities when they are alone, when they feel completely free from others scrutinizing them: "walking around in the world of darkness like a beast, and uncovering the secrets of the nearly twenty residents of this building one after the other. Saburō [Gōda] felt insurmountable pleasure just at the thought of it. He found life worth living for the first time in a long while."³³ His fascination with the sight of his neighbors in their "unwatched" state reflects the modern view of the body as "a sort of unwilled speech, an utterance whose code is in the possession of a figure of authority rather than controlled by the enunciator."³⁴ The Freudian concept of the unconscious, recently promulgated through translations, also supported the idea that the unconscious and the actions that it prompts one to perform present a no less authentic, if not more authentic, version of oneself. Perhaps the interwar urbanites keenly guarded their secrets because these theories made them feel that they were truly losing their grip on their body and subjectivity. Gōda's adventure in the attic eventually escalates from mere spying to murdering one of his neighbors—a man who posed no threat or annoyance to Gōda. His only "fault," in Gōda's eyes, was leading a completely transparent life, without secrets, his private life not differing from his public life. In his analysis of the text, the critic Matsuyama Iwao explains Gōda's seeming lack of motive as hatred for a person who failed to give Gōda excitement.³⁵ Seeing others lead double lives trains Gōda to expect them to provide him with exciting secrets, and when someone does not live up to his expectations, he creates another diversion by plotting and executing that person's murder. Gōda's actions imply the extreme length to which such individuals go to realize the desire to uncover other people's secrets, and that there is no remedy for the bored but active mind that seeks constant stimulation.

Gōda's actions after he finds the secret entrance to the attic and peeps into other residents' lives also suggest a new relationship mediated by seeing that does not confine the seer and the seen to the relationship of powerful and powerless. Contrary to Abe Isoo's prediction in *Chūō kōron* that possessing someone else's secret would lead one to abuse one's power over that person, Gōda's knowledge of other people's secrets does not necessarily prompt him to seek further gain. His viewpoint from the attic gives him a vantage point similar to that of the watchman in the middle of Jeremy Bentham's panopticon: he can see what all the prisoners do without being seen by them.³⁶ In theory, Gōda can blackmail any of the residents, as seeing puts him in a position of power over them. However, Gōda does not take advantage of the information; instead, "thinking" about the act of seeing excites him just as much as, if not more than, the nature of the secrets he witnesses. Gōda also does not forget to dress up for the occasion:

> He started with making his "wandering in the attic" even more interesting. He did not neglect to dress up like a typical criminal—body-hugging, dark brown wool shirt, matching tights—if possible, he wanted to dress all in black like the "Female Thief Purotea" that he once saw in a movie. But he possessed nothing of the sort, so he made do with what he had. He also wore *tabi* and gloves, though there was no danger of leaving behind fingerprints in the attic, as the woodwork there was still too rough. He also wanted to carry a gun, but since he couldn't get one, he made do with a flashlight.[37]

From this passage, there is little sense that Gōda's enjoyment comes from a feeling of superiority over the people he observes. Rather, his paying attention to his clothes so that they will fit the occasion suggests that he watches not only the residents under his feet but also himself as he is engaged in the act. Just as when he hides in his closet to watch his own room with the mind-set of a thief, dressing up as a criminal in a movie and acting like one gives him the sensation that he is in the world of make-believe. Being a witness to the extreme discrepancy between the inner and outer lives of his neighbors is not enough to satisfy him: for his pleasure to be complete, he has to play the part of the "wanderer in the attic" and live up to his own expectations of the scene and his secrets. The desire for supremacy over others by visual tailing takes a backseat to another desire to engage in the play of the detective-criminal while stepping back and enjoying the sight of the entire picture.

Modernology, Sherlock Holmes, and the "Tell-Tail" Story

Gōda's desire to observe others and their secrets finds another manifestation in modernology, an academic outlet for the obsession to watch. Modernology was a new field of inquiry established by Kon Wajirō (1881–1973) and Yoshida Kenkichi (1897–1982), as well as their colleagues in the days immediately following the Great Kantō Earthquake in 1923. Although the earthquake devastated many residents of the flourishing capital, for Kon and his colleagues it was a convenient, ground-clearing event that provided an opportunity to witness the regrowth of the city from the ground up.[38] Kon writes: "I would like to apply the same methodology the anthropologists use for primitive cultures to discover their special features. . . . While the cultures of primitive peoples are recorded and analyzed, the civilized peoples *(bunmeijin)* are left unstudied."[39] Prompted by Tokyo's seeming return to its primitive state through the earthquake, these urban ethnographers went quickly out onto the streets to document all facets of Tokyo's recovery and the *modan* culture that flourished there.

In contrast to archaeology, the study of the past, modernology concerned itself with the study of the present: its proponents recorded the minute details of urban life ranging from the behavioral patterns of shoppers in large department stores to the closet contents of students from out of town. Although the modernologists were made up of those who were considered "academics," it was not because of their work in modernology: Kon Wajirō, for instance, was a professor of architecture and industrial design at Waseda University by the time he undertook his study of the city in 1923. Kon's contemporaries considered modernology to exist on the fringes of serious academic work, and such an ambiguous status often worked to the modernologists' advantage as they circulated their findings in the mass media, taking such forms as cartoons and photojournalism.[40] Despite its general popularity, modernology faced two dilemmas from the beginning: one originated in the taxonomical issues of their data, and the other came from their employment of tailing as one of the main methods for data gathering—and the act's inherently pleasurable nature.

One obvious way to study urbanites and their lives is to ask them questions directly. For instance, if the topic is the behavioral patterns of female shoppers in department stores, one could gather data by interviewing them on-site. In "Geshukuzumi gakusei mochimono shirabe" (A Study of Boarding Students' Belongings) and "Shinkatei no shinamono chōsa" (An Investigation into the Domestic Property of New Families), for example, modernologists collaborated with volunteers to collect their data. At other times, however, they often preferred to observe their subjects quietly, without drawing attention to themselves.

In these reports, the modernologists' conduct overtly resembles that of detectives or tails in contemporary detective fiction. In the report "Shinjuku Mitsukoshi madamu bikōki" (An Account of Tailing a Housewife in Mitsukoshi Department Store in Shunjuku; 1927), modernologist Iwata Yoshiyuki trails behind a beautiful young woman as she enters the store on a rainy afternoon. At the beginning of the report, Iwata suggests to his readers: "Once you read my account of tailing, I am confident that you will get a rough idea of what shopping means to this woman. Everyone reveals his or her own vice, personality, character, and even economic class, when they behave unconsciously. I hope all of you reading my report reflect on your own behavior and laugh as you read my account."[41] Iwata's goal is to see on the street what Gōda saw unfold within the walls of supposedly private space: by observing the woman without her knowing and using the information her body unconsciously volunteers, he aims to discover more about her than she knows herself and possibly turn her into a consumable object of entertainment.

Iwata's methodology—certainly central to all modernologists—begs some questions about appearance and identity. Namely, does one reveal everything about oneself while unaware of being watched? Is appearance not but one facet of one's identity? At the beginning of his study, Iwata describes the woman's appearance in detail: as soon as his tailing starts, the readers are informed that she wears her hair in a bun, sports relatively heavy makeup, and drapes a Western coat over her kimono. She also carries an umbrella in her right hand, and her handbag is wrapped in a purple cloth (seemingly to keep it dry in the rain). These elements of her appearance suggest to Iwata that she is a housewife. However, as he never interviews her directly, he has no way of confirming it throughout his investigation. In fact, this forces him to recategorize his specimen: "To be honest, I had [originally] been tailing her thinking that she was an unmarried woman (*reijō*)."[42] It is only after seeing her look into the displays of pickled vegetables and meat with an air of familiarity that he concludes that she is a housewife: "At this point [as she stopped and looked at the vegetables], I was completely astounded and had to admit that she is a married woman."[43] Even after being convinced of her marital status, he remains unsure about her economic status as he witnesses her negotiate the fee for a taxi ride. Although he previously assumes that she is of the petite bourgeois intellectual class, as he takes into account the amount she bought and the way she negotiates with the taxi driver, he is more inclined to speculate that she is actually from a higher economic class.[44] As long as Iwata takes into account only the outward signs of the woman's identity, his categorization is inconclusive at best: if she had stayed in the store a little longer, and indicated visually that she is a single woman (e.g., by looking wistfully at a wedding gown display), Iwata might have swung back and speculated that she was not a married woman.

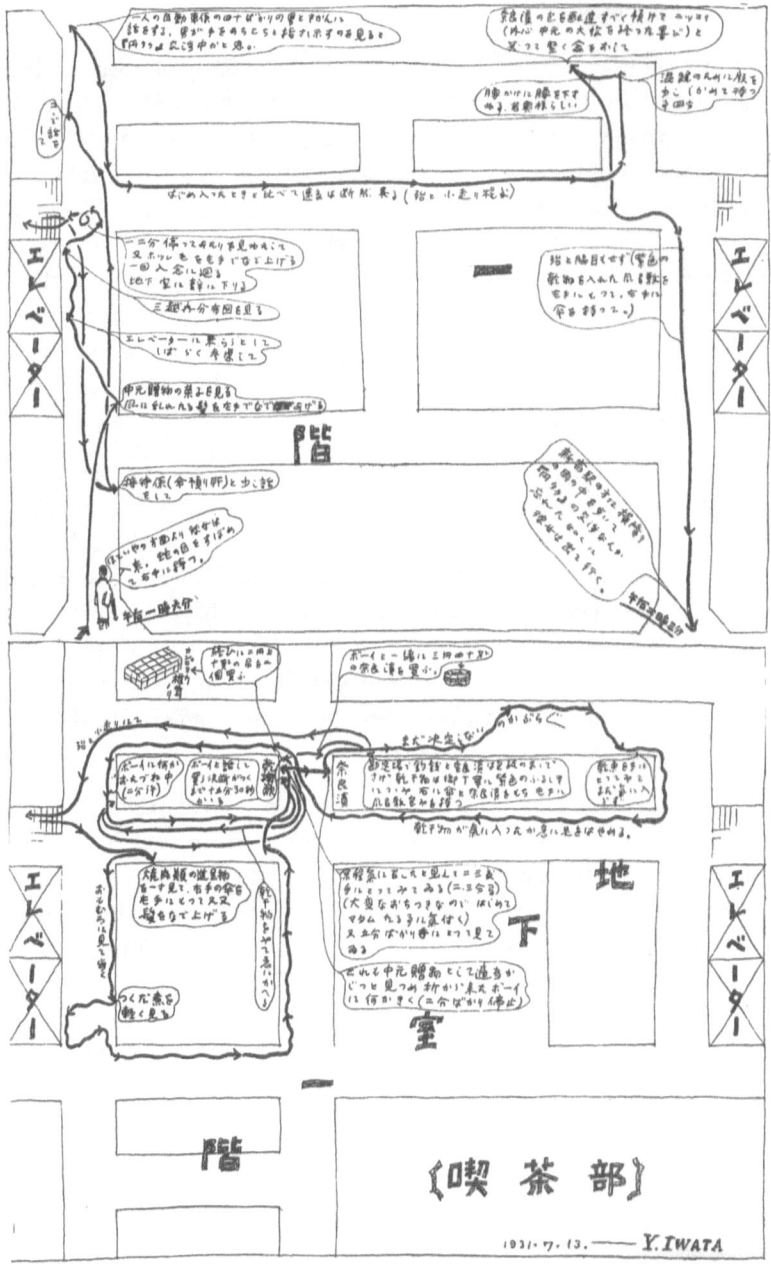

A map of a woman's shopping trip to a department store by modernologist Iwata Yoshiyuki. Iwata tails the woman in question for a little less than an hour (1:06 p.m. to 2:03 p.m.) on July 13, 1931. He drew a picture of her in this diagram (center, on left side), at the entrance of the store, and traces her movements by an arrow on the first and basement floors. Iwata, "Shinjuku Mitsukoshi madamu bikōki," 38–39.

With such an overreliance on visuality, modernologists such as Iwata stand in for the figure of the Holmesian detective, a representation that was missing from contemporary detective fiction. In attempting to figure out a person's identity and past from the visual clues he or she unconsciously displays, Iwata resembles the classic detective as embodied by Sherlock Holmes when the sleuth accurately describes Dr. Watson's recent sojourn in Afghanistan in "A Study in Scarlet" (1887).[45] This story of transatlantic revenge was available to Japanese readers through various translations by the 1920s. As Watson guesses that his new friend had been told of his recent expedition, Holmes answers:

> I *knew* you came from Afghanistan. . . . Here is a gentleman of a medical type, but with the air of a military man. Clearly an army doctor, then. He has just come from the tropics, for his face is dark, and that is not the natural tint of his skin, for his wrists are fair. He has undergone hardship and sickness, as his haggard face says clearly. His left arm has been injured. He holds it in a stiff and unnatural manner. Where in the tropics could an English army doctor have seen much hardship and got his arm wounded? Clearly in Afghanistan.[46]

The detective's success lies in his ability to process telltale visual signs of a person's identity and reconstruct them in such a way that they tell a cogent story about the person. In much the same way, the anonymous narrator in Edgar Allan Poe's "The Man of the Crowd" (1839) finds himself in a similar situation when he sees an intriguing stranger, an old man, in the crowd, and decides to follow him to figure out more about him. However, what he sees in the old man does not neatly fall into place and articulate a unified identity. After tailing the old man for a while, the narrator concludes that the old man is a master criminal who knows how to navigate the crowd and work it to his advantage. The narrator says to himself: "This old man . . . is the type and the genius of deep crime. He refuses to be alone. *He is the man of the crowd.* It will be in vain to follow; for I shall learn no more of him, nor of his deeds."[47] In this comment, the narrator acknowledges both the presence of an element of identity that escapes visual representation and the complexity of human character.

In contrast, Iwata is less willing to give up his quest to decipher, in the manner of Holmes, his object of study through her physical manifestations, perhaps because of the false encouragement from the veracity of hard data and owing to a certain misogyny that emerges here and there throughout his study. The only concrete information Iwata finds out through tailing is numerical: he records that it took this woman fifty-seven minutes to complete her shopping, twenty-three minutes and thirty seconds to browse and decide which pickled vegetables to purchase, all while stroking her hair eight times.[48] In deciphering the mystery of the woman's social identity, he processes all that he knows as stereotypical characteristics of this type of woman. Despite Iwata's confidence, however, the ultimate uncertainty of his judgment risks distorting the entire body of data and reveals to us the limit of what one can know about someone else through tailing.

Other modernologists also had a hard time resisting the same urge. Kon Wajirō and Yoshida Kenkichi, cofounders of the discipline, succumb to a similar desire in their foundational work "Tōkyō Ginzagai fūzoku kiroku" (A Record of the Customs in the Ginza, Tokyo; 1925). While this work articulates Kon and Yoshida's academic goal to record all aspects of *modan* culture as they are and honor urban diversity, they also corrupt the information that they gather when they rely too heavily on appearance in sorting out their data. When classifying the pedestrians in the Ginza, they establish categories such as men, women, students, shop assistants, laborers, children, and miscellaneous. In deciding who falls under what category, they only infer from people's clothing and never actually ask the pedestrians about their actual social status. To retain critical distance from their data, the modernologists only tail them, both visually and physically: "When men and women, the objects of our data collection, encountered us modernologists in charge, most of them took no notice of us. Among those we observed, soldiers in uniform tended to notice and turn around, and students often looked at us dubiously."[49]

Kon's method of data collection assumes that people wear not only their feelings but also their identities on their sleeves. By taking such a view on the relationship between appearance and identity, Kon risks corrupting his data at the point of the initial gathering. For instance, he purports to dissect the fashion of students and laborers and illustrate their diversity in the subsection titled "Gakusei oyobi rōdōsha no fūzoku" (The Fashions of Students and Laborers).

However, because Kon himself exercises his subjectivity—in basing his study upon his stereotypes of students and laborers—his data represent not the fashion of the actual students and laborers but those who dress like students and laborers. Classification of data posed problems for Kon from the beginning: "Before we collected this data, we wondered how to make categories. In the end, we decided to focus on the prominent features as it was our interest to have the data classifiable by all of us."[50] As Kon and his fellow modernologists visually tail their objects and make them universally classifiable data, they truncate their idiosyncrasies, which may be more significant evidence of what the individuals are really about. Iwata's study of the housewife shopping in the Ginza, carried out two years after Kon's seminal work, suffers from the same pitfall when it adopts Kon's idea of appearance and identity. Kon's descriptions in other subsections—on topics such as hairstyle, gloves, and fabrics—allow him to depict the multiplicity of urban culture and identity that is more complex than all-Western versus all-Japanese, and "shift discussion away from conceptions of alterity into acknowledgment of difference."[51] The sincerity and meticulousness in these subsections express more eloquently than anything else that Kon really cherished the diversity and complexity of urban fashion and *modan* culture. However, by focusing on deciphering and standardizing visual clues demonstrated by the urbanites, Kon inadvertently oversimplifies the data and betrays the complexity of urban culture—the very nature of city life—that attracted him to undertake the study in the first place.

The taxonomical dilemma in modernology is similar to what the pioneers of Western law enforcement faced in the nineteenth century when they developed the famous "Rogues Gallery," a collection of mug shots of delinquents. When the Western means of identification—fingerprinting, body size, facial features, for instance—were imported to Japan, methods of collection, classification, and storage became major concerns. When Ōba Shigema (1869–unknown), an expert in the field of *kojin shikibetsu* (individual identification), published *Kojin shikibetsu hō* (How to Differentiate Individuals; 1908, expanded version 1910), the compilation of his research on penal systems all over the world, he needed to explain how to take measurements and samples in detail and with illustrations, while also volunteering for a mug shot.[52]

During the late nineteenth and early twentieth centuries, both

Western and Japanese police forces were transitioning from investigative methods based on intuition and experience to those guided by science and method. The technology of fingerprinting as a tool for identification was perfected in the British colonies by a group of English scientists during the same period. The transition initially required the building of a large body of data cataloging crimes and criminals, similar to what Sherlock Holmes calls the "brain-attic," where he "stock[s] all the furniture that he is likely to use, and the rest he can put away in the lumber-room of his library, where he can get it when he wants it."[53] As soon as each case is solved, Holmes or Watson makes entries for all the parties involved in his various indexes. Their database is composed with a single audience in mind: themselves. However, as the number of potential users of such data expands, the making of a universally user-friendly system based on objective standardization becomes a pressing need. In the case of the Rogues Gallery, the idea that no two people share exactly the same physical attributes (unless they are biologically related) gave rise to the idea of storing photographic images of offenders; however, the same idea also gave them the problem of not knowing how to organize the pictures as easily retrievable information. In an attempt to

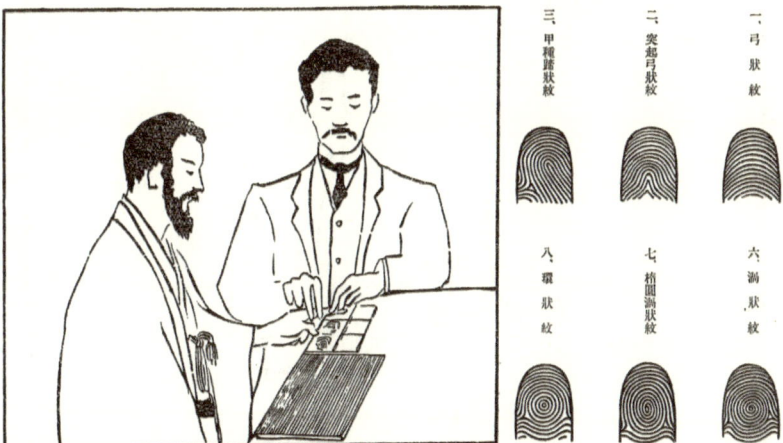

Forensic scientist Ōba Shigema categorized fingerprints into nine types, six of which are shown here. This illustration of a police officer in a Western suit fingerprinting a suspect dressed in a kimono accompanied detailed instructions on how to obtain fingerprints properly to ensure the accuracy and quality of the prints and to standardize the process. Ōba, *Kojin shikibetsu hō*, 25, 83. Courtesy of the Hōgakubu kenkyūshitsu (Law Library) at the University of Tokyo.

Following Alphonse Bertillon's method of identification, Ōba took various measurements of a suspect's body parts, such as his height. Throughout his book, officers appear in Western garb and suspects in kimono, as if to insinuate the Western origin of these identification techniques and their application to the Japanese body. Ōba, *Kojin shikibetsu hō*, 173. Courtesy of the Hōgakubu kenkyūshitsu (Law Library) at the University of Tokyo.

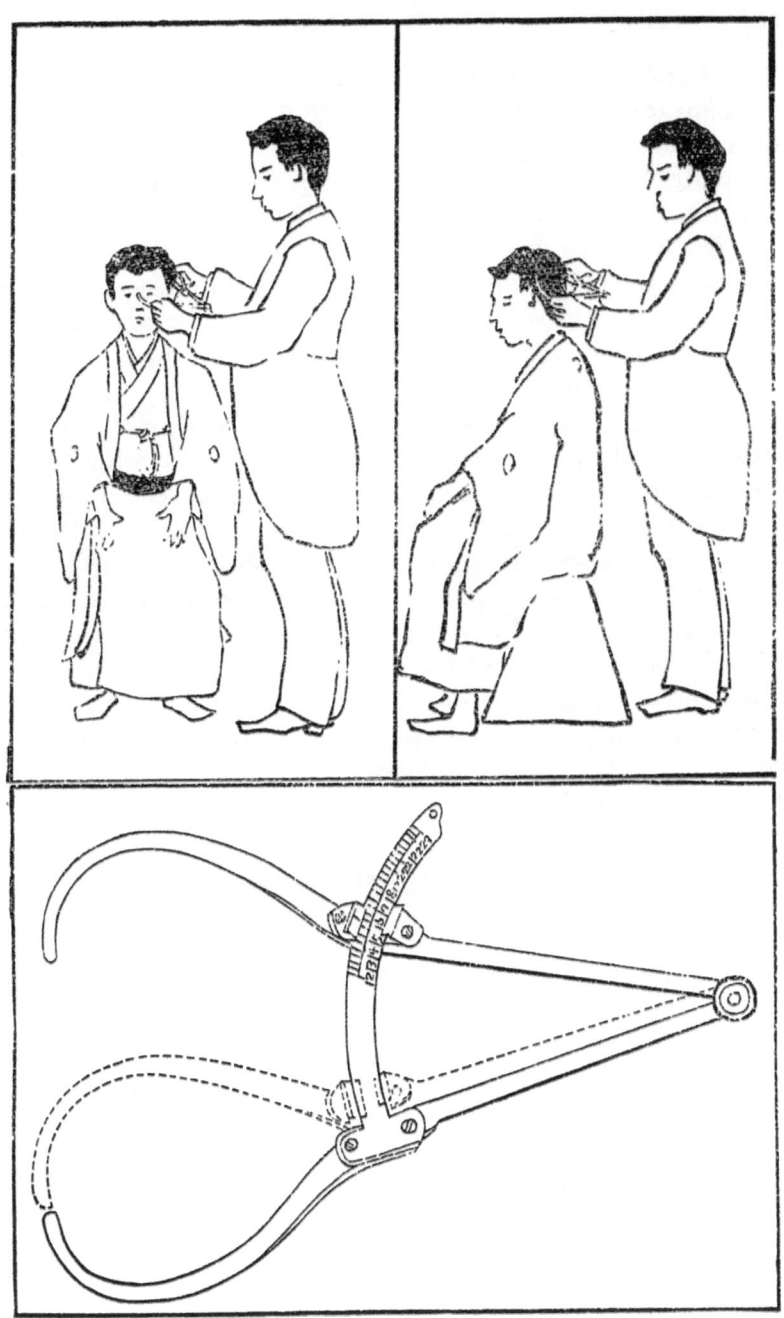

Ōba illustrates the method and device with which to measure the size of a suspect's skull. Other important measurements included sitting height, circumference of the skull, and the lengths of the right ear, left leg, left middle finger, and left pinky. Ōba, *Kojin shikibetsu hō*, 177, 178. Courtesy of the Hōgakubu kenkyūshitsu (Law Library) at the University of Tokyo.

fix this problem, the idea that the individual body is nothing more than "the realization of a limited number of measurable types"[54] justifies the authorities' establishment of classification standards so that any officer appointed to a particular case—with varying degrees of experience and intellect—can take advantage of the database. Kon's endeavor is very similar to this. When making categories, the goal of modernology of reporting the everyday life of the present for future generations seems to take precedence over faithfully recording the details of that everyday life, no matter how conflicting or insignificant they may seem.

In addition to the taxonomical dilemma, modernologists were also concerned with the excessively pleasurable aspect of their study and tailing. Their anxiety comes from not one but several sources. Over the two hours that Iwata tails the young woman, he is alarmed a few times that she has noticed him. One foreseeable consequence for him if she spots him following her is the corruption or loss of these particular data: as soon as she realizes that someone is watching her, she is likely to change her behavior accordingly. Another ramification, perhaps more serious, is to be accused of a sort of voyeurism. Although not always respected or strictly enforced, the *Keisatsu han shobatsurei* (Police Laws for Criminal Punishments) of 1908 had officially outlawed what we would now call "stalking," imposing upon the offender a maximum sentence of either thirty days in jail or a twenty-yen fine.[55] While such acts as peeping were seen as both innocuous and tolerable in earlier times, the decree recognized certain ways of seeing as not only sexual but also potentially harmful, and proscribed them. Rather than being preoccupied with the criminal aspect of his conduct in light of such laws, Iwata appears intent on visually decoding a woman whose appearance he rates "eight [out of ten]."[56] In the essay "Kōgengaku sōron" (On Modernology; 1931), Kon Wajirō confesses that he and his associates are sometimes accused of enjoying their work too much.[57] Since other modernologists never chose to undertake such studies of young housewives, it is reasonable to assume that Iwata's study was largely motivated by and carried out because of his personal interest in the topic and the woman.

Although Iwata does not make his romantic attraction to the woman explicit in his writing, another contemporary writer depicts a scene in which an individual engaged in modernological research unexpectedly encounters a sexual sight during his data-collecting session. In the short story "Kaidan" (Staircase; 1930), Unno Jūza (1897–1949) portrays a young student, Furuya, who experiences an adolescent sexual awakening when he inadvertently catches a glimpse of a female student's pale calf from underneath a staircase at a busy train station as he helps his modernologist friend study the demography of train passengers.[58] Quivering at the sight of the female student's "pert breastlike calves," Furuya articulates the sexual excitement that Iwata may have felt when the modernologist recorded "I say for certain that the color seemed to be light pink" and found not being able to know the exact color of her underwear "disappointing" *(zannen na koto ni)*.[59] While modernologists may stand on the street to record urban life with the utmost dedication to their discipline, their eyes sometimes catch things that make them forget their original mission. Ultimately, the traces of enjoyment in their works tell us more about them than anything about the objects of their gaze.

While Kon seems to laugh off the accusation of frivolity, for Yoshida Kenkichi, the other cofounder of the discipline, the criticism raises a legitimate concern. When Yoshida incorporates tailing as a method of gathering information, he exercises more caution in controlling how his study might appear. In "Ren'ai kōgengaku" (Modernology of Love), he tails six young couples on their dates. Just like Iwata, Yoshida avoids directly interviewing them, even if it means that he and his readers will forever be in the dark about the true nature of the couples' relationships: "Even if the 'boyfriend' in my study turns out not to be one, what is recorded in my study will reveal an aspect of modern love life as it unfolds."[60] One of the potential complaints Yoshida foresees is that there are more "graphic" scenes in which modern love life shows itself, implying something like outdoor sex *(gekkō wo abita ren'aiteki fūkei;* literally: "moonlit scenes of love"). To this, Yoshida simply counters by saying that "such research risks sliding into the realm of curiosity hunting" *(ryōkiteki shumi)*[61] and might cease to be the academic study that Yoshida wants to publish. What is behind his comment is his fear of an involuntary association with cultural trends such as the so-called *ero-guro-nansensu* phenomenon that favored all things erotic, grotesque, and nonsensical.[62] By making a point about his intention not to make it an *ero-guro* piece, Yoshida prioritizes one particular reading of modernology as serious scholarly research above all others. His declaration, however, also implies that his audiences were already trained through other media such as detective fiction both to look at tales of tailing as curiosity hunting and possibly derive pleasure from such accounts of tailing.

Yoshida's apprehension that his academic work would be misunderstood stands somewhat at odds with the way the modernologists, including Yoshida himself, designed their works to be consumed by readers. The modernologists try to efface their presence in the collection of the data so as not to corrupt it. However, as the urbanites acquire knowledge from their studies, the one-time objects of study are bound to reshape their self-image. This is especially true when the findings of the modernologists were made public. Most, if not all, modernologists did not exclusively target professional academics as their audience: rather, they were interested in disseminating their findings to the widest range of readers possible, and so published them in general-interest magazines with large circulations. Yoshida was no exception to this view. Kon and Yoshida's first major work on urban *modan* culture, "Tōkyō Ginzagai fūzoku kiroku" (1925), was published in the highly influential women's magazine *Fujin kōron* (Housewife's Review). In 1927, Kon and other mod-

Modernologist Yoshida Kenkichi identifies six dominant fashions from the data he previously gathered from observing couples in the Ginza. Yoshida Kenkichi, "Ren'ai moderunorojio," 56. Courtesy of Yoshida Kanoko and Shiozawa Tamae.

ernologists put on an exhibition of their works at the Kinokuniya Bookstore in Shinjuku, one of the most comprehensive bookstores in the heartland of post-earthquake urban commercial culture.

On one hand, the modernologists were aware that they needed to let their subjects—modern urbanites—act normally so that they would reveal their natural behavior; a good detective avoids leading suspects and instead observes them until they betray their true characters or intentions. However, as the modernologists dissected the city's cultural topography and disseminated their findings, they risked compromising their original intention of being faithful recorders of modern life. Although the academic aspects of their efforts required them to attach meaning to their findings, they ceased to be innocent bystanders once they engaged in such interpretation.

Such a risk is already inherent in the way readers typically consumed modernology. One way audiences may have enjoyed the subject was vicariously, by following along on the adventures of tailing that they could not participate in themselves, as their physical mobility, employment, and conscience prevented them. Or, they may have enjoyed locating themselves within the data, finding out where in the various demographic categories they fell. Kon, for one, encourages such a reading by inviting his young audiences to identify their families within his data.[63] The modernologists on the street act as a sort of a time-lapse camera: their job is to render visible what previously remained invisible or unnoticed by others. As audiences locate themselves within the data, they realize that they had been secretly watched, and according to the modernological schema of consciousness and behavior, this knowledge will affect the way audiences will act from that point on. They may look at others on the street to locate them in the data, or they may learn to police their own behavior. In this way, modernological findings shaped the urbanites' self-image from within (that is to say, by situating themselves and their findings within the culture of the city), and promulgated the "detective-like" way of seeing that had already been prevalent among them.

Although raising the self-awareness of urbanites seems to contradict the modernologist's preference for "tailing," this cultural awakening was one of the original missions of the discipline. Kon argues that "without being studied, civilized subjects take pride in their customs and in their unconsciousness and unawareness think it is absolute. I can see this attitude in people's facial expressions as they walk on the street. The unconscious collective *(muishiki na shūdan)*, the city streets and houses are filled with them. They evoke in me the feeling that 'I have to study them.'"[64] Kon's manifesto, when put in context with the methodologies used in Iwata's and Yoshida's works, reveals a contradiction within modernology: while modernology aims to make urbanites—or Tokyoites, to be precise—aware of the peculiarities of urban life and to relativize their culture through their research, the authenticity of their research relies upon the same people being unconscious and uncritical of their own behavior. Tailing works when the person who is being tailed is not aware of it: otherwise, it is only as revealing as a conventional interview, a method considered by the modernologists not as efficient as catching someone off guard.

When the modernologists resorted to tailing for data gathering, it was not without some dilemmas and internal conflicts. However, these issues did not prevent contemporary readers from being fascinated by modernology as an opportunity to look at themselves anew. As a city grew larger and its culture more complex, an attempt like modernology to render it comprehensible for its inhabitants became necessary and popular. In striving to achieve objectivity and in placing utmost confidence in the visual clues of their study materials, the modernologists best embody the faith in the outward manifestations of identity and criminality as exemplified by certain fictional detectives. They should also have known, however, that looks sometimes do not reveal everything, and that even Sherlock Holmes, the master of deciphering visual clues, falters against those who know not only the language of vision but also techniques to manipulate it. Most famously, Irene Adler in "The Scandal in Bohemia" succeeds in disguising herself as a man and defeats Holmes at the game of visual deception. The cross-dressing anonymous adventure-seeker from Tanizaki's "Himitsu" and the pleasant young journalist turned big-time robber Matsumoto from Kōga's "Kohaku no paipu" would also have been able to trick the modernologists' watchful eyes and be spared of accurate categorization if they had indeed been walking on the real streets of the Ginza. While Holmes willingly acknowledges his defeat, the interwar modernologists seem reluctant to let go of their faith in the supremacy of visuality over all other ways of cognizance, and hesitate to give up the pleasure of tailing.

Tailing the Tail, Tailing Oneself

Those who subscribed to modernology may have found pleasure in discovering themselves among the data gathered by tailing or any other methods. Similarly, Gōda and other characters who find themselves suddenly starring in a detective fiction derive pleasure from seeing themselves in the act. However, when some literary characters who become addicted to the act find their own faces on those whom they tail, their confidence in their autonomy comes tumbling down. In some cases, the consequences are significantly more serious than the corruption of data.

A man called "T," an acquaintance of the narrator in Ranpo's "Hitori futayaku" (Playing Two Roles; 1925), is another avatar of the bored urban dweller. However, unlike Gōda, who was a bachelor, T is married to a beautiful wife. But his marriage does not stop him from having extramarital relationships with other women, and his infidelity is a constant source of marital strife. Fed up with his wife's jealousy, T one day decides to catch *her* having an affair. In order to plot this, he puts on a disguise and becomes the man with whom his wife will cheat: "I'm sure everyone feels this, but if you spy on your wife interacting [sexually] with another man, it must feel strange."[65] T goes to tremendous lengths just to experience this unknown but promisingly enticing sensation. One night, he puts on the disguise and sleeps with his wife. As he departs in the morning, he leaves behind a cigarette case with different initials from his, indicating another owner. The next morning, his wife is surprised to find it and realizes that the man she slept with the night before was not her husband, but she says nothing about it.

T continues this bizarre affair in which his wife does not seem to realize the true identity of the stranger. His curiosity is satisfied, but eventually he finds himself with a new predicament: the wife falls in love with the stranger and out of love with T. The narrator asks: "What used to be fake jealousy is now becoming genuine, if one can call his [T's] feelings such. His jealousy had no target. Who is he jealous of? The wife kept herself pure of any other man's touch. T is his own rival in love."[66] T, the original, competes with his double, a supposed reproduction of himself, in order to win his wife's affection, and it is the copy who is in the lead. Although T originally intended to spy on his wife's sexuality when she takes a different partner, the situation eventually forces him to reveal more about the dynamics of his own lust than hers: "Although he used to take little notice of his wife's beauty, now he finds her the most attractive woman in the world. Thinking that someone has stolen her from him (though it is actually himself), he feels insurmountable envy. His wife gazes wistfully into the distance, and he thinks that she is thinking about her lover. He is consumed with envy. He has done irrecoverable damage. He is ensnared by the trap he himself set up."[67] It is a trap, but a sweet one nonetheless, as the incident allows him to renew his interest in his wife. By assuming a different identity and a new point of view, T is able to find his wife attractive. Looking at her is not exciting enough; he has to play voyeur and tail to feel aroused, even if the object of his gaze remains the same.

His jealousy eventually elevates to a point where he abandons his original identity by leaving his wife, getting minor plastic surgery, and coming back to play the role of the stranger permanently. He is no longer in control of his tailing: the act of tailing has taken over his life, and the rival, created only to be tailed, chases T out of the scene. In doing so, T plays out what René Girard describes in *Deceit, Desire, and the Novel*: "The desire according to the Other is always the desire to be the Other. There is only single metaphysical desire but the particular desires which concretize this primordial desire vary ad infinitum."[68] In choosing to abolish his original identity and assume the new one completely, T becomes the "other," from whose position he can enjoy the setup of his previous life.

Copying someone else's role is also what T's wife learns in order to become and stay the coveted object in this triangle of desire. At the end of the story, when the narrator runs into the couple years later, T reveals that his wife had actually always known that it was all her husband's doing. T says to the narrator: "I thought I deceived her well, but it was I who had been deceived all along. She told me that she realized my prank right from the start, but decided to play along as it was harmless and rather helped our marriage. I thought it went too well."[69] T's wife is aware of the mimetic nature of her husband's desire and works it to her advantage. Her knowledge of its dynamic also allows her to keep an eye on her husband—something she was unable to do before—while he indulges in extramarital philandering. As T and his wife make love, he spies on both her and his rival, and from the latter he learns how to love his wife. At the same time, his wife learns through tailing him visually and sensually how to manage his contorted desire without ever leaving home. In addition to illustrating the difficulty of marriage, the perverse love life of T and his wife lets us catch a glimpse of the disintegration of the subjective viewpoint. For bored urbanites in interwar Tokyo, the "I" refuses to be confined to one viewpoint, as such a confinement only intensifies his (or her) boredom. To stimulate and satisfy their desensitized senses, they first need to externalize their desire and sensation.

But such tampering with the idea of the self sometimes brings devastating consequences when the externalized part takes on another identity and a mind of its own. Despite the double extramarital affairs and lack of conjugal communication, this story of mimetic desire has a happy ending: T succeeds in becoming the other, and he and his wife become a self-contained unit of love. However, another tailing aficionado from Ranpo's 1930 story "Ryōki no hate" (Beyond the Bizarre) is not as blessed in his marriage. Aoki Ainosuke is a young man bitten by the boredom bug in a manner similar to Gōda and T: Aoki's family inheritance made him rich enough not to work, and the most beautiful woman he had ever met became his wife three years earlier. He seeks strong stimulation of all kinds in his life—culinary, carnal, and cultural—but nothing alleviates his deep feeling of ennui. Although he is based in the provincial city of Nagoya, he keeps another house in Tokyo and regularly visits Shinagawa Shirō, a close friend from university days who is now a successful businessman in the capital.

One afternoon, Aoki strolls alone through a crowded festival held in one of the major shrines of Tokyo, hoping to get some cheap thrills from the freak shows—a dying culture but nonetheless a fixture at local fairs. However, Aoki spots something more exciting in the crowd: his square friend Shinagawa, who would frown upon such tasteless spectacles from the past. Intrigued, Aoki decides to follow his friend, supposedly to catch him at the most awkward moment possible. As Aoki tails Shinagawa, he whispers to himself: "Looks like he's doing his share of curiosity hunting. He must've kept it a secret even from me because it is an embarrassing taste. You usually admonish me, friend, but we're just the same."[70] Aoki smiles to himself, because he feels that he has discovered his friend's weakness, and the feeling of dominance grows as he visually figures out his friend. As Aoki tails Shinagawa, he sees his friend enjoy a horse show and an acrobatic performance under the big top, both considered lowly entertainments. At one point, Aoki sees Shinagawa hide something behind a bush. No longer able to contain his urge to pop in front of his friend and see the look of surprise on his face, Aoki decides to greet him. However, the man Aoki was tailing vehemently denies that he is Shinagawa. Dumbfounded and still suspicious, Aoki goes back to the bush where the man hid something, and finds six wallets. They are telltale evidence of the man's, and possibly his friend's, shocking identity: a pickpocket.

Later on in the story, some movie footage accidentally confirms that the pickpocket at the festival is not Shinagawa. He is only a look-alike. While the discovery excites Aoki, as the mission of finding the pickpocket again distracts him from his chronic boredom, Shinagawa is not as thrilled at the thought:

> "You [Aoki] can remain carefree about this, but for me it's such an annoyance. Think, there is one more person just like me somewhere in the world. It's a horrible feeling. I'd want to beat him to death if I ever meet him. There's something more frightening. According to you, he's a criminal. Picking someone's pocket is a petty offense, but what if he commits something more serious, like murder? I look just like him, so I'm not entirely immune to some mix-up. I can neither stop his crime nor predict it. What if I don't have an alibi? It's really scary if you think about it. We don't know who he is, and that makes it scary. In addition, we also have to think about the following scenario. I may not know him, but he may know me. My picture is printed in my magazine, and he is more likely to recognize me than I him. . . . When a criminal finds someone who looks just like him, imagine what sort of horrendous schemes he comes up with! Can you imagine? If I had a wife, it would be easy for him to steal her from me, too."[71]

The threat of being made a cuckold by one's double is a real one, as T from "Hitori futayaku" would be quick to point out. However, as Shinagawa himself mentions, he is a single man. In addition, even if Shinagawa's worst fear comes true and his double indeed commits a grave crime like murder, there were some technologies available in this period that could exonerate him. The texts on criminal science written by professionals for the general public, such as Ōba Shigema's *Kojin shikibetsu hō* and some works of detective fiction such as "Shimon" (The Fingerprint; 1918) by Satō Haruo (1892–1964), informed their audiences that fingerprints could be used to implicate the criminal as well as acquit an innocent party.[72] However, fingerprints are not as easily recognizable as facial features; although they might be able to ultimately prove Shinagawa's innocence in a court of law, they cannot protect his reputation as a public figure during and after the trial. What he is worried about is a sort of identity theft, in which someone else posing as him usurps his identity and reputation to commit crimes. Although the victim may be able to clear his or her name in the end, it will be a messy process. Seeing one's double completely independent of oneself inevitably leads to a fundamentally disturbing question of identity and existence: who is the real Shinagawa Shirō, he or I?

Shinagawa's concern reaches a new height when Aoki succeeds in locating Shinagawa's double in a seedy flophouse in a residential area of Tokyo, and invites Shinagawa to meet him there. While strolling in the Ginza, Aoki encounters a mysterious gentleman turned pimp who eventually takes him to this shack. The location and the structure of the house situate it in line with other "uncanny spaces" that also appear in the pre–Great Kantō Earthquake writings of Tanizaki Jun'ichirō and Satō Haruo. Just like the seedy shack to which the nameless protagonist of Tanizaki's "Himitsu" is taken by his lover, and the house at the end of a cul-de-sac to which the protagonist of Satō's "Roji no oku" (In the Alleyway) is drawn, the house Aoki visits serves as yet another "wormhole" through which visitors can escape to a parallel world that is creepier and more exciting than the one in which they live. These spaces exist within the parameters of the familiar and everyday, but often lock away secrets behind an impregnable facade. From the outside, the structure to which Aoki is taken is just another traditional *hiraya* (one-story house) standing in a quiet part of Tokyo; inside, the house has a hidden attic in which affluent and lustful lovers can engage in casual trysts. The arrangement has an appeal even to Aoki's dry sense of fun:

> "I get it, I get it. Someone must have added this secret room. Great idea. Looking from outside, it is a regular one-story building, so as long as the authorities find nothing wrong downstairs, they would never find out anything that goes on in the loft. No one would ever dream that there is a windowless room in the attic."[73]

But being one of the sexual participants in the secret room is not exciting enough for Aoki, who developed a taste for voyeurism from his habit of tailing: he proposes to the mistress that he peep on others' escapades through a hole from next door. In his preference for voyeurism over participation in actual sex, Aoki resembles Gōda and T, for whom the eye is the primary erogenous organ. Aoki invades the bedroom retaining the gaze of the tail: "The experience of having shaken with fear in the darkness is well worth the twenty-five yen I paid. Look at the elaborate structure of the house. It's straight out of detective fiction."[74] The secret makes the forgettable flophouse a crucial prop in Aoki's imaginary adventure, in which he plays a different character from himself. Just as for Gōda it takes the relocation of his viewpoint from the middle of the room to the closet to become a "character in a detective story," Aoki needs to change his role from the party engaged in the sexual act to the party who watches others engaged in it in order to experience the most intense sensation of pleasure. The latter position, though indirect, allows him to assume not one but two roles in this bizarre performance.

Aoki's little adventure takes a wild turn when he finds out that Shinagawa's double also frequents the same house. Aoki proposes to Shinagawa that they together observe the double and his conduct. Ironically, to carry out this mission, the real Shinagawa is forced to wear a disguise with tinted glasses and a fake moustache. The elaborate disguise pays off, as Shinagawa's double treats them to a fantastic spectacle that is beyond belief: unlike the real Shinagawa, unmarried and with a reputation as a stick in the mud, the double turns out to be a stallion; he plays a horse for his one-night lover and engages in hard-core sadomasochism with her.

Shocked, Shinagawa is unable to watch the entire episode, as he is tormented by the striking resemblance between himself and the man whose most intimate moments are laid bare in front of his eyes. However, the resemblance does not appear to be the only source of concern for him. After all, his double is not engaged in anything illegal per se: his partner, though perverse and violent, appears to enjoy her time with Shinagawa's double. Throughout the story, Shinagawa is described as Aoki's moral foil—serious, square, and career-oriented.

The seeming emphasis on Shinagawa's moral character also appears to be an attempt to make him a person free of secrets, the most powerful kind of being in a society where digging up dirt on private as well as public figures was a fact of life. But can he really be free from vice? The diffusion of the psychoanalytical view of the unconscious gave everyone reasons to watch their conduct. Behind the seeming proliferation and diversification of entertainment, the outlets for more sinister kinds of desire, such as sadomasochism or homicidal impulses, became increasingly limited in this period. The question of how to control such desires was a pending one for interwar urbanites: peeping into public bathhouses, a seemingly harmless act of everyday life in earlier times, is now seen not only as a misdemeanor but also as a preliminary step to a more serious crime such as rape or murder. Many of the first-person narratives of crime from the same period attest to this belief, the best example of which is the priest in Watanabe Keisuke's "Sei akuma" (Saint Devil), who uses the diary in which he chronicles his demonic fantasies as a safety valve to release his pent-up desires. Drawing on Dorothy E. Sayers's theory on the cathartic effect of detective fiction, Ranpo discusses in the 1933 essay "Tantei shōsetsu to katarushisu" (Detective Fiction and Catharsis) the function of detective fiction as a vehicle for readers to unleash their "antisocial desires" and vicariously enjoy committing crimes "in order to keep a healthy mind-set."[75] Before resorting to tailing or crime, Ranpo's boredom-stricken characters, including Gōda Saburō, experiment with reading detective fiction to alleviate their ennui.

Shinagawa, however, is neither bored nor in need of a cathartic remedy such as detective fiction. Exactly how he had been taking care of his antisocial desires is not told in the story, but no matter what he was doing, it successfully kept him in check and allowed him to maintain the facade and identity of a balanced, socially adjusted businessman. If, unlike Aoki, Shinagawa had been the type who took pride in being able to control his unconscious desires and appear "normal," which it seems he was, witnessing his double perform the horrendous acts of perverse sex would have been devastating. Not only do his efforts to keep the monster in the closet end in vain, it is as bad as if he had actually been engaged in the acts he thinks his society condemns. People can hardly control the unconscious when it is part of them: how can Shinagawa possibly control his unconscious when it takes a body of its own? Unlike T, Shinagawa is not inspired to learn from his double how to indulge in his deviant sexual acts. While his double may be able to affect his life, Shinagawa is not able to influence or control his double's conduct. When Shinagawa later accidentally receives an amorous letter in his double's place, it announces the merging of their identities: "It is clearly a love letter from a married woman to Shinagawa Shirō. [Shinagawa speaks:] 'I have no idea who this woman is. But it is surely addressed to me. *I* am having an affair with some married woman.'"[76]

His friend Aoki, however, looks at the scene a little differently. For him, the spectacle entails not only witnessing his friend's lookalike lose himself in his hard-core sexual antics but also seeing his otherwise very together friend tremble in fear: "Dr. Jekyll and Mr. Hyde! Shinagawa Shirō might be a businessman serious to a fault, but maybe a devil resides in his heart and takes him over once in a while, as a kind of Mr. Hyde."[77] Although Aoki knows that the two are completely different individuals, he indulges in the fantasy that his friend leads a double life. The conflation of the lives of Shinagawa and his double, although false, will create "secrets" for his otherwise faultless friend and make him vulnerable to moral critique.

The story itself, which the author later admitted was written in a nonchalant and unsystematic manner, eventually disintegrates into a hodgepodge tale of tailing: Aoki starts to suspect that his beautiful wife is also part of the flophouse sex ring and is having an affair with either Shinagawa or his double, or both.[78] As with T and his wife in "Hitori futayaku," the imagined presence of another man in their marriage makes his wife more desirable to Aoki: "He was consumed with jealousy. He found his wife more and more attractive. Though she is a harlot, he knew she was beautiful. The fact that he was tailing her as a detective tailing a thief excited his flair for the bizarre. He found tailing a kind of sexual act."[79] For Aoki, tailing is no longer foreplay that leads to fulfilling sex but an act that replaces actual intercourse.

The story ends with the somewhat nonsensical revelation that a mad scientist, overconfident in the automatic omnipotence and ethics of science, manufactured the doubles of Shinagawa and others by plastic surgery.[80] For those who are willing to allow Ranpo certain artistic responsibility and conscience, the ending steers the story toward science fiction, a genre that existed adjacent to detective fiction or even overlapped with it at times. The figure of the "mad" scientist intoxicated with power clearly exists beyond the ordinary idea of what is possible, and betrays the supposed fairness in detective fiction as put forth by S. S. Van Dine and Ronald A. Knox.[81] The hastily put together whodunit also appears to be nothing more than a desperate attempt of a time-pressed author to meet the deadline and satisfy his editor. Behind the carelessly inserted temporary conclusion, the real solution to the quandary of city life—what to do when one finds one's double—remains unanswered.

Urbanization and the Depth of Reality

An urbanized city, a natural disaster, a new academic discipline, and a burlesque house—all erased the relationship between the past and the present, oneself and the surrounding world. The job of the detective in such a world is to magically reclaim this relationship, but his task is constantly undermined by the arbitrariness of events and the limits of his perspective.[82] Only upon the successful completion of this task, just as Matsumoto in "Kohaku no paipu" is able to navigate the city both before and after the earthquake, can one gain the coveted prize. On the other hand, the dilemmas of the modernologists best attest to the difficulty of this task, and reveal how, in the context of the city, reality is nothing but an amalgam of an infinite number of these incidents and interventions, where nothing is what it appears to be.

Reality gains depth not only when the city develops physical complexity through urban growth but also when the modern subject develops a case of extreme self-awareness in response to the opaqueness of daily existence.[83] Such heightened self-consciousness necessitates an externalization of one's desire in order for one to feel pleasure. The complexity of urban life makes a chance encounter between an urbanite and his double possible, but what makes the city dweller see himself in the stranger is his self-consciousness that has been trained to objectify his own body and desire. What he discovers, however, is not always pleasant: as he plays spectator to his own body, he finds that his physical identity now hosts multiple, previously unknown layers of desire. In the process, his own body becomes just as mysterious as the city. Shinagawa is horrified at the sight of "himself," not only because his double is lecherous and perverse, but also because he witnesses that a part of him—his hidden, repressed desire—now belongs to a different reality, a different system of representation in which he has no option but to be submerged in a shared identity with his double. When Shinagawa disguises himself in order to observe his double, or when he receives a love letter addressed to his double, such a merging is gradually taking place. In these stories, tailing is a dangerous act precisely because it is a technique that drags the tail more and more deeply into a world where the satisfaction of omniscience is denied while giving him an indelible thrill and the impression that his actions render the world more comprehensible.

What emerges from the analyses of these literary works and modernological reports is not only an image of people addicted to tailing but also one of people who are overwhelmed by the conditions of urban living and who are willing to believe that the physical attributes of others reflect their inner character. But such a misconception—that appearance corresponds to content—is constantly disproved in the face of the abyssal darkness of the city.

2. Eyeing the Privates: Sexuality as Motive

Cutting up Beauties

In Edogawa Ranpo's 1930 work "Majutsushi" (The Magician), Hanazono Yōko, the daughter of a wealthy business owner, is kidnapped by a crazed killer. As amateur detective Tamamura Jirō, her fiancé, searches for her, he stumbles upon a bizarre show in a little theater:

> The tuxedo-clad emcee came on stage and delivered the prologue: "The next act is the most popular one of our troupe, a wondrous magic trick, something our leader learned while in Europe, the magic of taking apart a beauty *(bijin kaitai jutsu)*. Our leader will cut up a beautiful woman, her arms, legs, and neck, then put them back together and revive her. She will smile to you after dying once. This is the magic of taking apart a beauty." . . . And the dismembering of the nude doll began. The clown with a smiling mask struck a blow downward on to her thigh with his broadsword. Bright red blood spewed out. One leg of the beautiful girl rolled forward on the stage. A hint of a groan from her gagged mouth. There is no way for a doll to groan. There must be someone behind the curtain doing her voice—Jirō thought so to himself, and jumped with astonishment. Oh no, he said to himself, that body, that voice, everything about that nude doll resembles Hanazono Yōko.[1]

Jirō's worst fear is later confirmed when he finds out that what he thought was a nude doll is indeed his beloved Yōko. By the deranged killer's elaborate scheme, he is made to witness his lover's horrendous execution.

What is even more horrendous, however, is that she was not the only young woman who met this fate in this era. This chapter examines fictional as well as real images of female victims and killers, the two dominant modes in which interwar Japanese women could be involved in crimes. Focusing on the instances of intersection between the discourses of crime, sexuality, and gender reveals how women sought to rise to the position of the subject—most prominently as detective or killer—in these discourses. As detective fiction secured its position as the most popular genre among the readers of modern urban literature during the 1920s, a curious pattern was starting to appear. In stories by Ranpo and other popular detective fiction writers, beautiful young women were not only slaughtered but also dismembered, with their body parts showcased in Ginza department store displays or used as stage props in theater performances. The *moga* (short for "modern girl"), the new representation of the young urban female consumer much like American flappers, often were the deranged killers' preferred targets of attack.

To trace the depiction of women in interwar detective fiction is also to chronicle the *moga*'s struggle to escape the position of the victim in the killing. Through seemingly frivolous acts of *oshare* (stylishness), romance, and murder, this heroine of Japanese interwar *modan* culture sought to exercise her subjectivity and define her own existence within the confines of her body and everyday life. *Modan* life—in the forms of industrialization, universal education, and capitalism—took her out of the confines of the home onto the streets, only to be watched, stalked, and killed. In a society where people were starting to recognize the danger of being seen, the *moga,* owing to her visibility, occupied a precarious position. Her fear was real, as the sinister spectacle of dismemberment continued well into the 1930s. The violent acts did not stay within the realm of the imagination. On the streets of cities throughout Japan, people were terrified by the reports of gory crimes of dismemberment that would make even Hannibal Lecter flinch: in 1932, a dismembered male corpse was found in a sewer pipe in Tamanoi, an area in Tokyo known for unlicensed prostitution; in the same year, a severed arm of a woman and her headless torso were found in a barn in Nagoya.[2] Urban dwellers' anxiety was heightened as fiction imitated reality

Three *moga* strolling the Ginza. From "Machikado no kindaishoku: Hard to Please Occidental Sisters—The Modern Girls of Japan," *Asahi Graph*, June 8, 1927. Reproduced by permission of Asahi Shinbun.

and reality fiction. Whenever these incidents occurred and official investigations by the police became stalled, detective fiction writers were consulted by the newspapers as experts on grotesque crimes and were asked to speculate on the criminal's identity. The dominant contemporary cultural trend of the city was *ero-guro-nansensu* (commonly abbreviated as *ero-guro*), and the bodies of young women were certainly the preferred props to express the *ero* part.

Found alongside tales of slaughtered women are criminology texts that warned male readers about the dangers of deviant women and prescribed for women how they could become deviant. These writings vividly reflect this hodgepodge state of crime narrative. Faced with the gloomy outlook of urban life, the experts on criminal science, criminologists in particular, were asked to act as "detectives" who could answer not only the old question of whodunit but also the more complicated question of whydunit. In an attempt to solve the riddle, many criminologists revisited older Western as well as Japanese theories of deviancy and ended up focusing their theories upon female offenders and abnormalizing their sexuality. Such writings, indistinguishable from pornography at times, make the clumsiness of their endeavor most apparent. By unduly concentrating their attention on sexuality, this pseudoscientific discourse deemed women irrational, unaware, and overly sexual, possessing a "natural" inclination to commit crimes.

These attempts met with skepticism from some creators of detective fiction, another group concerned with the motivations behind criminal behavior. The middle and final sections of this chapter examine how detective fiction explored other ways in which women could rise to the position of the subject in the killing, as well as how a real tale of a notorious murderess was fictionalized in order to both question and fit the theories of female criminality put forth by contemporary criminologists. Two works in particular, Edogawa Ranpo's "Injū" (Beast in the Shadow; 1928) and Hamao Shirō's "Satsujinki" (Murderous Devil; 1931), showcase how the genre, perhaps closest to the science of crime, turned the findings of these criminologists upside down and transformed them into fodder for fiction. These authors played with preconceived notions of female criminality, sexuality, and genre conventions in order to write stories that extended beyond the confines of fiction.

The convergence of the discourses on sexuality and criminality reached a new level by the appearance of Abe Sada in the media in

1936. When the story of this good-looking ex-prostitute, ex-*jokyū* (café waitress), and ex–kept woman who murdered her lover and severed his penis made it to the news, her case became a real-life crime mystery in which all readers could participate. The media reports on her case, her own testimony, and her lawyer's defense at the trial all elucidate how the discourses on sexuality and criminality merged in the gaze projected upon her body that wished to fictionalize her case and her life to fit the preexisting mold of female criminal rather than alter that mold with her emergence. The discourse of women as immature, uncontainable beings helped reduce Sada's jail sentence; however, the court's adoption of this stereotype undermined her personal quest to become a killing *moga,* and women's overall struggle to murder someone on their own terms.

In addition to examining depictions of women in a particular literary genre in a certain social setting, this chapter also aims to uncover the dynamics of the merging of reality and fiction. At the first glance, fiction and reality seem to be engaged in a fruitful relationship of cohabitation: for instance, criminologists openly discuss using detective fiction as a source of information, and writers turn to scientific writings of crime for inspiration. However, tracing their interactions also allows us to see how, within this symbiosis, some authors generate instances of subversion and tension by creating characters who do not fit the preexistent criminological mold of female killers, and real-life female killers attempted to break away from this mold.

In the quotation at the beginning of this chapter, we witnessed a horrendous murder. Fortunately, the killer is uncovered at the end of the text by an able sleuth. What has been left unfinished, however, is to identify what was *really* being dismembered in the form of women's bodies in this scene and others similar to it. Answering this question will require us to play the role of private eye and examine how professionals of crime, be they detective fiction writers or criminologists, engaged in the activity of "eyeing the privates" to weave the discourse of criminality.

Moga Corpses for Sale: From Shopping to Chopping

The diversity of writings and imaging of women—ranging from active and beautiful to dead and chopped up—raises some interesting questions: Why did such graphic images of the female body emerge in the period when women are said to have taken a modest but steady step toward political as well as financial independence? How could they coexist, and, more important, how were they connected? Although Edogawa Ranpo, perhaps the most famous detective fiction writer of his generation, is known to have written many stories in which killers routinely dismember their victims, he repeatedly experienced creative conflict when writing such works.[3] His sinister spectacles always found a loyal readership, however, and many of his gruesome stories became popular movies.[4] The correlation between the arrival of women in the public arena and male anxiety has often been pointed out,[5] but little of what lies beyond this ungrounded anxiety has been discovered or even speculated upon.

The popularity of his works becomes even more perplexing when put in context with the emergence of the *moga*, a new image of women in the public arena. Known for her signature cropped hair and flowing Western dress, the *moga* was a widespread cultural phenomenon, and her youthful likeness was reproduced in all facets of modern life, ranging from department store walls and subway stations, down to little things like matchbox covers. However, she rarely turned up full of life in detective fiction. In the supposedly fictional world that exists parallel to reality, people find more than they bargain for in department stores. In "Issun bōshi" (Tom Thumb) from 1926, the killer advertises his crime by sending one arm of his victim, a young woman from a wealthy family, to her home and displays another as part of a doll in a Ginza department store.

Written a few years later, "Mōjū" (Blind Beast; 1931) also features a serial killer, a blind sculptor who is obsessed with making a statue of absolute beauty out of the body parts of real women. Seven succumb to his demonic scheme before its completion, and the lifestyles of the first three victims overlap with conventional images of *moga*: an actress from an Asakusa revue show, a café owner, and a young widow with a flair for adventure. After being killed, their bodies are dismembered and used in a series of grisly public displays: they become stage props, parts of a nude doll at a Ginza intersection, and unlikely weights for advertising balloons. Just like the mannequins placed in show windows, the body parts of the sculptor's victims function as the perfect showcase for the idea of crime for all to see.

But perhaps we find the archenemy of the *moga* in "Kumo otoko" (Spider Man; 1930), the master criminal in Ranpo's story of the same title. During the day, he poses as handicapped criminologist

Kuroyanagi; but by night, he is a blood-sucking serial killer who collects women's corpses. Unlike Ranpo's other killers, who hunt down their prey, Spider Man lures them to his lair by placing fake job ads in the paper. He rents a temporary office and posts: "A female clerk wanted. Seventeen to eighteen years old, charming lady to work as the receptionist of an art dealer. Competitive salary. Please come between hours three to five o'clock in the afternoon. Y-town, Inagaki Art Dealer in Kantō Building."[6] He is thoroughly familiar with the psychology of aspiring *moga:* as young women were still discouraged from working outside home in some circles, he knows that the *moga* responding to his ad would likely be coming in for their interviews without informing their families so that they can present their employment as a fait accompli. True to *moga* form, the first victim, Satomi Yoshie, a young woman with a strong aspiration for financial independence, does not tell her family of her appointment. Her silence ultimately causes her demise and delays the investigation of her disappearance. It is indicative of the difficulty women such as Yoshie faced in this period: as Spider Man knows, victims of violent crime, once raped, are unlikely to make the incident public. By the end of the evening, Yoshie is raped, murdered, and cut into pieces. Spider Man would kill two more *moga* before detective Akechi Kogorō finally captures him. As in the case of the Blind Beast, all Spider Man's victims are displayed in places of high visibility: in an aquarium tank, at a magic show, as models at pharmacies. Spider Man, in describing the purpose of his mission, quotes Thomas De Quincey and his famous essay "On Murder Considered as One of the Fine Arts": "Murder is art. . . . Young beautiful women are materials for my art."[7] Just as in the case of the Blind Beast's statue of absolute female beauty, the body parts of the Spider Man's victims serve as tools of self-expression for a deranged artist.

Why did such a dreadful scene of violence win so much popular fascination? For some insight, we can turn to Michel Foucault's theory of visuality and discipline in his discussion of public torture from *Discipline and Punish*. Through a spectacular recounting of the execution of Damiens the regicide, Foucault outlines the transition in Europe from a society of public execution to one of constant surveillance. For him, this step is neither forward nor backward: in the former, one is not watched at all but risks being ripped apart once one commits a "crime"; in the latter, one is constantly watched, but there is no prospect of horrendous torture or punishment even if one is accused of wrongdoing.[8] Although Japan followed a path very different from that of the West in pursuing modernity, it witnessed during the Meiji and Taishō periods a similar transition from violent execution to constant surveillance. Examining the visual images of *moga* and detective fiction suggests, however, that the *moga* got the worst of this deal: for them, operating in the public arena of modern life meant making themselves subject to intense public scrutiny. In addition, in the world of detective fiction they also faced the danger of being chopped up and subjected to ostentatious displays of violence usually reserved for premodern criminals. Probably the most famous of all so-called *dokufu* or "poison women"—morally corrupt women whose vices include murder (of men who get in their way)—Takahashi Oden (1848–79) was beheaded for killing a well-respected merchant three years earlier.[9] Her execution was extremely public: "The public knew how she sat, what she wore, her executioner's charm, and a dozen other details recounted through the eyes of a number of writers." Although this sort of spectacle may have been eradicated by the 1920s, the experience and training of deriving pleasure from such sight are likely to have lingered. Or, perhaps *moga* being repeatedly chopped up is one of the instances in which premodern "monsters," as Gerald Figal would put it, reared their ugly heads in the modern era when the Meiji suppression of the unsightly and backward eased.[10] These dismemberments may be fictional, but they figure prominently in *modan* culture. The gory acts performed by Ranpo's killers using dismembered body parts seem to have struck a chord with readers who felt a nostalgia for the thrills and chills of public violence of the past.

Equally "split" is the conventional and historical definition of *moga*, for the term has been applied to at least two very different historical figures.[11] One of these might be called the "shopping *moga*," an upper-class woman with disposable financial resources made available to her by a close male, usually a relative or patron. Her novelty lies in her up-to-date sense of fashion and ability to indulge in capricious escapades. The other is "working *moga*," a gainfully employed urban woman. Unmarried but sexually active, she earned her own living. While the latter did not enjoy as much idealized visual representation as the former, the actual number of shopping *moga* was minuscule compared to the working *moga*.[12] The shopping *moga* is the female heir to the culture of the post–World War I economic boom, whereas her working counterpart inherited much from the tradition of "new woman" *(atarashii onna)*, an image promulgated earlier by *Blue Stockings* magazine and leftist brochures. Their difference lies in their economic interests and life goals, and these things change according to a number of social, economic, and personal factors.

Yet, these two kinds of women were eventually meshed together in the course of interwar history by two forces: commercial design and the media. They prescribed for both types of *moga* what they should be rather than what they were, while showing others how to look at them. This gaze projected upon women's body can be described as "male" in the sense that it objectified women and confined their bodies in their femaleness.[13] Though this particular way of seeing is gendered in this case, a further analysis of Ranpo's works will reveal that one need not be biologically male to subscribe to such a view.

Alternatively, the gaze in question here may be close to what Benjamin called "the outcome of its (the collective consciousness's) dream visions" in his *Arcades Project*.[14] Benjamin's conception of the mass fantasy finds another articulation in Kitada Akihiro's study of advertisements, and my own treatment of interwar advertisements owes its theoretical framework to both of them. Building onto Benjamin's idea, Kitada argues that in the context of interwar Japan, advertisements existed in a space that was neither inside nor outside: in modernity, the subjects all are thrown into the space where the boundaries between outside and inside, advertisements and nonadvertisements, commodity and noncommodity are erased or blurred at best.[15] Kitada asks a crucial question in analyzing the advertisements as texts: "Do we ever scrutinize advertisements in our real life and analyze them? Rather, isn't it as if we never look at them seriously as to make sense of the advertisements, but we nonetheless find ourselves drawn into the world which they create as a whole?"[16] An advertisement first enters a person's consciousness as he or she is in the state of *Zerstreuung*, or "distraction" (as translated by Geoffrey Hartman), and serves as a "hypnotist's wake up call" announcing the subject's entrance to the world of *jibutsu*, or things, where consumers' vague fantasies are concretized as commodities.[17]

Some advertisements, however, perpetuate the state of *Zerstreuung* for the looker. This is especially true if they evoke associations between this state of distraction and the promoted commodity, as well as between the promise of sexual gratification and the endorser of the commodity. Advertisements for alcoholic beverages are good examples of this. In some of the most popular ads, women's bodies are used as endorsement tools in order to arouse consumers' commodity fetishism. Although drinking was a widespread stress-relieving activity among interwar Japanese women, the use of women as endorsers, and the selection of young and beautiful women in particular, seem to assume a predominantly male audience.

In one of the most famous advertisements in this period, a poster for Akadama port wine designed by Kataoka Toshirō (1882–1945), a nude woman coyly smiles at the audience.[18] The primary product for sale here supposedly is the wine she is holding. However, it is not clear from the woman's sexually inviting facial expression and nudity whether it is the wine or the woman's body that is available for enjoyment.[19] Similarly, in Machida Ryūyō's poster for Union Beer, the *jokyū*, an avatar of working *moga*, carries a bottle of beer to her customers upstairs.[20] She is likely to sell her sexual charm to entice her customers to drink as much as possible, as was routine for *jokyū*, who lived off not a fixed salary but their customer tips. In a similar vein, a poster for Kabuto beer, Union Beer's competitor, shows a woman standing at a distance from a table full of foreigners.[21] It is not clear whether this woman is one of the guests or a waitress taking a break, but in either case her exposed left and soon-to-be-exposed right arms evoke sexuality before thirst. The promoted product appears only at a distance. A tasty-looking beer could not sell itself; it had to be accompanied by an attractive woman who looked just as tasty. Although several contemporary literary texts as well as real-life biographical accounts from contemporary women show that alcohol was a pleasure enjoyed by both sexes, the overt adoption of the male gaze in these posters not only neglects women as potential customers but also confines them to a position that is neither that of producer nor that of consumer but rather an endorser or, if she is dead, endorsement tool.

As with posters with attractive women promoting alcoholic beverages, the choice of physically pleasing women on the part of killers and advertising executives certainly implies the main target audience as heterosexual male. One of Ranpo's works, though, suggests that one need to not be a man to be affected by such blatantly sexual visuality. In the 1934 work "Yōchū" (Mysterious Worm), beautiful women are again in danger. The three victims in this story are the reigning Miss Tokyo, a movie star, and a rising violinist, the three

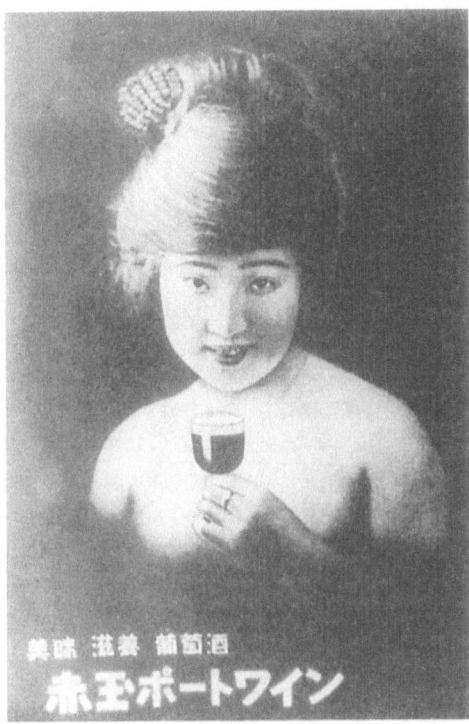

Poster for Akadama Port Wine (1922). This advertisement by Kotobukiya (the precursor of Suntory) was one of the first to use a young model in a suggestive pose to promote a product. Courtesy of Mainichi Shinbunsha.

most beautiful women in the capital. In the midst of fear following warnings that they are in danger, we see Tamako, Miss Tokyo, unexpectedly adopt the killer's gaze projected onto her. As she takes a bath at home, she is mesmerized by the beauty of her own nude body: "How can the human body be so beautiful?"[22] She also fondly remembers when a photo of her that she had no recollection of anyone taking mysteriously appeared in a magazine. As she washes herself, she stands in front of a mirror, next to a window, fascinated by the shadows and curves that her body creates. In her fantasy, she talks to the killer: "Mr. Blue-Glasses (as he was called by the authorities), do you really fancy my body?"[23] She then oscillates between being hopelessly attracted to her own body and blushing from having such a thought. Just like Gōda in Ranpo's "Yaneura," who dressed up for his part as a detective-voyeur even though he was not to be seen, Tamako accepts her part as an attractive young woman in someone else's fantasy and, though hesitantly, finds delight in that role.

In her adolescent narcissism, Tamako resembles the *shōjo* (girl), the postwar Japanese girl whom Jennifer Robertson deems "not-quite-female female" with her heterosexual inexperience but homosexual experience.[24] Building on this image of *shōjo,* John W. Treat explains that she is "presumably homosexual because the emotional life of the *shōjo* is essentially narcissistic in that it is self-referential, and self-referential as long as the *shōjo* is not employed productively in the sexual and capitalist economies."[25] Tamako at the time of the bath scene fits Treat's definition of *shōjo,* and her reliance on her governess, Tonomura Kyōko, also suggests the validity of Robertson's suspicion of her homosexual experience.

Tamako's days as *shōjo,* however, are numbered, as the male gaze is mixed with her more narcissistic gaze and forces her to enter both sexual and capitalist systems of exchange. As Tamako is intoxicated with the curves of her blossoming body, the embodiment of *shōjo* grace, another person watches her from the window: the man with the Blue Glasses himself. Tamako's fate is sealed when she, though unconsciously, allows herself to adopt his gaze upon her as her own. Soon afterward, her body is put on view in a shop window in the Ginza as a mannequin, for everyone to admire.[26]

If Ranpo had ended his story there, "Yōchū" would have been a mere adaptation of his earlier works. What makes "Yōchū" more than a mere rehash is the originality in the identity of the killer. While killers in his earlier works have all been male, in this story Ranpo gives this glamorous task to a woman: Tonomura Kyōko, Tamako's former governess. After her arrest, she confesses that she had been treated unfairly because of her physical repulsiveness, and the trauma caused by it prompted her to attack beautiful women and gather everyone in Tokyo in front of the store window where she placed victims' bodies.[27] By saying so, she implies that a one-dimensional view of women triggered the murders, as it was unjustly imposed on her. Her twisted reaction to that imposition, however, suggests that she too seems to have learned to judge people by their appearance, just like the people who wronged her. Kyōko has internalized the male gaze in an inverted way: rather than destroying the value system that tormented her, she derives pleasure from tearing up what that system values and shocking its proponents by putting women's remains on display. Just as the Blind Beast wished to create a statue embodying absolute female beauty, and Spider Man desired to make a gallery graced by forty-nine beautiful women, Kyōko aims to create a work of art that reflects her own suffering through the suffering of others: "Although it was illogical, her [Kyōko's] enemy was all beautiful women. She was obsessed with the idea of the total eradication of all beautiful women from the face of the earth."[28] With Kyōko, we see the danger of objectifying women reach a new level: murder and dismemberment of women becomes a routine for a killer to follow, even in the absence of concrete logic to back up his or her actions. Self-expression using female corpses becomes an acceptable mode of communication for someone who considers him- or herself a kind of avant-garde artist.[29]

For women who previously lived in the domestic sphere, relegated to the shadow of men's achievements, seizing every opportunity to gain visibility in the public arena was certainly important. However, there was much harm in being seen in one way and one way only. The killer reconstructed the female victim's identity, without any input on her part but just as he saw her. The images of female corpses in Ranpo's works highlight the danger of not being able to control one's own image in the city, where sometimes appearance is the only facet of identity that can be recognized. The grisly tales of dismemberment work as a sort of X-ray view of the fanciful advertisements featuring the *moga:* they are designed to function as metaphors that reflect larger societal trends, hidden cultural dynamics, and reality. The fanciful image of the *moga* and her corpse in detective fiction were two sides of the same coin. For *moga,* being cast as an actress in the play of modern life was enjoyable, but when consumerism forced everyone, including the *moga,* to equate the female body with commodity, there was no way she could buy the power to command her own image without costing herself an arm and a leg.

Discourse on Female Criminality

Detective fiction writers were by no means always satisfied with serving as mirrors of society. The relationship between a number of detective fiction writers and scientists of crime best articulates this point. As Ranpo experimented with a female serial killer who kills women, another group interested in women who kill, criminologists, explored the motivations and methods of female killers. Inheriting concepts such as Cesare Lombroso's "criminal type" and Richard von Krafft-Ebing's "abnormal sexuality," this group sought the answer to whydunit as well as whodunit by analyzing the bodily traits of female offenders.[30]

As discussed in chapter 1, Japanese criminologists—influenced by theories of Western criminology, sexology, and psychoanalysis—disseminated the idea that a certain urge to see (to peep on someone or stalk someone) should be considered a pathological symptom of abnormal sexuality and a legal deviance. In consequence, certain ways of seeing that compromise the object's privacy and status were being outlawed or came under state regulation. The right to spy on others and eye their privates became a privilege reserved for those authorized by the state: doctors and criminologists.[31] Often assuming the air of "experts," these scientists of crime fabricated discourses of sexuality and criminality that permeated interwar Japanese society with a certain credibility. They represented a new group of people who did not "cut up" women in the same way as deranged killers but were entitled to "cut open" their bodies. For them, the female body represented one of the last fortresses of premodern superstition, irrationality, and excess.[32]

Such a way of thinking about the female body had some precursors as early as the first few decades in the Meiji period. The account from the bizarre autopsy of a "poison woman" or a *dokufu*, provides clues as to how women's bodies, particularly their private parts, were observed in order to fabricate the discourse on their sexuality and criminality in later decades. Their findings were often published in mass general interest magazines such as *Kingu* (King) and *Shinseinen* (New Youth), as well as in professional medical journals, and were avidly read, as these writings often bordered on pulp rather than scholarly writing.

Some detective fiction writers recognized this popular fascination and turned the tables on everyone by inverting the perceived notion of female sexuality and criminality. While criminologists labeled female criminals (and to a certain extent all women) irrational and incapable of reasoning, two leading detective fiction writers let their female characters turn these dangerous qualities to their advantage in tricking their male competitors. Two characters created by Edogawa Ranpo and Hamao Shirō, in "Injū" (Beast in the Shadow) and "Satsujinki" (Murderous Devil), respectively, mislead male detectives by playing with preconceived notions of women and female criminality.

Serialized in 1928, "Injū" was one of the most popular stories ever published in *Shinseinen*, the most popular magazine for *mobo* (short for "modern boys," the male counterparts of *moga*).[33] In this story, the defiant female protagonist and killer, Oyamada Shizuko, manipulates the male fabrication of female sexuality and criminality to divert attention from herself. While Kyōko in "Yōchū" remained in relative obscurity until the end of the story, Shizuko occupies the central position throughout. Ranpo is one of the writers particularly known to peruse scientific writings on crime for material, be they texts on forensic science, investigative techniques, or criminology. He did not allow his creative work to be a mere reworking of scholarly theories, however. As we shall see, his "Injū" hosts more plays on theories of female offenders than faithful reiterations. Shizuko is matched with Samukawa, a detective fiction writer turned real-life detective, whose professional trade includes reading texts on perverse psychology. Their intellectual battle works as a microcosm of a gender war in contemporary criminology.

In "Satsujinki," Fujieda Shintarō, a usually capable private eye, loses sight of the real killer when he falsely suspects Akikawa Hiroko, the young woman who came to him for help when a vengeful killer set his eyes on her family. Written three years after the publication of "Injū" and at the height of so-called detective fiction debates *(tantei shōsetsu ronsō)* that erupted throughout the genre, "Satsujinki" plays with both the conventional notion of female offenders and Ranpo's character Shizuko. Both stories function as commentaries on contemporary criminology that has reduced women to being only capable of committing crimes of passion. The two texts offer instances of subversion as well as proof against the view of unilateral influence between fiction and reality in which reality not only inspires fiction but also dictates it.

The modern myth of women's criminality that Ranpo and Hamao tackle seems to have its origin in Takahashi Oden's autopsy held in early Meiji. Immediately following her execution, her body was taken to the hospital affiliated with the Metropolitan Police Office *(Keishichō)* and dissected by an army surgeon and three regular doctors. Some accounts of this autopsy reveal that these doctors focused their attention on Oden's genitalia during the procedure. Her bizarre autopsy is said to have been prompted by a newly emerging field of study called *zōkaki ron,* roughly "the study of (re)productive organs."[34] A cross between sheer superstition and legitimate study of anatomy, *zōkaki ron* was getting much scholarly as well as popular attention as one of the branches of science recently introduced from the West. After the autopsy, the primary operating surgeon, Osanai Ken (1848–85), made the following report on Oden: "Abnormal thickness and swelling of the labia minor. Over-development of clitoris. Enlargement of vagina."[35] For Osanai—a skilled physician who is credited with having performed the first operation in Japan with chloroform and even makes an appearance in *Shibue Chūsai* (1916), a novel by Mori Ōgai (1862–1922) about a doctor of Chinese medicine in late Edo period Japan—such physical abnormalities explained Oden's violent nature: after all, she ruthlessly slit her victim's throat and left him in a pool of his own blood, and it took several blows for the authorities to execute her as she kicked and screamed in resistance.

However, while Osanai found physical evidence that seems to correspond to Oden's "abnormal" psychology, another witness to her autopsy, the assistant army surgeon Takada Tadayoshi, found contradictions between various preconceived notions of her body and what he saw: "Since she had such an active sexual life, I imagined her to have a polyp somewhere, but there was no such thing. . . . When we cut her stomach open, since she was such a bold, daring woman, we expected her to have a gigantic gallbladder. But, I remember that it was not much bigger than that of a regular person."[36]

The scandalized reports of her autopsy made newspaper headlines, creating a media frenzy.[37] As reflected in Takada's perplexity (or disappointment) and the autopsy's popular reception, the revelations about Oden's autopsy caused the Meiji populace more confusion than clarification on the mystery of female deviancy. Their confusion reached its peak when they learned that the doctors also bottled Oden's genitalia after the autopsy. The infamous jar was rumored to have been collected in the University of Tokyo hospital.[38] While the court determined that Oden's crimes, robbery and murder, were financially motivated, the early generation of would-be criminologists turned her case into a tale of wild female sexuality. In *fuwake* (dissection) in the Edo period, criminals' bodies were given to doctors for educational purposes. Oden's autopsy was carried out because the authorities believed that they could find in her body a deeper reason for her criminality than determined by the court. The contemporary Meiji fervor for science and faith in rationality prompted the doctors, perhaps the front line of Meiji Enlightenment thinking, to cut Oden open in a more drastic way than that in which she cut her victim's throat. What they generated from Oden's body, however, was not a clear answer to her criminality but a discourse that established a loose connection between the physical characteristics of one's body and one's actions. Although Oden carried out her crime with finesse, even masquerading as the victim's wife to delay the discovery of the crime, the autopsy disqualified her from having a brain capable of planning and self-control. The Meiji doctors, precursors of modern detectives, chose to eye her privates, and by doing so deprived her and other female criminals of motivations more complex than sexual desire.

The overemphasis on gender and sexuality in Oden's case, however misdirected, became a trend in Japanese criminology in the following decades. In 1916, Terada Seiichi published *Fujin to hanzai* (Women and Crime), a monograph dedicated to the topic of female criminality. His study resembles an annotated list of comprehensive factors that push women to criminal deeds, including general items such as social, economic, and psychological factors, as well as miscellaneous and minute things such as season, alcohol consumption, regional superstition, and physical appearance. His book is written from the perspective that women have an innate criminal tendency different from men's and that their criminality can be explained through tangible elements. For that reason, he appears deductive rather than inductive, ignoring facts that do not fit his preconception and making a nondelinquent woman seem nothing short of a miracle.

This deductive tone lived on beyond Terada. Fifty years after Oden's autopsy and fourteen years after Terada's book was published, another criminologist, Nozoe Atsuyoshi (dates unknown), still discussed women in similar terms. In 1930, he declared: "To men, women's sexual desire remained an enigma, something unknowable. This 'secret' evoked sexual charm and lust. This enigma called 'women' is now solved by criminology."[39] He opened his *Josei to hanzai* (Women and Crime) with a blunt statement: "The psychology of a female offender is tightly connected with her physiognomy" and went on to argue that menstruation stimulates women's imagination and criminal inclination.[40] Nozoe's text is filled with pejorative statements about women: he holds women responsible for their lack of objectivity,[41] deceitfulness,[42] and excess sexuality.[43] Because of a woman's status as a sexual being, menstruation, pregnancy, and menopause are all potential crime triggers for the female criminal. According to Nozoe, women are more suited to petty crimes such as gambling and tax evasion, though at their most evil they certainly are capable of murder.[44] The absence of female philosophers, according to Nozoe, is not evidence that they had been excluded from that particular branch of knowledge but is simply a reflection of their inability to comprehend things objectively.[45]

In the second half of his book, Nozoe attempts to support his theories with rich case studies of women with deviant sexuality and criminal tendencies drawn from Western as well as Japanese sources. It is also the part where one sees traces of heavy censorship. The sections titled "Crimes of Indecency" *(waisetsu zai)*, "Unnatural Acts, Illegal Relationships" *(fushizen na kōi, fuhōnaru kankei)*, and "Perverse Instincts" *(hentaiteki honnō)* are filled with long omissions and blanks as the censors found many details of his examples unprintable. Sometimes, his sentences are so heavily censored that they cease to mean anything. "Perverse Instincts" presents the case report on a certain forty-five-year-old middle-class woman: "She really loved X at home. This X would jump onto her XXX and XXX, and like XXX. She would pet the belly of this X on her XXX until it XXX, and then she would lean against a chair and XXX, XXX, XXX."[46] In addition to such heavy censorship, Nozoe's deductive view of woman, with its utter misogyny, is even more surprising considering that his text was part of *Hanzai kagaku zenshū* (Complete Works of Criminal Science), a prestigious fifteen-volume anthology on the science of crime. The list of authors for this anthology included Takada Giichirō (dates unknown), Furuhata Tanamoto (1891–1975), Kominami Mataichirō (dates unknown)—a veritable who's who of the field. Nozoe's work shows the proximity not only of discourses of criminality and sexuality but also of pornography and certain branches of science.

Prejudiced criminologists like Nozoe represent a different kind of threat to women from deranged killers: they do not necessarily kill women, but instead portray them as inherently dangerous potential killers. For criminologists who believed in the sexual origin of human criminality, women represented what the Enlightenment—both Meiji and Western—could not change: that rational thinking and the hopeful view of progress passed through their bodies without ever affecting ("correcting") them. Women's bodies aroused anxiety because they are painful reminders of the limits of Enlightenment thinking.

Both bigotry and violence are equally detrimental to all women aspiring to be something more than accessories to male self-expression

女性と犯罪

女性と×××××は、クラフト・エービングに従ふと、×との××だけに限られてゐる。マシユカに依ると、巴里の或る秘密なクラブで、そこの女達が入場料を拂つた好色家連中の前に現はれる。そして、よく馴らされた×××××と××するのである。

これは四五年前の實例で、名は特に秘して置くが、或る中流家庭の四十五歳になる既婚女が、次のやうな事を自白した。即ち、彼女が、「自分の家の×に對する可愛さの熱情が非常に烈しかつた。この×は彼女の×××間に飛び込んで、彼女を××、こんな工合にして×××××。彼女はこの×を自分の×××××××、×××××××するまでその腹を撫でて遣り、それから彼女自身は身を椅子の凭れに投げ掛け、××××××××××、××××××××××××××、×××

或る女は×××××××、そのため二三年經つた後、精神病院で死んでしまつた。

又或る下女があつて、この下女は××××××××、××、××××××××。これを行ふために、彼女は×××。

— 348 —

A typical page from *Josei to hanzai* by Nozoe Atsuyoshi. The strings of Xs show how heavily the text was censored. Nozoe, *Josei to hanzai*, 348.

and foils to male intellect. Such women eventually found allies in detective fiction. As Ranpo described the ways in which the game of visual tailing presents danger to women, he also used his writing as an arena in which he could seek ways for women to turn to their advantage the preconceptions imposed on them. Whereas Meiji doctors and Taishō-Shōwa criminologists disqualified Oden and later female offenders from being capable of planning and executing complex crimes, Ranpo allows his female protagonist Shizuko to be precisely that in "Injū." She is a truly "modern" criminal in the sense that she neither copies men nor improvises through "feelings" in her transgressions: she is aware of the preconceived notions of her gender and knows how to turn them on their head in order to cover her culpability.

In the course of the story, we see that this content young wife of a well-respected industrialist is able not only to plan his murder but also to carry it out with impeccable precision. One day, while strolling the galleries of the Imperial Museum in Ueno, the narrator Samukawa meets a beautiful young woman, Oyamada Shizuko. Shizuko recognizes Samukawa's face, as she is a fan of his detective stories. As they nurture their friendship, Shizuko confides in Samukawa a concern regarding Hirata Ichirō, an old lover who holds a grudge against her. Hirata is also supposed to be the same person as Ōe Shundei, a detective fiction writer with a taste for cruelty who is a rival to Samukawa. Shizuko claims that Hirata has been watching her every move, even when she is at home. As she receives some letters confirming Shundei's presence within her house, her husband, Rokurō, a wealthy businessman, is found dead in the Sumida River wearing a wig. After a careful investigation, Samukawa concludes that Shundei is the only possible culprit. As Samukawa carries out this investigation, Shizuko starts a clandestine affair with him. Samukawa breaks off this liaison, however, when he realizes that Shizuko is the real killer. Although Shizuko's eventual suicide temporarily convinces him of the accuracy of his conclusion, the story ends with Samukawa living in torment as he suspects that he might have falsely accused her and driven her to take her own life.

Such open-endedness makes the theory that points to Shizuko as the murderer one of the strongest, but not absolutely so. It is known that Edogawa Ranpo intentionally left his story that way, despite pressure from his editors.[47] By doing so, he proposed a riddle to two parties: readers (detectives outside the story) and Samukawa (within the story).

One of the lengthiest and most elaborate preparations Shizuko has to complete before the murder is the concoction of Ōe Shundei, a mysterious detective fiction writer, renting a room and writing stories under his name. Samukawa describes Shundei as possessing a penchant for narrating stories from the criminal's point of view, however graphic and shocking it may be.[48] Writing detective fiction, and being successful at it, implies Shizuko's familiarity with the conventions of the genre. The rivalry between Shizuko and Samukawa starts before the murder of Shizuko's husband, when they were both writing detective fiction. Samukawa confesses that he always became jealous when Shundei received more praise than he did: "To tell the truth, every time his [Shundei's] works received praise, I felt indescribable jealousy. I felt childlike antagonism. I constantly wished to outsmart him no matter how."[49] The choice of Samukawa as her confidant, lover, and ultimately rival seems a logical one for Shizuko, who takes pleasure in the game of crime through her intellect and sexuality. For Shizuko, writing detective fiction served as a kind of practice for plotting an actual crime.[50] In contrast to the dismembered female victims in Ranpo's other stories, Shizuko exercises her subjectivity in shaping her masquerade and disguising her true intentions.

Shizuko uses Shundei not only as a cover to lay out her fantasies but also to divert suspicion from herself and give credence to her concerns. In order to convey the urgency and vulnerability of her situation, she shows to the narrator one of Shundei's threatening notes, in which Shundei chronicles the intimate details of her daily life. In contemporary psychoanalytical terms, Shundei manifests the tendencies of scopophilia, or voyeurism: it is a sign not only of perverse sexuality but also of criminal tendencies. Shundei writes: "Ever since I found you again, I've been following you like a shadow. You can never see me, but I watch you at home, outside, without a minute of interruption. . . . I may be watching you tremble with fear, from a corner with squinted eyes."[51] Shundei sees without being seen. As in Ranpo's other works, for a woman to be watched secretly is a prelude to her imminent death. By painting Shundei as a voyeur and using the established cliché of the genre, Shizuko can insinuate to the narrator that she is in danger without having to produce material evidence.

In concocting the persona of Shundei, Ranpo incorporates his real works and reputation in the story. Just like Ranpo, Shundei likes to stroll in Asakusa, sometimes wearing a disguise. In addition, the names and content of the works that Shundei supposedly has written all make obvious allusions to Ranpo's works. Shundei's "Yaneura no yūgi" (Playing in the Attic) evokes Ranpo's "Yaneura no sanposha" (A Wanderer in the Attic); "Issen dōka" (One-Sen Copper Coin) alludes to Ranpo's debut work, "Nisen dōka" (Two-Sen Copper Coin); "Panorama kuni" (Land of Panorama) sounds awfully close to "Panorama tō kidan" (A Strange Tale from the Island of Panorama). These titles mean little within the story, but they serve as red herrings for learned readers who take into account information outside the text in figuring out the whodunit.[52]

The text extends itself beyond the realm of fiction in more than one way. Texts of criminology, forensic science, and investigative methods as well as casebooks were important as sources of inspiration for detective fiction writers and as tools to make their fiction more authentic and realistic. In "Injū," Ranpo lets Samukawa use the case study from a real text on criminal investigation written by Nanba Mokusaburō, one of the leading authorities in the field on a par with the authors of the aforementioned *Hanzai kagaku zenshū*, if not even more prestigious. Samukawa says: "One day, I remembered a case in Nanba Mokusaburō's *Saishin hanzai sōsasho* that was very similar to this case (the death of Shizuko's husband, Rokurō). I often turn to this book for inspiration to write my own detective fiction, so that's why I remembered an individual case inside."[53] The comparison between his case and Nanba's case, however, enlightens Samukawa only to falsely rule Rokurō's death an accident.[54] In the same way that detective fiction writers read texts written by professional crime fighters to make their stories more credible, professional crime fighters read detective fiction for real-life knowledge. Kashida Tadami published *Hanzai sōsa hen* in 1936, as part of the anthology *Bōhan kagaku zenshū* (Complete Works of the Science of Crime Prevention). To keep themselves abreast of crime and investigation techniques, Kashida recommends that his students read detective fiction:

> Famous detective fiction pieces—especially the Western ones—are often based on reality and imbued with the newest scientific knowledge, so they are good guidebooks for investigators. What you find

in these books can be applied later to actual cases similar to them. I read Conan Doyle as a student, and learned a great deal from his main detective Sherlock Holmes.[55]

As the communication between tales of fictional crimes and reports of real crimes becomes frequent, and the discrepancy between intended and actual consumptions widens, the contours of the genre start to fade. Fiction about crime and the science of crime reinforce each other: the former comes to help in the fight against inventive criminals, while the latter can provide literary inspiration.

The relationship between detective fiction and scientific writings on crime did not always remain cooperative, however. Ranpo further overturns the contemporary criminological discourse on women by making Shizuko emphasize her psychological as well as physical frailty to Samukawa through the revelation of Shizuko's inclination for masochism. Looking pale and fragile, she embodies delicate beauty when Samukawa meets her the first time: "All the lines of her face—eyebrows, nose, neckline, and shoulder—suggested delicate gracefulness."[56] In contrast to her overall physical appearance, Samukawa also sees a bright red welt on the nape of Shizuko's neck. He finds it startlingly mismatched, but does not directly question her about it. He discovers where it came from after the death of Rokurō, when she invites him into a sadomasochist sexual relationship with her. As Samukawa discovers the passive nature of Shizuko's sexuality, he feels an "insurmountable desire" *(kokoro no taegataki nayamashisa)* to whip her.[57] As she draws Samukawa into the pleasure of sadomasochistic sex, he soon starts to "take mysterious pleasure in whipping her delicate body and seeing red welts rise on her pale skin."[58] Although Samukawa plays the more active role in their union, he seems to be the one losing his grip on his sexuality.

Shizuko's use of her sexuality as a weapon to make her opponent lose his foothold serves as a critique of the prevalent view of female sexuality and masochism. The early Taishō criminologist Terada describes masochism as an extension of normal female sexuality: "Since women assume the passive role in a sexual relationship, masochism is most often observed among women, while rare among men."[59] At the same time, contemporary criminology suggests that all crimes are sexually motivated, and a faulty extension of that theory is that a person of passive sexuality is not likely to be an aggressor in a crime. Allowing Samukawa to know her sexually gives him the illusion that he had witnessed a truth about her and female sexuality: "For the first time in my life, I thoroughly tasted the violence and the fierceness of a woman's passion. Shizuko and I returned to our carefree childhood, and ran through the large, haunted houselike shack as if we were two hunting dogs entangled in each other."[60] As Shizuko emphasizes the doubly passive nature of her sexuality (she is a woman and a masochist) and literally allows him complete access to her body, she implies that she is not an aggressor and has nothing to hide.

Samukawa gets one chance to crack the case open, however, and he uses that chance. After a passionate lovemaking session, it hits Samukawa that despite his earlier conclusion, Shizuko is the real killer. Curiously, the theory of Shizuko as the killer comes to Samukawa when his unconscious takes over and draws him into a daydream *(hakuchūmu)*. As he points the finger at her, he tries to confine her in her gender: "Some time ago, some critic called Shundei's works filled with skepticism unique to women, that his works were like shadow beasts moving in darkness. I now know that this critic was right."[61] Being a faithful student of contemporary perverse psychology, Samukawa diagnoses Shizuko as a sufferer of hysteria and locates the pathological origin of her criminality there: "Because I am a man, I can never fully understand why you wished to commit such a terrifying crime. But books on perverse psychology say that hysterical women often write threatening letters to themselves. There are many cases like that both in Japan and overseas."[62] Although Ranpo does not specify the text Samukawa refers to, it is quite possible that Ranpo had Terada's book in mind, as it also mentions examples of all that hysterical women will do to prove the product of their wild imagination is real:

> Even though it is not true, she would say that she was raped by a man, a thief entered a neighbor's home, a fire broke out in the neighborhood.... In worse cases, in order to make her account more credible, she would elaborate her evidence. For instance, she would injure her genitalia or stain her hands and feet with blood to prove that she was raped, or limp as if she could not withstand the pain. Other times, she would pretend to commit suicide. After leaving a note to her family, she would pretend to throw herself off [a cliff], or pretend to swallow some poison and dye her mouth red and pretend to have coughed up blood.[63]

Using gender difference, Samukawa establishes an unbridgeable gap between Shizuko and himself while reducing all her actions to pathological symptoms.

When Shizuko has a sexual relationship with the very person she aims to outsmart, she resembles many of the female characters in hard-boiled fiction, a newly emerging subgenre of Western detective fiction. During the late 1920s and early 1930s, European dominance in the field of translated detective fiction was slowly being replaced by its American counterpart. In the midst of this transition, the works of Dashiell Hammett, with an array of seductive femmes fatales, made their way to Japan through literary translations and film adaptations.[64] One of Hammett's most admired femmes fatales, Brigid O'Shaunessy of *The Maltese Falcon* (1930), bears a curious resemblance to Shizuko. Just like Shizuko, Brigid starts a sexual relationship with Sam Spade, against whom she competes to get the coveted golden falcon. For women like Brigid and Shizuko, having a sexual relationship is nothing more than a false declaration of their sincerity and an attack on one-dimensional views of the female psyche.

The two characters adopt almost identical strategies of persuasion after being accused of wrongdoing by their lovers. As he unravels how she carried out her crime, Shizuko tries to convince him of her weakness. She repeatedly claims that she is scared of the way he talks to her and of the topic of murder.[65] She also tries her best to distract him:

> "The way you talk gives me the creeps. Let's stop such morbid talk. I don't want to talk about it especially in a dark place like this. Let's talk about it some other time, and just have fun tonight. As long as I'm with you, I don't have to think about Hirata [Shundei]."[66]

She also appeals through her sexual charm: "I don't want to waste our precious time on such a scary story. Don't you want these lips of fire? Can't you hear my heartbeat? Hold me, hold me."[67] She also entices him to whip her as before.[68] When all her attempts fail and he exposes her entire scheme, she silently sways back and forth. Samukawa describes: "[Shizuko], now naked, clung onto me. She pressed her cheek hard against my chest, so as to make me feel the warmth of her tears."[69] Finally, she falls completely silent: Samukawa describes how he "took her by her shoulders and shook her lightly. She couldn't raise her head, perhaps because of the shame and guilt. She remained motionless and silent."⁷⁰ This is the moment when Shizuko is at her weakest: male reason outdid female cunning when it allowed itself to be taken over by the unconscious.

In a similar vein, Sam Spade in *The Maltese Falcon* accuses his new lover, Brigid, of shooting his former partner, Miles. Brigid uses the same strategy of persuasion through sexuality and evocation of memories of their sweaty lovemaking sessions: "But—but, Sam, you can't! Not after what we've been to each other."⁷¹ Just like Shizuko, Brigid's plea involves some tears:

> "This is not just." She cried. Tears came to her eyes. "It's unfair. It's contemptible of you. You know it was not that. You can't say that. . . ." Brigid O'Shaunessy blinked her tears away. She took a step towards him [Sam Spade] and stood looking him in his eyes, straight and proud. "You called me a liar," she said. "Now you are lying. You're lying if you say you don't know down in your heart that, in spite of anything I've done, I love you."⁷²

Brigid and Shizuko are both murderous women who have killed men in the past. Yet, they demonstrate a great ability to play weak, frail women who cannot control their tears.

There is, however, still one difference between Shizuko and Brigid. Whereas Brigid eventually admits to killing Miles during Sam's inquisition, and tries to sway him despite his knowledge of it, Shizuko never admits to killing her husband. Samukawa leaves her at their rendezvous shack and hears of her suicide the next day.

In taking her own life at the end of the game she started, Shizuko fits the mold of the classic femme fatale, especially as characterized by Slavoj Žižek. She, like Brigid O'Shaughnessy, comes to embody "a radical *ethical* attitude, that of 'not ceding to one's desire,' of persisting in it to the very end when its true nature as the death drive is revealed. It is the hero who, by rejecting the femme fatale, breaks with his ethical stance."⁷³ Samukawa's attitude after Shizuko's death attests to the validity of this statement. Although he was once so confident, Samukawa is tormented by this event to the point that he loses confidence in his theory of what transpired: "It has been six months since Shizuko died her tragic death. Hirata Ichirō [Ōe Shundei] never appeared again. My irreparable suspicion grows day by day."⁷⁴ What he refers to as "irreparable suspicion" here is his self-doubt over having accused Shizuko of murder. He hypothesizes that if indeed Shizuko was the person she appeared to be—frail, masochist, and, most important, in love—she may have committed suicide because of a broken heart, having been accused by the very person she loves. Or, if she did kill her husband, it may have been because she fell in love with Samukawa. In either case, Samukawa feels equally responsible for her death. What is implied in his hypotheses is that he may have killed her indirectly by driving her to suicide. Just as there was no concrete evidence to tie her to the killing of her husband, there is nothing to completely exonerate Samukawa from his own possible wrongdoing. The sense of unbearable uncertainty and the haunting possibility of having hurt someone unknowingly are both familiar sensations for the heroes of the hard-boiled detective novel, as such heroes "can never be quite sure if she [the femme fatale] enjoys or suffers, if she manipulates or is herself the victim of manipulation."[75] If Samukawa could be convinced that Shizuko fell victim to her own game, he can exit the world of deceit. However, because Shizuko conceals with her death the real account of what happened, she forever deprives him of that possibility.

Shizuko entices a detective fiction writer to play the game of whodunit and abandons the game without allowing him ever to leave it. And because of her silence, the puzzle remains as hopelessly difficult as the mystery of female criminality itself. For Shizuko, allowing access to her body does not entail allowing access to her secrets, just as access to Oden's genitalia did not guarantee an understanding of her inner motivation. Although Shizuko loses her life in the rivalry, she emerges the winner in her struggle against Samukawa, who is left in a hellish uncertainty, where even rational thinking cannot save him.

Hamao Shirō's "Satsujinki"

The theme of the struggle between the female protagonist and the male detective also runs through Hamao Shirō's "Satsujinki." The story of serial murders in an urban mansion serves as another example of the will to fight the criminal mold that reality tries to impose on fiction. Just as "Injū" was a smash hit with its readers, "Satsujinki" also fascinated both general readers and Hamao's fellow writers.[76] Alhough reputed to be one of the best *honkaku* (authentic) detective fictions of its time, "Satsujinki" is full of parodies and pastiche: it takes as subtexts several works from the contemporary "canon" of detective fiction, two of which are none other than Ranpo's "Injū" and S. S. Van Dine's *The Greene Murder Case*. In "Satsujinki," a misogynist private detective sets himself up for failure when he falsely suspects his client, a beautiful young woman with a flair for criminology and detective fiction. Just like Ranpo's "Injū," "Satsujinki" undermines various texts of contemporary criminology that put forth outrageous claims about female criminals. The information from these texts enters "Satsujinki" as red herrings: consequently, the more one subscribes to the arguments of these texts, the harder it is for one to pinpoint the killer.

Fujieda Shintarō, the detective in the story, is a retired judge in his mid-thirties who now has a one-man private investigation service of some repute. His profile as a former judge implies that his professional training should have included extensive exposure to the science of crime, and works of criminology in particular. In fact, as an agent of law, he is one of the target readers of such material. As he chats with his friend Ogawa Masao, who assumes the role of "Dr. Watson"—narrator and associate in investigation—Akikawa Hiroko, the beautiful daughter of a wealthy industrialist, visits their office in the Ginza. Hiroko is concerned about her father's recent strange behavior after receiving mysterious threats. Seeing him take no action despite the possibility of danger for her family, she comes to seek help from Fujieda.

Described as having misogynist tendencies, Fujieda gives Hiroko a relatively cold reception for someone in her situation: while he is never rude to women per se, he holds the explicit policy of "Don't Trust Women; Don't Fall in Love with Beauties." He makes no exception for his client, assuming an overcautious attitude toward Hiroko even though she shows no signs of wishing to seduce him. In the opening scene and throughout the story, Hiroko remains a beautiful woman but without sexual charm. When she walks into Fujieda's office, Ogawa is immediately taken in by her "quiet beauty" and "intellectual appearance rare among women."[77] Fujieda is not so quick to let down his guard. As if to avoid the pitfall of his predecessors whose skills were marred when they fell for the charm of their female clients, he remains aloof throughout their initial interview. While Hiroko does not show any signs of romantic interest, her status as damsel in distress implies that she is available for a romantic and/or sexual relationship. Ogawa may be smitten with Hiroko, but Fujieda counters her unintentional temptation with an asexuality that is firmer than hers.

Fujieda's unusual caution continues as their initial interview is interrupted by the delivery of a message for Hiroko. She immediately becomes alarmed that the sender knows she is in the office, and she is shocked to see the same red triangle as the one on the threatening notes her father has received. She is mortified at the thought that someone was watching without her knowing it, even though she took great pains not to be tailed. Ogawa tries to console her, thinking that even though she appears strong, she too is a typical "vulnerable young woman."[78] As will be later revealed in the story, Hiroko is an aficionado of detective fiction; she understands that for a young woman to be watched secretly means taking a step closer to death. On the other hand, Fujieda unaffectedly explains to her that it is only a prank. Fujieda's unexpected calmness can be explained if Fujieda had encountered accounts of hysterical women who write threatening letters to themselves, just as Samukawa in "Injū" did. The message indeed turns out to be sinister: it urges Hiroko to return home immediately. After Ogawa escorts her home, Fujieda suggests to him: "Why do you think they knew Hiroko was here? Don't you find it strange?" He continues: "Her family seems to possess a strange, mysterious secret."[79] The more Hiroko appears beautiful, filial, responsible, and, most important, in danger, the more Fujieda seeks her real identity elsewhere, as if he thinks she will show her true colors when she is caught off guard.

Fujieda's distrust of Hiroko grows from a mere extension of his more general misogyny to a professional skepticism when he learns that she is an avid reader of detective fiction. His realization comes soon after the murder of her mother, the first of many killings in this case. Just like all the others who were present at the house that night, Hiroko is called in by the investigative team as a potential witness and suspect. During this interview, Hiroko's attitude changes from that of a scared girl to a defiant woman. When the police ask her about her alibi, Hiroko answers that she was reading S. S. Van Dine's *The Greene Murder Case*.[80]

Considered one of the masterpieces, Van Dine's 1928 work was one of the most popular Western detective fiction texts in the early 1930s. In this work, the members of the Greene family are killed one by one. Fujieda immediately recognizes the similarity between the fiction and the case at hand, and suspects Hiroko for her strange bedtime reading. He says to Ogawa, "Didn't [her choice of] *The Greene Murder Case* imply something to you? Yesterday she was afraid that something might happen to her family, especially to her father. That's why she came to see me. She received this strange letter and went home pale. That same night she was reading *The Greene Murder Case* of all things."[81] To all who know that the killer in *The Greene Murder Case* is one of the daughters of the family, the basis for Fujieda's implication is clear. While he finds it "unimaginative" *(ude ga nai)* to plot the killing exactly as it is laid out in a novel,[82] he takes Hiroko's testimony as a sort of declaration of war. As the reader will later find out, Hiroko mentions the text only in an attempt to give Fujieda verbal clues into who she thinks is the killer, but he is too busy suspecting her to notice.

As Fujieda's suspicion of Hiroko is ignited, all subsequent interaction between Hiroko and Fujieda becomes a sort of verbal sparring, especially when they discuss detective fiction. Ada Greene, the culprit of *The Greene Murder Case,* was an adopted daughter of the family. In one of the high-tension conversations, Hiroko reveals to Fujieda that one of her two younger sisters, Sadako, was actually adopted: Hiroko's mother took her in years before at her husband's request. Hiroko also confides in Fujieda that there was a dispute between their parents regarding the allocation of their children's inheritance, and their mother was opposed to giving an unusually high sum to Sadako and her live-in fiancé, Date, a powerful lead that gives Fujieda a glimpse into the relationships within the household. However, Fujieda is more interested in finding out about Hiroko's opinion on *The Greene Murder Case* than Sadako's true identity, even in the same conversation:

> [Fujieda] "You love detective fiction, don't you?"
> [Hiroko] "I do. I usually don't like American ones much, but I make an exception for Van Dine."
> "How did you like *The Greene Murder Case*?"
> "I thought it was good. It's just that I could spot the killer before [Philo Vance, the detective] could."
> "That's clever of you. People have a hard time figuring that one out."
> "Well, [Ada Greene] was not a biological daughter. It's obvious when there is an outsider living in the family."[83]

Frustrated with the detective unwilling to help her, Hiroko offers her own theory, suggesting Sadako as the killer. For Fujieda, who is already biased against her, Hiroko's endeavor may seem nothing more than an effort to divert attention from herself, even though such directness in communication contradicts his own image of the killer as an artist.

Through the rivalry between Fujieda and Hiroko, Hamao asks a number of important questions about literary influence between two sharply different traditions. Is Hiroko the killer, like Ada Greene? Is this story a mere copy of *The Greene Murder Case*, ending in the same way? The answer depends not only on the specific clues presented within the story but also on the extent to which the reader values the originality of the author's text.

Hamao further plays with the preconceptions of his stubborn detective by giving him a chance to browse through Hiroko's library with Ogawa. The room, described by Ogawa as "fitting for a beautiful person [like her]," is filled with mesmerizing red herrings for Fujieda. The top bookshelf holds art history books in German, representing Hiroko's interest in the arts. On the second shelf are books in Japanese on literature, music, and fine arts. Another shelf is dedicated to detective fiction: five books by Van Dine, almost all the works of Sherlock Holmes, novels by German authors, followed by the accounts of real crimes by Kingston Pearce and others.[84] The selections in Hiroko's library indicate that she possesses the sensibility for both crime and art. Since Fujieda describes the killer as an artist many times before this scene, the reader can surmise what is going through his mind without his voicing it. When the detective and his sidekick next speak to Hiroko, their conversation digresses to a murder case in the West:

> [Fujieda] "You have Jesse Tennyson's *Murder and Motives*. Have you had the chance to read it?"
> [Hiroko] "Yes."
> "I believe Tennyson discusses the case of Constance Kent. A terrifying murderer, isn't she?"
> "Oh yes, the girl serial killer."
> "There are some scary women out there. They look as if they wouldn't kill a fly, yet they commit the most horrendous murders . . ."
> "Indeed. They say women look like a bodhisattva on the outside while they are demons *(yasha)* on the inside. The more beautiful, the more insidious." Hiroko laughed with her beautiful eyes wide open.[85]

Hiroko professes to know about not only the most horrendous crimes committed by women but also the stereotypical view that wants to see physical beauty as an outward sign of a woman's criminality, as well as its possible cover. Earlier in the story Fujieda reminded himself of his motto, "Don't Trust Women; Don't Fall in Love with Beauties," but here Hiroko does the reminding for him. To someone who suspects her of wrongdoing, she appears a formidable adversary who challenges the male detective. But to an unclouded mind that sees her as who she is—a woman in danger who loves her family—she appears simply frustrated with the detective who does nothing but question the legitimacy of his client's ordeal. Her dissatisfaction will later prompt her to present her own version of a whodunit. Soon afterward, the police arrest Hiroko, and it is only then that Fujieda reveals to Ogawa that she is not the killer. Ironically, Hiroko is also erased from the story as soon as she is taken off the list of suspects: even at the end of the story, we only hear a rumor of her becoming the respectable head of her household.[86] Fujieda is not able to handle Hiroko: as soon as she suggests that she too can play the game of rational thinking, she is chased away from the spotlight. Fujieda's unwillingness to accord Hiroko her justified role—that of co-investigator—symbolizes the possible larger societal attitude of denying women the actual ability to master their bodies and emotions.

Both "Injū" and "Satsujinki" offer critiques of monolithic and simplistic views of female offenders as well as fiction's subordinate position to reality. They also lay out the tension within detective fiction between the obligation to follow the rules of the genre and the urge to reinvent them. As Hamao introduces the killer midway through the story and as a detective, he also breaks some of the "rules of detective fiction" put forth by Van Dine himself and Ronald A. Knox.[87] The Western hard-boiled novel is said to invert the conventions of both the whodunit and the romance.[88] Similarly, Japanese romance, or *ren'ai shōsetsu*, was showing moralist and conservative tendencies during the interwar period.[89] It can be said that Hamao and Ranpo played with the rules not only of their own genre but also of the Japanese romance, with a parade of perverse sexuality and extreme gender biases. These two works attest to the oppositional stance of detective fiction in relation to criminology, and their popularity reflects the presence of audiences who enjoyed seeing such tension and blurring of boundaries being played out in the rivalry between female offenders and male detectives.

Abe Sada: Pathologized Body and Fictionalized Scandal

Ranpo played with the boundary between reality and fiction by incorporating himself into the story as a decoy; Hamao parodied some preconceived notions of female criminality by presenting a chauvinist detective who is blinded by his own stereotypes. Both works have at their foundation the belief that women criminals can rise to the position of the subject by going against the grain of criminology, driving home the point that female sexuality and criminality are more complex than theorists make them out to be.

One woman, who lived her adult life in and out of the sex industry, came very close to embodying these notions. Her crime connects reality and fiction while cutting off something else. On May 12, 1936, a stylish playboy type in his forties and a good-looking woman of about thirty checked into a *machiai*, an interwar precursor to the modern-day "love hotel." After a weeklong hedonistic stay, the man was found strangled with his penis and testicles cut off. On one of his lifeless thighs were scrawled the bloody words "Sada Kichi futari kiri" (Sada Kichi Alone Together) and on the other was the character "Sada." The authorities eventually found out that the victim was Ishida Kichizō, the owner of a restaurant in Nakano, and the woman was Abe Sada, one of his former employees. When she was finally arrested at an inn in Shinagawa, she flaunted an "actress-like smile" to the journalists. The public was also excited to learn that she was carrying Ishida's penis in her *obi* at the time.

Immortalized in Ōshima Nagisa's 1976 movie *Ai no korīda* (released under the English title *In the Realm of the Senses*), Sada is the last heroine of interwar culture.[90] The idiosyncratic nature of her crime makes her appear an inappropriate window on this period in history. However, many elements of her testimony indicate that her life was almost too common, and she too is a product of her time. For instance, while Sada is not usually recognized as a *moga*, her escapade in the Ginza the day before the murder suggests that she was at least familiar with the phenomenon and their behavior. Sada's day out in the flashiest area of Tokyo is sprinkled with the most notable symbols of interwar *modan* culture.[91] With her visit to Shiseidō and her Western lunch washed down with coffee, Sada is no less a *moga* than the countless other women who aspired to this image in this era. She distinguishes herself from others by chopping up someone else, instead of being chopped up. While explaining herself during

Newspaper spread showing Abe Sada and her famous smile as she is taken into custody by the police. The large captions read (from right to left): Stayed at an inn in Shinagawa without skipping town—Used the alias Ōwada Nao—Female Heroine of Grotesque Murder—"We can't stay together"—She killed him as he slept—"Because I loved him"—She responded to the officer with a smile when she was arrested. *Asahi Shinbun*, May 21, 1936. Courtesy of Asahi Shinbun.

the trial, she claims her agency in designing the crime. She emphasizes that she bought the knife used to sever Kichizō's penis a few days prior to the incident, indicating the premeditated nature of her violence. Those who were in a position to judge her, mostly male, did not allow her such a privileged position and turned her act into another "crime of passion."

With *ero-guro* culture and detective fiction at their height, Sada represented to her contemporaries a classic female enigma and her case a juicy whydunit. Between the disclosure of the incident in May, Sada's arrest, and the trial in December, people engaged nationwide with the case through the media. Developments were reported every day in every major newspaper and gazette like a serialized novel. *Yomiuri Shinbun* hosted an examination of Sada's psychological profile by Kaneko Junzō of the Metropolitan Police Office even before she was arrested.[92] After the discovery of Kichizō's body on the morning of May 19, Sada managed to remain ahead of the authorities for two full days, until she was arrested in Shinagawa. During the initial stage of this (wo)manhunt, she was described in the press as anything from a *bijin jochū* (beautiful housemaid) to an *yōfu* (enchantress) who combined the "audacious nerve of a poison woman" *(futeki na dokufu dokyō)* and the "characteristics of a modern vamp" *(kindai vanpu kishitsu)*.[93] A newspaper article even described her as the Shōwa version of Takahashi Oden.[94] While Sada was on the run, the police distributed twenty thousand photos of her in cities where she was known to have resided, and eager readers called the police with tips on her whereabouts. One "Abe Sadako" was mistakenly taken into police custody.[95] After the real Sada was located, notables from all walks of life offered their opinion of the case in various magazine and newspaper features, including the doyenne of modern Japanese feminism, Hiratsuka Raichō, and the physicist-poet Ishiwara Jun.[96] Through such public discussions and widely available clues, Sada's case was turned into a semifictionalized "true crime" story to be consumed as a sort of detective fiction.

The contemporary public's association of Sada with Oden is not surprising, as Oden by this period had been established as the prototype of deviant woman in modern Japan. In the process of this association, Sada's crime also appears to have been fictionalized and shaped to fit the mold of Oden's legacy. However, there is one important difference between their fictionalizations. In Oden's case, there were two competing fictions: her insistence that she killed out of revenge versus the explanation, promulgated by Kawatake Mokuami (1816–93), Kanagaki Robun (1829–94), and the Meiji doctors who examined her, that blamed her sexuality. The first makes Oden a heroine in line with Edo morality, whereas the latter condemns her as a woman of questionable conduct. In Sada's case, however, the media portrayal of her and her own self-portrait overlap for the most part. The media initially concocted the image of her as an enchantress based on her crime. Her conduct after her arrest does not really give the impression that she wished to prevent the media's further distortion of her image: rather, it seems that she made comments and gestures that only enhanced this image. As she was taken into custody, she flashed a now-legendary smile at the journalists. Her photo was often accompanied with the line "Can I have *it* back?"—the request she reportedly made to the police. On being asked why she killed Kichizō, she proudly said, "Because I loved him." She never spared praise when speaking of Kichizō's skills in bed:

> "I've never met anyone like him. There was nothing bad about him. I never wanted to cling to a man who wanted to desert me, but I could never forget him. I once stayed away from him for two days in a house in Shimoya. It was only for two days, but I couldn't get a wink of sleep then."[97]

When asked why she cut off her lover's penis and testicles, she answered, "Because they are the most precious things to me."[98] During her interrogation, Sada repeatedly declared that she was not afraid to be put to death and even insisted that she deserved it. What emerges from these simple and perhaps damaging comments is her desire to convey the truth about the relationship while weaving a tale of love rather than an emotionless crime report. As long as the media elaborated the narrative of a sexy, passionate woman in love, Sada willingly interpolated that narrative.

On the other hand, Sada did not enjoy being deemed a mere pervert, even though her own comments and conduct betray her. First and foremost, she was adamant about her identity as a lover—the one who loves—in relation to Kichizō: for her, a sadist in love is different from a pervert whose carnal desires are nothing more than the manifestations of her pathological symptoms. Ironically, the narrative of Sada as pervert was woven at the hands of her defense lawyer,

Takeuchi Kintarō, who made sincere efforts to spare her a harsh long sentence. The contemporary media were well aware that the outcome of the trial hinged upon how well Takeuchi could portray Sada as a "normal woman" *(futsū no onna)*.[99] In defending her, Takeuchi chose to make his client everything contemporary criminology deemed a female offender to be.[100] Takeuchi turned her body into a wayward physical abnormality and her crime a crazed woman's fantasy.[101] In the process, Sada did not become a "normal woman," but a "normal woman" became a possessor of a body for sexual perversion.

In order to explain Sada's supposed "abnormality," Takeuchi usurped the existent connection between Sada and Oden, and forged a similarity between their bodies:

> The famous Takahashi Oden, the poison woman of a hundred dynasties, suffered from a physical defect. As that defect prompted her to commit her crimes, the defendant has a physical defect she cannot master by her will. In addition to her mental defect, she had this bodily defect. As it was the trigger for her crime, we should rid her of any criminal liability.[102]

It was shocking for Takeuchi to bring up a physical deficiency of Sada's body, considering that she had mentioned earlier during her testimony her previous visit to a doctor. Feeling alienated from her own body through a constant sense of sexual frustration, Sada went to a doctor to get examined. To her surprise, the doctor told Sada that there was nothing "wrong" with her body and it was normal for human beings to be irritated in a period of abstinence. His recommendation for her was to enter a serious marriage *(majime na fūfu seikatsu)* and distract herself by reading erudite books on spiritual training.[103] Although one doctor gave Sada a "normal" body, Takeuchi took it away from her and instead gave her a deviant, abnormal body, while in the process reinforcing the myth about women's bodies and their sexuality.

To strengthen his defense, Takeuchi elaborates the unusual nature of Kichizō and Sada's sex life by painting Kichizō as a "sexual pervert":

> Kichizō was a pervert *(seishin ijō sha)* who took pleasure in being maltreated *(ijimerareru)*. Sada is another pervert who enjoyed both bullying and being bullied. It must be one in a million for people

with these qualities to find each other. Kichizō and Sada present yin and yang, even and odd, a puzzle not meant to be solved, and they were drawn to each other. Only the playfulness of the god of Fortune triggered this incident.[104]

What is implied in this series of binary metaphors is that Kichizō was as much of a sexual deviant as Sada, and his death was an inevitable result of their chance union. Takeuchi's explanation bears a striking resemblance to another statement used to explain the tragic consequences of a couple engaged in a sadomasochistic relationship. The difference was that this incident took place in fiction. In Ranpo's "D-zaka no satsujin jiken" (The Murder on D-Hill; 1924), the wife of a secondhand bookstore on D-zaka is found brutally murdered. After some investigation, the detective, Akechi Kogorō, solves the case, ruling it "murder based on consent":

> "The owner of the nearby noodle shop was an extreme sadist, a sort of descendant of the Marquis de Sade. In a twist of fate, he found a female masochist a store away from his. The wife of the used bookstore was a female masochist, as perverse as he was. With skills reserved only for the sick like them, they were having an affair without anyone's knowing. You know why I said it was a murder based on consent. With their pathological desire, they could barely be satisfied with their spouses. That's why we found fresh wounds and bruises similar to hers on the wife of the noodle shop owner. But needless to say, he wasn't satisfied and neither was she. So when they found each other right under their noses, it's not hard to understand that they had a mutual agreement. But in the end they suffered from another twist of fate. By the combination of their passive and active powers, their shameful conduct escalated. That night, they caused this incident that they never wished upon themselves."[105]

Whether it was "the playfulness of the god of Fortune" or a "twist of fate," both Akechi and Takeuchi emphasize the accidental nature of the masochist's "murder." One possible explanation for this surprising resemblance between Takeuchi's defense and Akechi's ratiocination is that Ranpo and Takeuchi consulted the same or similar texts in elaborating their logic. Or, their similarity could indicate that Takeuchi read Ranpo's work and found this passage useful in formulating his defense for Sada. In either case, some level of genre-crossing reading is expected to have taken place. When an imaginary tale of perverse love is used to explain the dynamics behind a bizarre real-life incident, it enters the realm of reality. Sada's crime, too, enters the realm of fiction as its shocking nature is enhanced by the efforts to make sense of it.

Women, the "Chinamen" of Interwar Detective Fiction

Shizuko in "Injū," Hiroko in "Satsujinki," and Abe Sada in real life, all resist the imposed mold of the female criminal in claiming agency in their criminal deeds. One difference between Oden and Sada is that Sada was not executed but survived her term in prison and World War II. She was released in 1941 and even got married for a while, assuming a new identity—until her former self became known to her new husband. After short stints as an employee in a *ryokan*, she disappeared from the public eye in 1971. The narrative that gave her the identity of a woman of perverse sexuality may have shortened her stay in jail, but it forever confined her to that identity and that identity only, in much the same way as the victims of Ranpo's deranged killers were confined to the identities of endorsement tools. Sada became the poster child for uncontrollable female sexuality, and she could not convince society that she was rehabilitated or that her sexuality was just one facet of her identity.

Ronald A. Knox suggested in his "Detective Story Decalogue" that "no Chinaman must figure in the story," because Western audiences have the "habit of assuming that the Celestial is over-equipped in the matter of brains, and under-equipped in the matter of morals."[106] As one can perhaps see in Knox's expression "Chinaman," somewhat pejorative even by the standards of his time, Knox recognizes a different kind of logic, a different kind of rationality at work among non-Western subjects. Introducing a "Chinaman," or more precisely making him the culprit, disrupts the promise of fairness in the game of detection, as neither the reader nor detective may be able to understand his motive. Japanese criminologists of the interwar period seem to have thought of women as overequipped in the matter of privates, and underequipped in the matter of brains. Their murders and postmortem embellishment of their corpses became a part of an imaginary modern urban landscape. Within the same urban setting, Ranpo sought more active ways in which women could participate than the criminologists permitted them, and Hamao poked fun at the latter by pointing out the silliness of their overtly simplistic view of female deviancy. The contention between criminal science and detective fiction reflected in these works also influenced the discussion and the consumption of real-life criminal incidents, among which Sada's case is the primary example.

Some criminologists and detective fiction writers fed the all-too-neat loop of women and criminality, but others—Ranpo, Hamao, and Sada—questioned the legitimacy of this dynamic by exploring new ways in which women could act as criminals. In the process, the supposed boundary between what is real and what is imaginary was destabilized: detective fiction could no longer strictly be considered "fiction." After appearing in his own detective story as a red herring, Ranpo transgressed the supposed boundary between fiction and reality by commenting on real cases such as the Umetarō murder (a case involving an elaborate cover-up) (1931), the Lindbergh kidnapping (1932), and the aforementioned Tamanoi dismemberment case (1932). Eventually, Ranpo himself cited the gory overlapping of fiction and reality in the Tamanoi case when he decided to take a leave from writing in early 1932. Immediately, one reader questioned the timing of Ranpo's departure and wrote to the police: "Edogawa Ranpo is the killer. It is extremely suspicious that he stopped writing upon the occurrence of this case. I advise that the police detain him immediately."[107] It would have been predictable for this anonymous tipster to say upon reading "Injū," "Edogawa Ranpo is Ōe Shundei"; it is quite another issue when he says, "Edogawa Ranpo is the *real-life* Tamanoi butcher."

From the standpoint of literary history, newspaper reports on Sada elucidate the dilemma (in its worst form) that concerned many detective fiction writers in this period. As I have briefly mentioned, taking place at the same time as Sada's case was the so-called detective fiction debate *(tantei shōsetsu ronsō)*, in which the key players of the genre expressed their concerns and solutions to resurrect the genre that was growing more popular than ever but at the same time losing its originality. From this point of view, the dismembering we witnessed at the beginning of this chapter can be understood as not only a metaphor for the violence enacted upon the female body but also the figurative dismantling of the entire genre of detective fiction. The conflation of fictionlike real crime cases and real crimelike fiction, together with the common labeling of all nonnaturalist, avant-garde writing as detective fiction posed a huge problem for many

Newspaper spread reporting on the Tamanoi dismemberment case. The article details how the crime scene is now a small tourist attraction and that people are now curious as to how hard it is and how long it takes to cut up a human body. The page features a composite sketch by popular cartoonist Tsutsumi Kanzō and a profile of the killer(s) by Edogawa Ranpo. "Dismembered Body Attracts Interest," *Asahi Shinbun,* March 17, 1932. Courtesy of Asahi Shinbun, Hirai Ryūtarō, and Tsutsumi Naruki.

writers and evoked in some the need to rigidify the contours of the genre—an endeavor that in itself was rife with contradictions and conflations.

The abuse of science was not a phenomenon confined to the discourse of gender. Behind biased scientists of crime like Nozoe, other scientists were committing crimes in the name of science. Science became a motive for murder, and some detective writers used the allure of their genre to transmit to their readers messages of alarm against this trend.

3. Mad Scientists and Their Prey: Bioethics and Murder

The Emergence of Mad Scientists

Japanese detective fiction of the early twentieth century challenged its own generic norms by blurring the boundary between fiction and reality, between legitimate academic endeavor and vulgar thrill. Behind this haze at the periphery of detective fiction, the dichotomy between hero (detective) and villain (criminal), the genre's central setup, was also being undermined. Prominent but deranged agents of science—such as research scientists, engineers, and doctors—started to appear more often as serial killers than as models of scientific morality. Such sinister representations of scientists are somewhat at odds with both the contemporary state ideology toward and the popular understanding of science. The latest advances in forensic science such as blood-type analysis and fingerprinting were often featured in both Japanese and Western detective fiction as indispensable tools that allowed detectives to figure out "whodunit." In most early texts, science was the detective's ally in the pursuit of truth and justice, as we see later in this chapter.

Why, then, did these scientists come to embody a new menace to the human pursuit of happiness, in the very genre in which they previously commanded so much respect? Popular images of white lab coats and frizzy hair aside, these scientists appear "mad" in that they are portrayed to act with a fanatical devotion to scientific advancement and stop at nothing to realize this goal. To these brilliant but warped minds, even human life becomes expendable in the name of science.

Some authors of interwar Japanese detective fiction challenged the widespread embrace of scientism—the unconditional faith in science and its agents that had been prevalent in Japan since the Meiji period—and suggested that science could function as an instrument or motive for crime, as well as a weapon against it. Such an inversion not only points to the creativity of detective writers in questioning and overturning conventional perceptions of scientists and their pursuits but also underscores the fundamental ethical ambiguity of scientific endeavor in the 1920s and 1930s. As these "mad scientists" appear and reappear, the tales of their crimes come to form a sizable cluster within the genre.[1]

This chapter focuses on the subgenre of what I call "mad scientist murders" within the larger stream of interwar Japanese detective fiction. Through an overview of the popular sentiment toward science during this period and a discussion of four key works by four authors, I explore how these authors used the motif of the mad scientist and his uncompromising attitude toward his work to criticize the widespread overconfidence in the promise of science and suggest the possible incompatibility between science and ethics. Contemporary Japanese Marxists, who are perhaps more widely recognized as having been preoccupied with the emergence of science and technology in this era, shared with detective fiction writers a concern with the monopoly of certain knowledge and skills by a select few whose training lacked an ethical component.[2]

Scientists undoubtedly were privileged elites in modern Japan, and the government had played a crucial role in establishing their position since the early days of the Meiji period: it lured promising students to careers in science through everything from raising the prestige of the discipline through generous funding to exemption from military service.[3] To show how the image of science and scientists developed, I summarize the government's attitude toward science in the period leading up to the early 1920s, before the introduction of the motif of the "mad scientist" as a criminal type by Kozakai Fuboku (1890–1929), himself a man of science. I discuss key texts from the 1930s by Yumeno Kyūsaku (1889–1936) and Oguri Mushitarō (1901–46) and describe how they dealt with the question of "science without conscience." I close with Unno Jūza (1897–1949) and his 1937 work "Hae otoko" (The Fly Man), in which we can find one of the earliest problematizations of the fascist obsession with creating the "perfect human being" by harnessing the power of science. These four authors contributed regularly to *Shinseinen* (New Youth), perhaps the most important literary publication in the modern, urban culture of interwar Japan, and avidly read each other's works. They sought to temper the popular craze for science and offered a sobering and even disturbing view of science run amok.

The history of science in Japan has enjoyed considerable critical attention: James Bartholomew's *The Formation of Science in Japan: Building a Research Tradition* traces developments in the systems of education, research, and application of science from the Tokugawa period to the early twentieth century; Mizuno Hiromi's recent dissertation, "Science, Ideology, Empire: A History of the 'Scientific' in Japan from the 1920s to 1940s," shows how the high status of science and scientists withstood the growing rhetorics of spiritualism and fascism before and during World War II. In contrast, cultural responses to such contemporary scientific developments have not yet received the same scholarly interest. The texts discussed here are no exception: despite their popularity among contemporary audiences, they are undeservedly neglected. Given the relative scarcity of secondary sources on these texts, my analysis relies heavily on close readings of these stories while making reference to what little Japanese and English scholarship exists. My goal is to complement the studies on the history of science in Japan by shedding light on cultural responses to various government policies and real-life incidents.

In addition, in order to conceive of the literary endeavors of these authors in a global context, dialogue between Japanese and Western texts dealing with the issues of ethical ambiguity in science and medicine demands attention. A comparative analysis of mad scientist murders in Japan and pulp fiction from the same period in the West reveals that Japanese interwar mad scientist murders share traits with the "scientific romance" of H. G. Wells as much as with their direct genre counterparts, Western detective fiction. Similar to the Wellsian scientists in works such as *The Island of Doctor Moreau* (1896) and *The Invisible Man* (1897), the Japanese mad scientists play god and tamper with the bodies of their experiment subjects. In the last decade of the nineteenth century, Japanese audiences had been introduced to the work of Wells, along with other founding fathers of Western science fiction such as Jules Verne.[4] The example of Yumeno and the film *Das Kabinett des Doktor Caligari* (The Cabinet of Dr. Caligari;

1919) attests that depictions of mad scientists in other media such as film also inspired Japanese authors in this era. As Hiroshige Tetsu points out, the struggle to situate science in relation to other social values was not a problem unique to Japan.[5] Tracing the stylistic and thematic parallels between the works of Japanese and Western authors suggests a unidirectional but nonetheless selective and discriminating cross-cultural communication between two brands of pulp fiction originating in different geographical locations and helps us situate the dilemma of the ambiguous ethicality of science in a global context.

Attitudes toward Science

Within the first few years of its inception, the Meiji government made the promotion of science—and the importation of technology in particular—a top priority, as this knowledge was immediately pertinent to the industrialization and militarization of the country. The government established the Ministries of Education (Monbushō) and Engineering (Kōbushō) in 1871, with the former ministry playing a crucial role in reforming the various educational institutions it had inherited from the old regime.[6] The government was especially eager to update Japanese technology in the field of medicine: many medical professionals, mostly German, were recruited to train Japanese students in the fields of ophthalmology and surgery, the two branches of medicine in which Japan lagged furthest behind.[7] These efforts soon paid off: although Japanese scientific education relied heavily on so-called *oyatoi gaijin* (hired foreigners) during its early years, by the late 1880s most national universities were populated almost completely by Japanese faculty members. Around World War I, the government took the initiative to systematically fund various scientific research projects, which had previously been financed by donations from private foundations.[8] Despite several international and budgetary crises, this trend grew under the Meiji and subsequent Taishō governments.[9]

The government's promotion of science trickled down to the masses both directly and indirectly, making the field a promising career choice for an aspiring youth. The two giants of the Meiji literary world, Natsume Sōseki (1867–1916) and Mori Ōgai (1862–1922), were both touched by the larger societal enthusiasm for science. Born to a family of doctors, Ōgai was educated at the University of Tokyo, the center of medical studies in modern Japan, and went on to a successful career as a military doctor whose training included a sojourn in Germany. Even Sōseki, by training a scholar of English language and literature, often expressed frustration with literature: he saw it as the pursuit of spectral *(yūrei no yō)* intangibilities and wished that it were as "cosmopolitan" *(kosumoporitan)* as science.[10]

Following the advancement of science in Japan as well as in the rest of the world, the subdiscipline of forensic science was also making progress by leaps and bounds. Criminal investigation based on intuition *(kan)*, for which the only training was years of experience, slowly gave way during the late Meiji and early Taishō period to investigative techniques based on science and method. The technology of fingerprinting as a tool for identification was perfected in the British colonies by a group of English scientists in the late nineteenth century. After some twists and turns, fingerprinting was introduced to Japan in the early 1900s as a viable and official method of identification. The authorities started collecting fingerprints of inmates in 1908, initially with the purpose of finding repeat offenders. The fingerprint was first used as evidence for conviction in 1911, in a robbery case in Kanda, a downtown area of Tokyo.[11]

The growing fervor for science and progress continued into the Taishō era, with both popular literature and school textbooks echoing and amplifying this sentiment. Satō Haruo (1892–1964) used fingerprinting as one of the central themes in his 1918 short story "Shimon" (Fingerprints). As the narrator's old acquaintance R. N. loses his grip on reality because of years of opium abuse, the knowledge that "no two fingerprints are identical" stands as the last pillar of certainty in his ever-disintegrating world. The reliability of the technique, confirmed over and over by his collection of sixteen books on the subject, allows the dying madman to find the killer, a Hollywood actor named William Wilson who was suspected of being a German spy. Without the technique of fingerprinting, R. N.'s conclusion that Wilson indeed committed murder in a Nagasaki opium den would be no more reliable than the hunch of a delirious drug addict. This piece of scientific knowledge serves as the last thread connecting reality and imagination for R. N. Science offers precision and comfort, not only for a man dying from drug overdose but also for a nation faced with an increase in crime brought about by the decay of traditional law enforcement.

Other writers participating in the genre of detective fiction were quick to exploit the omnipotent aura of science, and many contemporary Japanese translations of Western works highlight the widespread fascination with scientists and experiments. In the 1890s, Mitsuki Harukage (unknown–1915) introduced the works of the British writer Richard Austin Freeman (1862–1943) to Japanese readers through his loosely adapted translations. Freeman's most famous creation was Dr. Thorndyke, a tall Englishman trained as doctor, lawyer, and detective who carried a signature green briefcase full of medical equipment.[12]

Although Japanese translation was not kind to the name of Freeman's protagonist—Thorndyke became "Kureta hakase" (Dr. Kureta, which is a play on "thorn" and "dyke")—it enhanced rather than distorted the detective's godlike image as revered spokesman for science. Just as Thorndyke squared off with Sherlock Holmes on the pages of the *Strand* magazine, Freeman's meticulous barrister-doctor boasted a popularity comparable to Sherlock Holmes among Japanese readers, as the works of Freeman and Sir Arthur Conan Doyle reached Japanese audiences at roughly the same time.[13] Future detective fiction writers such as Kozakai Fuboku and Edogawa Ranpo (1894–1965) avidly read the translations of Freeman's "inverted" detective fiction, in which the killer and his modus operandi are revealed to the reader at the very beginning of the story. Ranpo paid homage to Freeman by adopting the inverted narrative structure in his own works, "Shinri shiken" (The Psychological Test) and "Yaneura no sanposha" (A Wanderer in the Attic), both published in 1925. Much like the viewers of the *Columbo* series of television mysteries, the readers of Freeman's works derive pleasure not from guessing "whodunit" along with the detective but rather from watching the detective use method and science to unravel a solution they already know. The popularity of this formula, in which science always allowed Thorndyke to get his man, highlights the aura of infallibility that came to surround science and its practitioners.

This glorification of science was also instilled in young Japanese minds through more direct means, teaching students that sometimes scientific discovery should take precedence over ethical concerns. Among the materials found in the standard elementary school curriculum was an account of the discovery of Jennerian vaccination that emphasized the virtue of putting progress ahead of ethics. In 1796, English doctor Edward Jenner performed perhaps one of the most controversial human experiments in the modern era. Jenner, along with his contemporaries, knew that milkmaids who contracted cowpox never got smallpox. But this assumption was never scientifically confirmed as fact. So when a milkmaid with cowpox came to him, he intentionally passed the disease on to James Phipps, his gardener's son, by scratching the boy's skin with a contaminated piece of metal. When Jenner saw James recover from the cowpox, he gave the young boy smallpox. James failed to contract the disease, and what had been empirically suspected—that those who get cowpox do not contract smallpox—was proved as a fact through human experimentation.[14] It is undeniable that Jenner's invention indirectly contributed to the complete eradication of the disease in the 1970s. However, he received split reviews from his contemporaries regarding his achievement, as the method through which he determined the relationship between cowpox and smallpox and perfected the vaccine were questionable from an ethical point of view because it involved humans.

In Japan, Jenner's ethically ambiguous experiment was regarded highly. He epitomized the unrelenting scientific and progressive attitude that Meiji Japan wished to make its own. Jenner's smallpox vaccine had been known to Japan since the early nineteenth century, when information about the technique arrived in 1801 or 1802, through Nagasaki, via China and Russia. Philip Franz von Siebold, one of the most famous foreign doctors in the last years of the Tokugawa era, successfully vaccinated a number of Japanese in the 1820s.[15] Knowledge of the smallpox vaccine, therefore, was no longer new to the Japanese by the early twentieth century. Jenner's discovery was not new, but the evaluation of his actions as commendable was a Meiji phenomenon. Interestingly, the educational value of Jenner's experiment was not viewed as scientific: the anecdote was placed not in a science textbook but in a *shūshin* (ethics) textbook. As early as 1904, Jenner made his first appearance in *Jinjō shōgaku shūshinsho* (Standard Textbook for Ethics), a fourth-grade textbook, and was firmly rooted in the genre of biographies of great men *(ijinden)* in standard textbooks until the elimination of the subject of *shūshin* from the school curriculum altogether in the postwar era.[16]

Even prior to the inclusion of Jenner's life story in *shūshin* textbooks, the Japanese scientific community commemorated his crowning achievement in 1897 by commissioning a statue from Tamamura Kōun (1852–1934) and displaying it in the garden of the Tokyo

National Museum—the equivalent of a "hall of fame" for scientists.[17] This was by no means the first statue in honor of the controversial doctor: others still stand in the cathedral in Gloucester (his native town) and in London's Trafalgar Square (it was later moved to Kensington Gardens). Both English statues depict him as a mature man of resolve: in the Kensington Garden version, he sits pensively wearing a robe. He holds a rolled-up document and looks as though he is still contemplating the big decision. In the Gloucester version, he stands holding a piece of paper, his stern expression suggesting that he has just made a momentous decision (probably to vaccinate a patient to test if his theory is true). In contrast to the statues erected in his native England, Jenner's statue in Tokyo depicts him as a youthful, almost boyish figure, pensive in perusing a book—perhaps to allude to the relatively immature state of Japanese science.[18] The plate affixed to the base of the statue explains in highly formalized Chinese characters Jenner's contribution to humankind.

Also, it was appropriate that the Japanese statue portrayed Jenner as a youth, as one of the primary audiences for his statue was schoolchildren on field trips to the museum. If these children had finished fourth grade, they would have read about him in their *shūshin* class. The *shūshin* textbook went through five editions, and each time the message of the Jenner story varied. From the first version, the lesson emphasizes the length of time it took Jenner to perfect his vaccine (clearly stated as twenty-three years in all versions), his endurance of the ridicule and criticism he received, the strength of his resolve (as he disclosed his determination to test his hypothesis on a human being), and his courage to have tested it on his son (clearly stated in all but the first version).

The fourth edition from 1934 offers by far the most detailed account of Jenner's life and the invention of the vaccine: it states that he is English and that he came to be aware of the connection between cowpox and smallpox as a young medical apprentice. Most important, this version explains Jenner's motivation as his desire to help the unfortunate. As a milkmaid explains to the older doctor that she would not contract smallpox because she had cowpox before, the young Jenner thinks to himself: "What a curious tale. Maybe there is some sense to what this woman says. If so, I shall study it and invent a good way [to prevent the spread of smallpox], and help save unfortunate patients like her."[19] But curiously, the obstacles for Jenner

Statue of Edward Jenner in Ueno, Tokyo, just off the main entrance to the Tokyo National Museum. Photograph by the author.

Statue of Edward Jenner in Kensington, London. Courtesy of Yuri Kawana.

are the ridicule *(azakeri)* of his peers and friends and their superstitious beliefs (for example, that children who received the cowpox vaccine would have cowlike faces and moo instead of talk) and never ethical concerns for Jenner's willingness to try his hypothesis on his patients—needless to say, a child.

In addition to Thorndyke and Jenner, another hero of science captured the imagination of Taishō Japan. In December 1922, upon the invitation of Kaizōsha, a new and ambitious publishing house in Tokyo, the world-renowned physicist Albert Einstein stepped off a ship in the port of Yokohama. Kaizōsha had recently invited

Illustration of Jenner performing the famous experiment on his own son in a *shūshin* (ethics) textbook. In Lesson 8, "Hatsumei," in volume 4 of *Jinjō shōgaku shūshinsho* (fourth edition, in use 1934–40), 34. Reprinted in *Fukkoku kokutei shūshin kyōkasho*.

two other notable figures from the West: the English philosopher Bertrand Russell in 1921 and the American feminist Margaret Sanger in early 1922. While these two visits were utter commercial failures, Einstein's was not. Far from it: people were thrilled to see the newly crowned Nobel laureate and his wife. The excitement surrounding Einstein's visit also launched a few new science magazines, including those that later became two leading interwar science journals, *Kagaku chishiki* (Scientific Knowledge), inaugurated in 1921, and *Kagaku gahō* (Science Illustrated), founded in 1923.[20] These magazines offered writers, including Kozakai Fuboku and Unno Jūza, the opportunity to showcase their knowledge of science by contributing essays and stories.[21]

With his unassuming appearance and general friendliness, the world's best physicist captivated Japanese audiences. Most important, Einstein inadvertently promulgated not the nitty-gritty of his theory of relativity but the image of scientists as "lovable" and at times even "holy" or above reality. Various nonscientist intellectuals observed Einstein and felt an imaginary sense of affinity: the children's writer Ogawa Mimei (1882–1961) described him as a "tender poet one would remember with nostalgia" *(yasashii, natsukashii shijin)* who bore some resemblance to Lafcadio Hearn.[22] Even the last skeptics against scientists as noble beings were won over by Einstein's fabulous career and disarming looks. Miyake Yasuko, a journalist married to a scientist, described Einstein's appearance as follows: "I used to think that all scientists were narrow-minded and restless with the shifty gazes of thieves, but Professor Einstein's eyes of grandeur and sublimity completely changed my view."[23]

Einstein's charm spurred many Japanese audiences to try to comprehend his theory. The Ōsaka Gakkō Eiga Kyōkai (Osaka Association for Education through Film) imported a German movie based on his theory of relativity *(Der Einstein-film),* while some former students of Ishiwara Jun, a leading Japanese physicist, wrote and serialized the play *Sōtaisei riron geki* (Piece on the Theory of Relativity) in the magazine *Shinshōsetsu* (New Novel) in 1923. The eagerness of the common people for anything about Einstein was so strong that at times it shocked the man himself, who with characteristic humility reportedly professed that "meaningless respect is like a loveless relationship."[24] The admiration for the person of Einstein and the eagerness of specialists to feed such frenzy indeed yielded little progress in terms of deepening the understanding of his theory, physics, or science in general. Einstein's scholarship was so erudite that even his fellow physicists could not understand parts of his lectures.[25] However, newspaper reports of the current king of science enjoying his stay in Japan—including a backstage visit at a Kabuki theater and a party with geisha—distracted people's attention from the glaring intellectual gap.

The cult of Einstein reached the point where university officials in Fukuoka preserved the blackboard on which Einstein had scribbled during a lecture and forgot to erase.[26] Although people in the provinces were clearly in awe, intellectuals in the capital were not immune to the aura of the Nobel Prize winner. Shikanogi Masanobu, a professor in the humanities who sat in on Einstein's lectures for six days, recalled: "I heard the quiet, serene sounds of his spirit. His thinking progresses steadily, quietly, like the melting of spring snow, without running, while sprinkling the meadow of knowledge with his jewels of mathematical equations."[27] Those who professed ignorance of

Albert Einstein being served by a geisha. No matter where the famed scientist went during his visit to Japan—arriving in Kōbe, arriving at Tokyo Station, visiting Gakushūin, viewing a kabuki performance—his every move was photographed and published in the press. *Tokyo Nichinichi Shinbun,* November 26, 1922, 9.

Einstein's scholarship, including Shikanogi, may have been playing dumb in the presence of the genius, but their worship of the world-renowned scientist appears willing and genuine—and not much different from the adoration showered upon the scientist by the general public. Einstein's visit also enhanced the popular ideas that science, though it remains beyond the common realm of understanding, is a positive force; that the agents of science, though they may appear unusual, are intellectually and even morally superior people; and that the ordinary standards of judgment do not apply to them. This creates a potentially dangerous situation: science is something for the masses not to understand but to believe.

In the shadow of this "Einstein boom," there were those who exploited this myth. The enthusiasm for anything scientific bubbled up into overconfidence in scientists and their methods and caused some real-life scandals surrounding ethical medical practice. In 1924, two years after Einstein's visit to Japan, Sakaki Yasuzaburō (1870–1929), a professor of psychiatry at Kyushu Imperial University, announced that he had found the ingredients for a sort of *elixir vitae*. Sakaki claimed that by stimulating a patient's thyroid gland, he could rejuvenate him: he claimed that in clinical trials he was able to make the patient's gray hair turn black, eliminate his wrinkles, and give his skin a healthy glow.[28] The newspapers sensationalized this discovery, and the general public went crazy about the prospect of eternal youth and immortality. While other, more sober scholars questioned the validity of Sakaki's assertions, the professor continued his experiments undeterred—including one in which he supposedly proved that tying the seminal ducts could prevent aging in men. Although many of his claims were dubious at best, Sakaki was no quack: he was respected as the head of the psychology department at the university and was married to the sister of the emperor's personal physician. His training included a medical degree from the University of Tokyo and a three-year stint in Germany as a government-funded student, during which he befriended Einstein. For music lovers, he is romantically known as the professor who founded the first Western-style philharmonic orchestra in Japan.[29]

In his obsession for finding the nectar of youth, however, Sakaki hardly appears to be the elite doctor he actually was. He aspired to obtain government funding to establish the National Research Institute for the Prevention of Aging (Kokuritsu rōsui yobō kenkyūjo), but the strange case of the Taishō *elixir vitae* ended when he and two of his colleagues were arrested for illegally selling their services in an unofficial capacity. The three were acquitted, but the investigation into this case revealed a considerable number of medical professionals willing to offer similarly questionable services to anyone willing to pay for them. The outrageousness and popularity of Sakaki's exorbitant claims illustrate not only the faith of contemporary society in the omnipotence of science, but also the unscrupulousness of certain scientists who were eager to exploit such confidence. The *elixir vitae* scandal brought to the fore the problem of popular ignorance about science and the danger of scientific advancement unchecked by ethics—a problem the Meiji government, in its pursuit of rapid modernization, had neglected to tackle decades earlier.

Kozakai Fuboku and "Tōsō"

Following the *elixir vitae* incident, even those who previously sought to enlighten the masses about the omnipotence of science realized the need to caution against such blind faith in science and scientists. Kozakai Fuboku, a researcher and practicing doctor when not penning works of detective fiction, was one such professional. Having received solid training in Japan as well as in America and Europe in the early 1920s, Kozakai was a reputable specialist in physiology and serology by the age of thirty.[30] He was also a detective fiction aficionado who routinely published crime stories as well as essays on forensic science and criminology. In his 1925 essay "Kagaku hatsumei no kyōi" (The Threat of Scientific Inventions), published a year after the *elixir vitae* incident, Kozakai warned his readers that they needed to remain realistic about the possibilities and limits of science: "Even though we ought to pay our utmost attention to the advancement of science, we should never think that science is omnipotent, or that science will allow us humans to achieve all our desires."[31] Kozakai called for such restraint presumably because he felt that scientists could often become too self-confident and greedy and lose sight of their original goal: the betterment of human life through science.

It is curious for such words of caution to come from Kozakai, because he actively promoted the heroism of an individual who put science ahead of common morality when he serialized "Jennā den" (A Biography of Jenner) in *Shōnen kurabu* (Boys' Club), a magazine for school-age children.[32] Kozakai narrates the life of Jenner as a great scientist who risked his social standing and reputation for the greater good of humankind. Rather than upholding prejudice and ignorance, Jenner preferred to know things through direct experimentation: the relationship between cowpox and smallpox was one such question. Contrary to most historical accounts, Kozakai reports that Jenner first tested the use of a lesser pox as a vaccine for human smallpox on his first-born son, Edward. If this was true, then Jenner's experiment with his gardener's son would have been unnecessary. Kozakai is aware of this possible contradiction and explains that "probably cowpox was not available" when Jenner first experimented on his son.[33] Jenner is not depicted as a cold-blooded scientist willing to sacrifice his "guinea pigs," but as a God-fearing human being torn between the conflicting demands of scientific research and his religious beliefs. Kozakai emphasizes that it is only when Jenner overcame the fear of killing the boy in the name of science that he found the courage to place smallpox on the arm of an unsuspecting little patient:

> May 14! A memorable day for the history of mankind. It is this day that Jenner decided to carry out the experiment. He woke up early and prayed to God. He was born to a family of clergy, so he always had the habit of prayer, but never did he pray from the depth of his heart like that morning. Thirty years after the idea first came to him, he experimented with his own child, and though that gave him confidence, this time he might end up harming someone else's child. Earnest were his prayers then.[34]

In Kozakai's account, Jenner never entirely suspends ethics: he is worried about the well-being of the child, though the setup of the experiment is such that he has to risk the boy's life, and his motive for doing the entire experiment is utterly selfless. In this story, science is a discipline of heroes, and one outstanding man makes all the difference: "The immunization for smallpox was discovered through the efforts of one man. . . . Is not the power of humankind great (*idai*)?"[35]

Such a positive attitude toward scientists and their experiments did not remain with Kozakai later in his life. By the end of the 1920s, Kozakai's fiction shows a significant change in his attitude toward unscrupulous agents of science and their behavior. In his last work, "Tōsō" (Conflict), published posthumously in 1929, Kozakai depicts the struggle between two academics who subscribe to opposing schools of thought about abnormal psychology and deviant behavior. They stop at nothing—even ethics—to prove the other wrong.

The willingness to test the limits of ethics in the name of scientific pragmatism made for innovative detective fiction. The story centers on the mysterious death of Kitazawa Eiji, a young wealthy industrialist found dead in his home. It is a case of apparent suicide, in which the victim has left a suicide note and dies of a seemingly self-inflicted gunshot wound. The note, a handwritten copy of a suicide note left by a certain "author A," is an obvious allusion to the writer Akutagawa Ryūnosuke, who had shocked the literary world a few years earlier by taking his own life.

While investigating Kitazawa's death, however, the police find out that his wife was cheating on him with a young novelist. Upon further investigation, the police discover evidence that hints at foul play: a gun in the novelist's possession is the same model as the one used in Kitazawa's suicide; and the complete works of author A, including the volume containing his suicide note, are also found in Kitazawa's room. Because of such circumstantial evidence, a cloud of suspicion hangs over the young novelist and Kitazawa's wife.

However, the truth of what happened turns out to have nothing to do with their illicit affair but everything to do with a battle for academic hegemony in the field of medicine. Two giants in the discipline of psychology, Professors Kario and Mōri, subscribe to rival schools concerning the relationship between physiology and human psychology. The looming question for them is the same as the dilemma embroiling contemporary criminologists: Why does one human being kill another? Or, more precisely, why do some resort to murder, while others do not?

Mōri is a proponent of the so-called brain school *(nōshitsu gakuha)*, which argues that all manifestations of abnormal psychology, including murder, are nothing but the results of brain malfunctions. In other words, no external stimuli can prompt one to commit an antisocial act such as murder. Rather, chemical imbalances within the brain are the only factor that can provoke one to commit the ultimate act, and such imbalances occur without the influence of any external catalyst.

On the other hand, Kario's "bodily fluid" school *(taieki gakuha)* explains the variety of human emotions, including homicidal impulses, through the imbalance of various secretions within the body.

In contrast to Mōri's theory, Kario argues that external elements can cause changes in the flow of humors, which can lead to extreme shifts in human behavior, especially in those with body types predisposed to be susceptible to wide mood swings. By applying the correct external stimuli, it would therefore be possible to induce violent acts such as murder.

The relevance of this academic conflict to the current mysterious death is revealed in a letter from the instigator of the entire incident, Kario, to Mōri, his rival, who also happens to be the forensic expert working on the investigation. When Kario met Kitazawa and found him to manifest every outward sign of possessing a body type capable of violence, he recognized the young man's potential as a subject for this behavioral experiment. Years later, when Kario sees the time is right, he uses hypnotic suggestion to make Kitazawa write a suicide note, then ultimately shoot himself—all the while making his experimental subject believe he is acting of his own free will. Although Kitazawa pulled the trigger, it is Kario who orchestrated his death: Kitazawa may have possessed the melancholic temperament to kill himself, but he would never have taken his own life if not for the scientist's ruthless experiment.

Kario admits his complicity in the death of Kitazawa to his professional rival Mōri, but his letter shows no sense of remorse or acknowledgment that his actions were unethical. He seems utterly unconcerned that he has caused the death of a man in the name of scientific advancement and does not expect to be prosecuted for the indirect murder he has committed.

Even more curious than Kario's lack of remorse is Mōri's reaction to his demonic rival's letter. After reading Kario's account of his murderous plot, Mōri describes his nemesis as a "prodigious scientist" *(tensaiteki kagakusha)* who is nothing short of brilliant:

> Dr. Kario is a genius. A genius whom I will never have the chance to surpass. As long as one is obsessed with academic conventions, one could never perform an experiment like his. In social terms, such a determination would be considered immoral. But if we want to overcome nature by science, we have to be willing to do something similar to what he did.[36]

Rather than denouncing Kario's ethical void, Mōri recognizes it as a value indispensable to the pursuit of scientific advancement. There is even a twinge of jealousy in Mōri's comments: the investigator seems to envy Kario's freedom from the conventional norms of right and wrong.[37]

In putting practicality and ability ahead of ethics, Kario also echoes the view of another mad scientist in Western pulp fiction, the title character in H. G. Wells's *The Island of Doctor Moreau*. Wells's key works had been translated into Japanese in the 1890s and were made available in the same sort of general interest youth-oriented magazines that actively published translations of Western detective fiction.[38] The Japanese translation of *Doctor Moreau* was made available to the reading public as early as 1924.

The story of Doctor Moreau is told by a young man named Prendick who is stranded on an unknown island. There he finds an obsessed doctor who reigns supreme among the beast-humans he has created. By the novel's climax, young Prendick fears for his own life and confronts Moreau and his assistant, Montgomery. Moreau tells Prendick that he manufactures new species: crosses between human and animals—horrendous creatures that run like pumas and talk like humans—invented through a series of vivisection and grafting. In horror, Prendick questions the doctor: "But, . . . I still don't understand. Where is your justification for inflicting all this pain?" Moreau remains unshaken at this accusation and articulates his intentions: "A mind truly opened to what science has to teach must see that it [pain] is a little thing." Moreau also echoes Kario and Mōri in "Tōsō" in his pursuit of "the extreme limit of plasticity in a living shape." Moreau disregards ethics: "To this day I have never troubled about the ethics of the matter. . . . The study of Nature makes a man at last as remorseless as Nature."[39]

Just as Mōri is taken in by Kario's determination, Prendick is momentarily charmed by the eloquence and determination of Moreau. After Moreau lays out the overview of his endeavor on the island, Prendick reevaluates the mad creator: "I looked at him, and saw but a white-faced, white haired man, with calm eyes. Save for his serenity, the touch almost of beauty that resulted from his set tranquility and his magnificent build, he might have passed muster among a hundred other comfortable old gentlemen."[40] Prendick's awakening to the nobleness of Moreau's appearance represents a dangerous moment when the agent of science appears more attractive than he actually is because of the firmness of his conviction and his devotion to a professional cause. Prendick shivers at the thought of admiring the madman, but there is no guarantee that the other audience of Moreau's speech—namely, the readers—experiences the same adverse reaction.

The narrator in "Tōsō" finds himself having to make the same sort of difficult decision as Prendick after Mōri, his academic mentor, and Mōri's rival Kario, pass away. Kozakai does not end the story with Mōri and Kario triumphantly overcoming nature and ethics in the name of science, and we catch a glimpse of his own dilemma as a scientist in this ambiguous ending. Soon after the Kitazawa incident, Kario dies of a stroke, and, upon hearing of the death of his professional rival, Mōri too withers away and dies. With the two scholars gone, the debate over the true meaning of fanatical devotion to a scientific cause—the value embodied by one while envied by the other—is also put to rest. The story ends with the narrator, Mōri's disciple, feeling "anxious" *(kokorobosoi)* as he is unsure of "when the discipline of psychology will be led splendidly *(hanabanashiku)* by people like them again."[41] This short passage gives us a glimpse into Kozakai's mixed feelings toward "mad scientists" and the reason why Kario is never completely denounced in the story.

Instead, Kario might appeal to those with certain expectations of heroism in science. The examples of E. S. Morse and Thomas Corwin Mendenhall showed Meiji Japanese how some great individuals can single-handedly further the cause of science. The suggestion of Kario's death as a "loss" is particularly significant given the prevalent feeling of marginality among Japanese scientists since the early 1900s with regard to their Western counterparts. Kario, though a man of questionable morals, could conceivably have led Japanese science out from the shadow of Western science. In his evilness, Kario embodies the extreme leader who can guide the movement for the "independence of science" *(kagaku no jiritsuteki hatten)* that many Japanese scientists had yearned for since the late 1910s. Although most scientists generally meant this as independence from Western leadership and technology, Kario takes it a step further and declares independence from morality.[42]

Within the story, there is no indication of the sort of ethical system that this young narrator will pursue in his scientific career. Since Kozakai passed away soon after the completion of "Tōsō," it is difficult to gauge what opinion he might have had later on if he had lived longer. As it was, the different depictions of devoted agents of science in "Jennā den" and "Tōsō" indicate that Kozakai was ambivalent about the ethicality of science in the late 1920s.

Yumeno Kyūsaku and *Dogura magura*

After Kozakai's death, a new generation of detective fiction writers influenced by his works took up the challenge of questioning the morality of science. Yumeno Kyūsaku was one such writer who used the fanaticism of scientists as an integral part of the plot in his magnum opus, *Dogura magura* (1935). Even before his career as an author of detective fiction, Yumeno dealt with the problematic nature of science and scientists as a journalist, reporting extensively on Sakaki's *elixir vitae* scandal in the early 1920s.[43] Of Kozakai's intellectual offspring, Yumeno offers the most critical view of scientific devotion as a possible virtue.

Dogura magura has long been considered a work written in isolation, detached from its historical and social contexts. Its birth as a self-published work *(jihi shuppan)*, its unique language, and its peculiar narrative structure all encourage this view. As Matsuyama Iwao has suggested, however, *Dogura magura* is a montage of elements of contemporary life, rather than a product of pure imagination detached from reality.[44] Yumeno's incorporation of the discourse on medicine, psychiatry in particular, attests to this view. Recent films were also a source of inspiration, as reflected in the several allusions to *Das Kabinett des Doktor Caligari,* a German expressionist film that created a sensation among Japanese intellectuals in the early 1920s.

Just as the strife between Kario and Mōri caused the death of an innocent bystander, the power struggle in *Dogura magura* between two psychologists, Wakabayashi and Masaki, drags a family of three into hell: one is killed, another is almost killed, and the third is committed to a mental institution. The scale of the experiment in *Dogura magura* eclipses that in "Tōsō": the academic obsession of the two doctors makes them launch a twenty-year experiment involving the Kure family of Fukuoka, a line with a history of a peculiar mental illness. The founder of the Kure family, a Chinese aristocrat from the Tang dynasty, became obsessed with painting scrolls depicting the decay of his recently deceased wife's beautiful skin. The intensity of his desire to witness and capture the range of human flesh (from beautiful to ugly) is present in his painting, and because of it supposedly all of his male descendants suffer from a homicidal strain of the Stendhal syndrome—a trancelike state induced by a work of art—in which a male family member sees the scroll and is compelled to kill all female members of the family. By providing this extensive background information, Yumeno expands not only the range of possible motives but also the origin of one's criminality: in addition to conventional reasons such as financial gain, revenge, elimination, jealousy, and simple blood lust, Yumeno suggests heredity as an unconscious motivation for crime.[45]

Over the years, the scroll in question comes to be hidden in a statue of the Buddha in a nearby temple. The Kure family has continued by producing only daughters and adopting sons-in-law for them to marry. However, when Masaki and Wakabayashi hear about the scroll and the family's accursed bloodline, they begin seducing one of the family's daughters. The two doctors are interested in the theory of "cell memory," the idea that the memories and feelings of ancestors can be transmitted to their descendants through a sort of memory-imprinted DNA.

After having affairs with the two scientists, the Kure daughter gives birth to a son, Ichirō. She tells no one, including Ichirō himself, that one of the scientists—Masaki—is his real father. Having realized her lover's true intentions, she spends her life running away from the man who made her conceive an experimental person. However, in spite of her efforts, the mad scientist hunts them down and shows Ichirō the scroll when he turns sixteen, and he kills his mother. The tragedy is repeated four years later when, the night before Ichirō is to wed Moyoko, his beautiful cousin, his father shows him the scroll. Ichirō is again possessed by a homicidal fit and almost murders his bride.

The story opens with Ichirō waking up in Masaki and Wakabayashi's mental institution, suffering from amnesia and trying to figure out who he is and who showed him the fatal scroll with the clear aim of murder. It is this unique setup that allows Ichirō to be detective, culprit, and victim all at the same time.[46] As Miri Nakamura notes, the two scientists turn Ichirō into "an inhuman automaton" that suspends all judgments when properly stimulated.[47] Kario from "Tōsō" turned a depressed man into a corpse, and Masaki and Wakabayashi transformed a genetically challenged child into a killing machine.

Although Ichirō had a direct hand in one murder and attempted to commit another, the real culprits are the two scientists, who had no qualms about creating a human being solely for the purpose of scientific experimentation and hurting others to gauge the validity of their theory. Ichirō's mother, Chiyoko, had high hopes for what her scientist lover could do for their child: before breaking off their relationship, Chiyoko pleaded with Masaki, Ichirō's real father: "I will give you the cursed scroll to be used as material for your research. Please study it, and use the power of science to break the frightening magical spell cast on the male members of my family. And protect my child from the curse. I beg you."[48] Ironically, Chiyoko confides the secret of the scroll to Masaki, believing that he, a man of science and rationality, can save Ichirō from the cruel curse that flows through his body, while Masaki (and Chiyoko's other ex-lover, Wakabayashi) aim to use her child to observe the real power of such an irrational phenomenon.

In portraying the exploitation of a mental disability by a figure of authority, *Dogura magura* shares its central premise with a film released in Japan a decade earlier that created a sensation among avant-garde filmmakers as well as writers. *Das Kabinett des Doktor Caligari,* originally conceived by Carl Mayer and Hans Janowitz and made into a film by Richard Wiene, is considered an expressionist masterpiece in its native Germany and received no less praise when it reached Japan in 1921.[49] As any complex narrative, the movie functions on many levels and does not allow itself to be reduced to one interpretation. The core of the film is the nightmare of Francis, a mental patient, who hallucinates that the director of the psychiatric institution takes Cesare, a patient suffering from a sleep disorder, to local fairs as a sideshow attraction while posing as Dr. Caligari, an eighteenth-century "mystic." The director, like Caligari, mastered not only the art of manipulating somnambulists but also turning them into tools of murder by hypnotic suggestion, in much the same way as Kario in "Tōsō."[50]

The film shows a scene in which the director first receives the new sleepwalking patient. He is overcome with joy:

> The irresistible passion of my life is being fulfilled. Now I shall unravel the psychiatric secrets of this Caligari! Now I shall learn if it's true that a somnambulist can be compelled to perform acts which, in a waking state, would be abhorrent to him ... whether, in fact, he can be driven against his will to commit a murder.

His fascination soon becomes an obsession: "I must know everything. I must penetrate the heart of his secret. I must become Caligari." In the film, the obsessed director sees the words "You must become Caligari" (Du musst Caligari werden) written on everything around him—rocks, trees, and even the sky—and the "divine" order eventually overtakes his sanity.[51]

The film was well received in Japan and became the must-see blockbuster of 1921. Two literary figures with a strong interest in cinema, Satō Haruo and Tanizaki Jun'ichirō, praised the film for fully realizing the possibilities of the medium.[52] Although Yumeno does not explicitly refer to the film as a source of inspiration, various elements suggest that he used the film as a reference in designing the world of *Dogura magura*. Like Masaki and Wakabayashi, Caligari is a man of science, standing for "an unlimited authority that idolizes power as such, and, to satisfy its lust for domination, ruthlessly violates all human rights and values."[53] Like the asylum director in *Caligari*, Masaki and Wakabayashi adopt a treatment method in which patients are free to move around the grounds of the asylum (*kaihō chiryō*), tested in reality by Kure Shūzō, the authority on mental illness in Japan who also was the personal doctor of the Taishō emperor.

The resemblance between the two stories becomes most apparent in the description of the other patients in the psychiatric institution. In *Caligari*, the hospital courtyard is home to a number of eerie figures: a girl who plays an invisible piano, another girl who cradles a doll in her arms as if it is her baby, an obvious Karl Marx look-alike who rants and gives impassioned speeches to nobody, a neatly groomed man constantly looking for something, and, beside him, Cesare, who is wide awake and stroking a flower. In the middle of the courtyard sits Jane, Francis's love interest, who seems to think she is a queen. In this scene, she bears an uncanny resemblance to the Virgin Mary, with the design of the courtyard floor appearing like rays emanating from her throne, her eyes fixed in a distant, vacant, but serene gaze. She wears a tiara that looks more like a halo than a crown, and sits in divine silence as a nun actually kneels before her in respect. When Francis asks for her hand in marriage, Jane replies, with a wistful gaze: "We queens . . . are not permitted to follow the dictates of our hearts."

Yumeno seems to mirror *Caligari* by surrounding Ichirō with an array of equally bizarre patients: an old man who labors day and night for no purpose, a crazy orator who detests all kinds of "walls," a girl who thinks she is the famous Russian ballerina Anna Pavlova, another would-be "queen" who sports a cardboard crown, and an old man who worships her, believing that she is the reincarnation of the Virgin Mary.54 Although some of these characters overlap with those in *Caligari*, they are not mere copies: the madness of the patients in Masaki and Wakabayashi's institution is due to the cell memory they inherited from their ancestors. But their "memory" also stands in for the new beliefs and ideologies that appeared in modern Japan, such as the desire for self-sufficiency through work *(jijo shugi)*, socialism, so-called new religions *(shinkō shūkyō)*, and the doctrine of art for art's sake *(geijutsu shijō shugi)*.55 These patients are not "mad" in the sense that they do not understand these values as others do, but they understand and embody them to a fault, in much the same way their own doctors personify a fanatical faith in science. When the mad scientists Masaki and Wakabayashi step into the courtyard and join these strange figures, the sinister microcosm of modern madness that Yumeno strove to create is completed.

Caligari and *Dogura magura* also adopt equally peculiar narrative structures, but they each create different effects, making different statements about madness. In the case of *Caligari*, which employs a multilayered narrative with a frame story and a main story, the emphasis is on the "supposed" truthfulness of the frame story. As if to further defeat the brokenhearted Francis, the asylum director appears in the courtyard, looking much less creepy and more dignified than when he was portrayed as Caligari. Upon seeing him, Francis screams, "It's Caligari!" But no one reacts to his warning: rather, it is the moment at which the frame story—the one Wiene reportedly added despite the objections of the original screenwriters—is brought to the fore.56 It was not the director who was crazy enough to pose as Caligari but Francis, who was mad to think that the director had assumed the identity of the manipulative maniac. To his disinterested fellow patients and the audience, Francis screams, "You all think I'm insane! It isn't true—it's the director who's insane!" He is subdued when he attacks the director, forced to wear a straitjacket, and then locked in solitary confinement.

Just as the end of Ichirō's ordeal is not forthcoming, the ending of *Caligari* gives the audience a sense that more harm is on the way, especially when the director turns to the camera and professes to know how to cure Francis. He does so with a hint of madness on his face—the type of madness we are now so used to seeing in people of his profession—as the movie fades out without offering any sense of reassurance. Francis may have been right about his false imprisonment; at the same time, the director may have been genuinely trying to help Francis by using his medical training. In a similar vein, the circular structure of *Dogura magura* discourages the reader from taking any one account, be it that of Ichirō or his doctors, as the absolute truth. One thing vaguely certain is that the end to Ichirō's suffering is nowhere in sight, and science is helpless to rescue him from his misery.

In the midst of despair, Ichirō is given one thing Francis does not have: while Francis is deprived of the chance to speak about his perhaps "unjust" imprisonment at the institution, Ichirō has the opportunity to confront both Masaki and Wakabayashi when he discovers the truth about their unethical behavior:

> "You two can please yourselves doing any research you like. You can live or die as you see fit for your science. But what about the innocent people of the Kure family? You toyed with their lives in the name of research? They didn't do anything bad to you. On the contrary: they trusted you, respected you, admired you, and relied on you, while you duped them, drove them mad, all the while making one of them bear a child for academic experiment. What do you do with their suffering and resentment? . . . Do you mean to say that, as long as you stay faithful to your academic research, you are exempt from everything else?"[57]

Ichirō's words are directed not only at the two doctors who imprisoned him but also at the entire enterprise of science: when such agents of science actively disregard the rights of their patients to their own bodies, their research ceases to serve any other purpose besides satisfying their own sadistic curiosity.

While the two doctors in *Dogura magura*—and Moreau in *Doctor Moreau*—decide to create and ruin a living being's life, be it human or animal, for the sake of scientific observation, other practitioners of science are willing to deprive a person of his or her life for the same purpose. In both cases, the agents of science take it upon themselves to weigh the needs of science against the rights of the individual—with the individual frequently ending up on the wrong side of the equation. It is perhaps this cavalier attitude that makes a "mad scientist" particularly dangerous: the conviction that he (or she) has the right to decide whether an otherwise uninvolved person should live or die in the name of science.

Oguri Mushitarō and "Kanzen hanzai"

We find a similarly dangerous agent of science in Oguri Mushitarō's "Kanzen hanzai" (The Perfect Crime; 1933), the author's debut work. Having spent nearly ten years in obscurity before finally winning a spot in *Shinseinen,* the same magazine in which Kozakai published "Tōsō," Oguri was more than ready for his moment in the sun. Staying away from other writers during this period of preparation also allowed him to produce works that were very different in style and taste from those of his contemporaries. "Kanzen hanzai" is no exception: set on the Sino-Russian border, this story boasts an entirely foreign cast of characters. It is a classic whodunit revolving around the murder of an itinerant Gypsy woman, Hedda, in a locked room. A Russian soldier named Zarov plays the detective, but he remains ineffectual throughout the investigation. The mystery is solved only when Elizabeth Laurel, an English doctor who was hosting Hedda, Zarov, and border-patrol soldiers, confesses her crime to him. She claims that her motive was to rid the world of the tainted blood that coursed through Hedda's veins. During Hedda's stay at the house, Laurel discovers that the itinerant Gypsy is one of the last descendants of the Dukes, a Polish family that had produced generations of criminals. Laurel becomes convinced that, for the sake of posterity, she must end the tainted lineage of Hedda and her forebears: "I received a sacred message from God. I had to make an important decision for the future of mankind."[58] Laurel first tries to sterilize Hedda, but when her attempt fails, she resolves to kill her. It is not up to Hedda to decide what to do with her body: Laurel volunteers to be the one who knows the significance of the contaminated blood and decides whether to let her ignorant (and unwilling) patient live, reproduce, or die.

Laurel also reveals to Zarov a tragic irony: the reason she chose to remain childless is that she too carries the cursed blood. In the name of humankind, Laurel takes Hedda's life, and then decides to end her own, thus ensuring that both afflicted lines will be terminated. From the start, Laurel is portrayed as physically repulsive, and to match her repugnant appearance, she proves she is capable of her own criminality—the product of both her "moral" cause and her "immoral" lineage—by ridding the world of another born criminal.

Perhaps most sinister, though, is how Laurel defends her motive for killing Hedda:

> [The murder I committed] may not be considered a crime in ten years, as I only carried out what was commanded of me by the sacred ideal that exists beyond the bounds of legality: eugenics, the study of improving mankind. We have to terminate all races *(shu)* that we cannot improve. I know that such a belief burns like fire in all conscientious doctors—including myself.[59]

Not only is Laurel a spinster and a doctor, but she is also a bona fide spin-doctor who puts a decidedly scientific slant on her motivation to kill. Laurel echoes the beliefs of contemporary eugenicists who were gaining momentum in medical and fascist discourse on the strong, desirable body. Just three years prior to the publication of "Kanzen hanzai," the first Miss Nippon contest was held and vague ideas about the ideal female body—fertile, strong, and aesthetically pleasing—came to be embodied by the ten finalists chosen. Jennifer Robertson's work illustrates how the contest and the winners offered their audiences and the eugenicists the "timely and timeless image of a eugenically superior national body."[60] Through the death of Hedda, Oguri asks whether her murder, the other side of the racial superiority achieved by eugenics, is justifiable.

Laurel and her genetic equivalent, Hedda, are the antitheses of Miss Nippon, whose "healthy beauty" *(kenkō bi)* emanated from her body with a promise of healthy offspring and future soldiers. Laurel and Hedda lack good blood, healthy bodies, and beauty—the three qualities described by Robertson through which Japan indoctrinated its own people and justified its policies.[61] The fervor to separate "us" from "them" illogically but successfully justified the idea that the inner character and potential of people are visible in their physical features. While the social and political implications of such an idea are frightening, the impact on detective fiction is also significant. Such a notion would violate one of the cardinal rules of detective fiction: a seemingly suspicious figure is never the real killer.

Chillingly, Laurel's prediction that in ten years her action would not be considered a crime came true in Japan within seven. Around the time of the story's publication, news reached Japan that Nazi Germany had legalized the sterilization of those who were "unfit" to reproduce.[62] The Meiji-born tradition of looking to Germany as a model in medical matters, together with the political proximity of Germany and Japan in the 1930s, encouraged the Japanese to follow the lead of the Third Reich. Despite strong opposition, the pro-eugenicists submitted a legislative proposal in 1937 calling for the legalization of eugenics in the interest of racial improvement *(minzoku yūsei hogo hōan)*. Although this proposal was not immediately ratified, its updated reincarnation was later implemented in 1940 as the National Eugenics Law (Kokumin Yūsei Hō), enacted in the interest of nurturing strong soldiers and healthy mothers as the prospect of a long, all-out war loomed more ominously than ever.[63]

In contrast to Yumeno, whose skepticism toward progress is made explicit through such works as *Dogura magura,* it is difficult to decipher where Oguri stood on the intellectual map in relation to science. Oguri has often been described by critics such as Ōishi Masahiko as a "pedantic" detective author who mesmerizes readers not with ingenious plots and tricks but by a display of spectacular erudition.[64] In addition to eugenics, Oguri touched upon issues such as the theory of hereditary criminality and predeterminist theories on the relationship between physical and psychological aspects of human existence in the 1930s. In his stories and essays, nothing points to him being pro-eugenicist: the writer who chose a life of poverty over material wealth is too much of a lone wolf to be lured into believing totalitarianism.

Perhaps an essay by Oguri from 1934 titled "Senja fuda kigen no kōyaku" (The Thousand Shrine Talisman: The Balm for Mysterious Experiences) can offer a clue. In it, he expresses a growing interest in *shinriteki gunshū* (mob psychology), which "locates the motive outside the individual *(kotai)* in detective fiction," rather than detective fiction that pits the criminal against the detective. Oguri is interested in how "a hypnotic suggestion *(anji)* and a mysterious force *(shinpiryoku),*" found outside the individual or even the collective, urge the implied party or parties to commit crimes.[65] Eugenics claimed that "a wide range of human physical, mental, and moral traits were inherited" and sustained an appeal to a wide range of audiences, both left and right, in many parts of the world in the early twentieth century.[66] In the case of "Kanzen hanzai," eugenics worked as a kind of pseudojustification and provoked a doctor to take an innocent bystander's life. The mid-1930s also saw the rise of other ideological forces that drove people to indiscriminate and impersonal killings: nationalism and militarism. When the fanatical devotion of the agents of science, itself a quasi-mystical force, finds convenient allies in these destructive ideologies, the mission to improve human beings or create new species better equipped for survival becomes an even more relentless pursuit of scientific advancement at the expense of human ethics.

Unno Jūza and "Hae otoko"

Just as the pro-eugenics argument charged ahead at full steam in 1937, the fundamental moral ambiguity of modern scientific endeavor became a central concern for Unno Jūza, another writer within the same circle of detective fiction aficionados as Yumeno Kyūsaku and Oguri Mashitarō. Whereas Yumeno dealt with the problem of scientists' fanatical devotion to the profession in *Dogura magura,* Unno showed in his works from the early 1930s the extreme lengths to which the mad scientist would go to secure a proper guinea pig for his research. In "Fushū" (The Possessed) from 1934, Unno depicts a mad scientist named Muroto, the most respected surgeon in Japan, who is obsessed with creating a human body that functions at maximum efficiency. His fixation ends up alienating him from himself and makes him operate on his own body. In the process, he creates not a superhuman but a horrible monster.

The story starts with his young and unhappy wife, Uoko, plotting her husband's murder with her lover, Matsunaga, in Muroto's remote laboratory. Muroto appears in the story as nothing short of an obsessed agent of science. Uoko goes to see him in his lab one last time before seizing the chance to kill him: "My husband, who was towering over the operating table studying carefully the corpse on it, looked up at me [on hearing me enter]. Between the white operation cap and a large surgical mask, I could only see his startlingly enlarged eyes."[67] His unusually intense gaze is the telltale evidence of his madness—and his undesirability as a husband. Soon after, Uoko kills him by pushing him into a deep well.

After Muroto's death, however, Matsunaga and Uoko are troubled by a string of strange events: Matsunaga, a banker, is falsely accused of robbing his own workplace and killing a guard, until the authorities discover that the thief stole not only money from the bank but the organs from the dead guard. The bank was completely sealed at the time of the robbery, save for a six-inch-square air vent. Within twenty-four hours, Matsunaga goes missing, leaving Uoko a note saying that he has been scarred for life. A series of bizarre events forces Uoko to suspect that Muroto is still alive, and her suspicion is further confirmed when she finds beside Matsunaga's note some ashes from the German cigarettes her husband used to smoke.

Soon after her lover's disappearance, Uoko is drugged and taken back to Muroto's lab, where Muroto disfigures the murderous lovers, grafting Matsunaga's face onto Uoko's head. What is perhaps even more frightening is that Muroto's overconfidence in his skills as a surgeon and the righteousness of his actions have allowed him to perform a gruesome experiment on himself, leaving him with one lung, half a face, and no stomach. He also cuts off all of his limbs, sacrificing mobility for the sake of optimal energy use.[68] After eliminating his original limbs, he uses more powerful synthetic ones magnetically attached to his torso. These new limbs enabled him both to escape the well and to enter the closed bank through the tiny vent. The radical physical transformation is also why the doctor ended all sexual relations with his wife, which made her suspect he was impotent. The case is only put to rest when the doctor dies from his own error (he starves to death when he mismanages the equipment that attaches the artificial limbs to his body), and his wicked scheme is exposed by the able private eye Homura Sōroku (Unno's clever play on the name Sherlock Holmes).

Because Muroto is already dead when Homura bursts into his lab, he spares the mad scientist a moral lecture. In another story by Unno from the same year, "Ningen kai" (Human Ashes), Homura takes a more unforgiving attitude toward a young engineer at a liquid hydrogen plant whose similar obsession with research ends up claiming six lives. At the end of this story, Homura reprimands the deranged engineer: "You are a man with an unforgivable hobby. You have forgotten God *(kami)*. When a scientist becomes oblivious to God, he is likely to end up like you."[69]

Homura reappears as the force to expose the wrongdoings of the agents of science in Unno's later works. While still working as a government engineer by day, Unno published two stories in 1937 that dealt with the theme of "improving the human body" *(jintai kairyō)*: "Jūhachiji no ongakuyoku" (Soaking in Music at 1800 Hours) and "Hae otoko" (The Fly Man). The former depicts the demise of a dystopian totalitarian regime that attempts to create perfect soldiers by brainwashing them with music, a sort of melodic propaganda. It is also the kind of story that crowns Unno as the founding father of Japanese science fiction.

"Hae otoko," on the other hand, adopts the form of detective fiction. The story tackles the problem of the unrelenting human desire to engineer a "superman" using the seemingly boundless power of technology. In this story, the murders in question include an unidentified corpse burned beyond recognition, a wealthy industrialist hung in his own home, and a judge who received a fatal gunshot to his head. Each murder was carried out in a sealed environment, suggesting that the investigation force is dealing with a classic locked-room mystery. These killings are so gruesome and illogical that detective Homura predicts early during the investigation that the culprit could only be a strange being at least eight feet tall who can also enter and leave any area through a small hole that barely allows a human head to pass. As the critic Nagayama Yasuo points out, this description of the killer alludes to Edgar Allan Poe's classic mystery *The Murders in the Rue Morgue*.[70] In *Rue Morgue*, too, there appears to be a superhuman killer who exceeds all conventional expectations of human behavior. After examining the evidence in the crime scene and testimony from various witnesses, C. Auguste Dupin, the story's detective, concludes that the unimaginable murders of a mother and a daughter are indeed the work of a nonhuman. In reaching this horrendous but logical conclusion, Dupin encourages his anonymous sidekick to rid himself of all preconceived notions in figuring out whodunit:

> You have properly reflected upon the odd disorder of the chamber, we have gone so far as to combine the ideas of an agility astounding, a strength superhuman, a ferocity brutal, a butchery without motive, a *grotesquerie* in horror absolutely alien from humanity, and a voice foreign in tone to the ears of men of many nations, devoid of all distinct or intelligible syllabification. What result, then, has ensued?[71]

Based on such evidence, Dupin eliminates the possibility that the killer is human and allows the impossibility that the grisly murders are the work of an orangutan.

In a similar vein, Homura Sōroku comes up with an outrageous physical description of the killer based on the material evidence. Even though the logically constructed profile itself appears highly unlikely, the culprit in "Hae otoko" turns out to be just what Homura imagined him to be: "an eight-foot monster who can go in and out of a locked room like smoke!"[72] The hideous creature, dubbed the "Fly Man," is the creation of Dr. Shiota, a mad scientist who is also the first victim. His obsession with creating a "superman" led him to obtain illegally the body of an executed criminal through a friend, a corrupted judge. Once Shiota gets the corpse, he revives him only to harvest parts of his body to make an efficient human body that does not waste energy but focuses it on his brain. The reasoning behind Shiota's plan is that by making the Fly Man's body more efficient, this new superhuman can devote nearly all of his resources and energy to his cognitive faculty—thus becoming a superior being of unprecedented mental power.

It is this corpse that is brought back to life to become the eponymous villain of the story. After escaping Shiota's care, the hapless monster takes revenge on the three men who took his life, toyed with it, and gave it back at will: the wealthy industrialist who falsely incriminated him in the colonies, the judge who gave him the unusually harsh punishment of a death sentence to pave the way for the illegal operation, and the scientist who chopped up his body and transformed him into a monster. Unno's Fly Man is as much a demonic construct of mad scientists as Yumeno's Ichirō: the agents of modern science, who have the skills and potential to help them, only exploit their condition instead.

By featuring artificially created "freaks"—an orangutan in Paris, a half-fly, half-human being in Tokyo—Poe and Unno show how changes in external social reality force us to stretch our imaginations in what we recognize as possible. In *Rue Morgue*, the ideology of European imperialism brings about the beast's transfer from his native surroundings to Paris, the heartland of civilization: such ideology occasions the Parisian sailor's trip to the Indian Archipelago and to Borneo in the first place. By having such unexpected culprits, Poe's *Rue Morgue* and Unno's "Hae otoko" tease out the two dominant narratives of modernity—imperialism and science, respectively—and the fantastic darkness that these modern realities create.

Such darkness deepens when the "monster" identifies his assets and takes control of his ability. Making use of his tremendous brain power, the Fly Man elevates himself from a mere violent killing machine to the level of an "intellectual" who understands the values of ridicule and parody. While Unno paints a sinister picture of science through Shiota's obsession and the Fly Man's misery, he also pokes fun at the achievements of science by focusing on forensics. Muramatsu, the prosecutor and the forensic expert in charge of the case of the wealthy industrialist, examines the body carefully. Muramatsu explains his findings to the police chief *(shochō)* Masaki, who appears less forensically adept:

> "Mr. Masaki, look at this. The trauma to the head was made by something sharp like a gimlet. Besides, we can see how the killer inserted the weapon once and pulled it out. It is a strange way to kill indeed."
>
> "I agree, Mr. Prosecutor. To have pulled out the thing shows some composure. He must be an extremely strong individual, or he wouldn't have been able to do this."
>
> "Yes. This is no ordinary method for murder."
>
> "Mr. Prosecutor, do you think the victim was strangled to death first, or stabbed first?"
>
> "Mr. Masaki, of course the injury to the head took place first. The amount of blood lost by the victim can attest to that. And," he pointed to the blood stain behind the victim's head, "the blood stain extends far, and there is a trace of [dragged] rope on the blood. This means the killer put the rope around him after he was dead."[73]

What is comedic in this scene is that Muramatsu, the prosecutor who eloquently reconstructs the crime, is actually the Fly Man in an elaborate disguise. He not only reveals his own modus operandi to the ineffectual police force but also makes fun of the enterprise of forensic science itself, as it provides only useless information for figuring out the profile of the killer. The Fly Man spoofs the role of the forensic scientist, who mesmerizes nonspecialists with his ability to reconstruct what transpired using clues that remain invisible to the untrained eye. It is the role that Thorndyke once so impeccably exemplified for Western and Japanese audiences. The Fly Man is equally capable intellectually, but he ultimately uses his talents to outsmart rather than assist law enforcement. In doing this, the Fly Man suggests that science, as knowledge (and technology), is not inherently ethical: it could end up in the wrong hands and aid in committing crimes that are harder to solve.

"Hae otoko" is a vendetta story of an unfortunate man who was subjected to a heartless experiment. The Fly Man, who no longer resembles a human being, harbors a resentment similar to that of Ichirō from *Dogura magura:* his murderous rage is fueled by his anger toward the irresponsible application of technology. His killing spree is stopped only when he engages Homura in man-to-man combat and is defeated. Unlike Western stories of mad scientists, "Hae otoko" does not feature the mad scientist giving an explanation of his rationale and objectives. The only sentiment Unno allows Shiota to speak directly is his regret:

> "Forgetting God, I have stepped into the study of evil *(ma no gakumon)*. I regret now that I have created the 'shrunken man' *(shukushō ningen)*. If I can, I want to kill him tonight before dawn. Doing so can erase my study and rid the world of his unprecedented superhuman violence. I have to kill him as soon as possible."[74]

The passage suggests the return of ethics to the mind of a mad scientist who tampered with divine power. Shiota, however, still seeks to play God as long as he believes that the annihilation of the monster is the only way to undo the damage.[75]

Mad Scientists, War, and Human Experiments

To trace the development of the subgenre of "mad scientist murders" within the flow of modern Japanese detective fiction is to witness a gradual shift in the articulation of motive from personal to impersonal, or from subjective to objective. The more "traditional" motivations of greed, jealousy, and simple hatred came to share the spotlight with more detached and clinical reasons to kill. Within the world of interwar Japanese pulp fiction, mad scientist murders are located at the intersection of science fiction and detective fiction. More precisely, it is where the two formerly indistinct genres begin to diverge. Whereas early detective fiction—original and translated works alike—may have served as an advertisement for science, the mad scientist murders of the 1920s and 1930s call for a more cautionary attitude toward the omnipotence and the fundamental ethicality of science.

The works discussed here were among the first in Japan to disseminate at the popular level the view of science and progress as illusions created and perpetuated by the ideologues of not only Meiji but also European enlightenment. The decades of the 1920s and 1930s saw, together with the rise of the pulps in both Japan and the West, the spread of the prejudice of pulp fiction as a vehicle for escapism: "a reputation that would be difficult for the mystery, the western, and particularly science fiction to live down."[76] Examining mad scientist murders within the discourse of ethics in science suggests that these authors, all educated professionals, gathered within the space of supposedly "lowly" pulp not only to express their own opinions but also to exchange sophisticated and potentially subversive ideas with others. It is ironic that detective fiction, a genre considered frivolous and disposable, offered an arena in which writers could voice their serious concerns about the world around them. As was the case with Yumeno and *Dogura magura,* the writers produced these works with little or no prospect of monetary reward. The mask of "pulp" that magazines offered was the perfect cover under which authors could invade the minds of readers when they were off guard in the relative ideological quiet of their "leisure" time. Rather than playing along with state ideology and popular faith in the positive aspects of science, a group of Japanese detective fiction writers used shocking plot twists, fantastic inventions, and deranged villains to provoke readers to contemplate the gloomy outlook for a future wrought by the potential madness of science without conscience.

It is no coincidence that this recasting of motive and the bifurcation of science fiction and detective fiction came at a time when science and technology played a growing role in the formulation of Japan's political and military ideology. The war effort in the 1930s and 1940s made real the human experiments Kozakai, Yumeno, and Unno prophesied in fiction years earlier. Experiments in creating or achieving "maximum efficiency" in human beings were no longer limited to the world of fiction: they became a part of everyday life for the entire population when scientists and the wartime government tinkered with ration levels to find the line between minimum nourishment and starvation.[77] Kyushu Imperial University, origin of the notorious *elixir vitae* scandal and home institution of the villains in Yumeno's *Dogura magura,* was also the site of vivisection experiments on captured American soldiers in May 1945.[78] Despite the efforts of the writers in showing readers the fictional horrors of runaway science, their vision of catastrophe was actualized in the all-too-real terrors of the atomic bomb; the mad scientist who takes apart human bodies without remorse came to life as the Japanese doctors and scientists involved in human experimentation projects such as Unit 731 in wartime China.

The doctors of Unit 731 in Harbin were perhaps the most sinister incarnations of these fictional mad scientists. One of the project's main figures, Yuasa Ken, confessed after the war that he went to Manchuria knowing that he would "have opportunities to vivisect" and described how he (and presumably others) became acclimated to the daily operations at the institute: "After one does it once, one grows accustomed to it. By the third time I was willing."[79] Another employee at the institute, Akimoto Sueo, studied at the University of Tokyo with a specialization in serology prior to joining the unit—exactly the same professional training as Kozakai Fuboku. The same educational background produced one mind that came to question the ethicality of science and another willing to turn a blind eye to its potential ambiguity and moral problems. War and nationalism exploited such precarious arbitrariness, and many scientists in limbo were more than willing to join the effort. As Tessa Morris-Suzuki points out, "Japan's wartime research exposed the deadly possibilities of modern technology when harnessed to the pursuit of national glory."[80] The mad scientist murders demonstrate that such "deadly possibilities" were already articulated by popular authors and were projected into the popular imagination as real probabilities in the years leading up to the war. They record what generally remains unrecorded and offer remarkable insight into the morally ambiguous image of science and scientists on the eve of war.

4. Drafted Detectives and Total War: Three Editors of *Shupio*

Living and Writing Total War

In analyzing the difference between premodern and modern military campaigns, sociologist Anthony Giddens argues that modern warfare can be described as "total war," in which every aspect of battle—including the organization of the army and the production of weapons—is touched by the principles of industrialization. As a result, victory depends on having abundant material as well as human resources for the long term: the side that first exhausts them loses.[1]

Japan first experienced this modern warfare in the late 1930s to 1945, when it found itself fighting battles on multiple fronts against the Allied powers. More than ever, citizens were regarded as resources, and living in a state of total war confronted them with a new and tremendous challenge. This was particularly true for writers: for the first time in Japan they were drafted specifically for their skills and were expected to serve the country in this capacity. Many made their way to the outskirts of the empire to report the bravery of the Japanese forces in combat. In addition, the call to duty did not end when these writers returned home: they were asked to continue to publicly support the war, and inspire their readers—who were also precious resources as future soldiers in the scheme of total war—in order for the country to achieve ultimate victory. Fulfilling the new task of state spokesperson was easier if one already agreed with, or was willing to be seduced by, the ideology of militarism and nationalism. Many writers were hesitant, at least in the beginning, to comply with such an overt request for propaganda. For those who refused to play any part in the government's brainwashing efforts, there seemed to be only two fates: to remain silent and cease to be a writer, or to voice dissent and be jailed.

According to the two most respected historians of Japanese detective fiction, Nakajima Kawatarō (1917–99) and Itō Hideo (1925–), the genre was facing a new threat from the authorities in the late 1930s. It was deemed not only useless but also harmful as a means by which to mobilize readers: detective fiction features Japanese killing other Japanese (when they should instead be killing enemy nationals).[2] The official genealogy of Japanese detective fiction regrettably and commonly discusses how Edogawa Ranpo, a well-respected leader of the genre, famously entered a period of self-imposed exile and spent his days organizing the legendary *Harimaze nenpu* (Cut-and-Paste Chronology of My Life), without the prospect of ever publishing it, while others, including postwar giant Yokomizo Seishi, opted for *torimonochō*—tales of old-fashioned criminal investigations set in the Edo period (1600–1868). Many others simply left the genre altogether because it attracted unwanted attention from the censors.

Because of this desertion, the wartime authorities are often accused of stifling detective fiction in this era by imposing a strict system of censorship. Nakajima and Itō both identified the beginning of the Pacific War as the end of interwar detective fiction, suggesting that the genre was made nonexistent as hostilities raged. The cancellation of the magazine *Shupio* in early 1938, the last stronghold of the genre in the publishing world, was the event that set the course for the genre's eventual disappearance from printed media during the war. Only a year earlier, Oguri Mushitarō, Kigi Takatarō, and Unno Jūza had joined forces to establish this magazine under the common goal of nurturing the genre of detective fiction by laying out its theoretical foundations, giving newcomers the opportunity to publish their works, and generally expanding the boundaries of the genre.[3]

For sympathetic readers and critics, the three author-editors were victims of wartime repression. On the other hand, the less forgiving see their decision to cancel *Shupio* as a statement of willing collaboration—political redirection from their former, relatively "liberal" views to fascist and nationalist stances—or at least abandonment of attempts to resist political oppression on creativity.[4] The official explanation that *Shupio* was having financial difficulties did not convince contemporary readers, especially as Oguri even noted in the magazine's last issue that the sales department had urged the editors to continue publishing.[5]

The hasty burial of their brainchild under suspicious circumstances is even more perplexing given that the three authors remained prolific beyond 1938. Kigi and Unno delved into science fiction *(kagaku shōsetsu),* a burgeoning genre that would get much attention during the war, while Oguri immersed himself in his so-called *jingai makyō* series (literally: stories from beyond the reaches of civilization), which was filled with wondrous creatures and fantastic adventures.

These are not mere examples of former detective writers taking refuge in other genres in order to avoid scrutiny; rather, a close reading of their wartime works reveals that they continued to use the techniques of intrigue and the allure of mystery in their new endeavors. Such an examination challenges the prevalent view that censors, publishers, and writers were bent on suppressing detective fiction in any shape or form, as the genre was deemed "seditious" and "unfit for times of crisis."[6] The elements of detective fiction present in works published during the war suggest that wartime censorship was a porous and imperfect system, and that authors could and did find loopholes in the grid of power and injected their works with thinly veiled critiques and messages. Their works urge us to question the nature of the wartime "ban" on detective fiction as suggested by Itō and Nakajima: the accounts of writers and censorship on other media suggest that it was not a "ban" based on a strict, top-down decree but one enforced more through voluntary cessation. A number of factors contribute to the genre's triumphant comeback in the postwar era: survival of the genre in other disguises during the late 1930s to early 1940s is certainly one important element.

Based on this view, the writings of the three *Shupio* editors appear not as products of coercion but as expressions of their limited freedom or negotiated agency. Using their works between 1938 and 1945, we can trace the state of detective fiction in what has previously been considered the genre's "blank years." A number of elements in the story "Kaitō-ō" (The King of the Mysterious Tower; 1938), the first serialization Unno undertook immediately after ending *Shupio,* dismantles the view that detective writers were forced out of the genre by the censors. Instead, "Kaitō-ō" suggests that Unno was willing to adopt the techniques, setups, and plots of detective fiction in order to achieve the ideal that he had been hatching for more than a decade: the promulgation of a new brand of science (namely, Japanese science) that could counter the dominance of Western science. Although he was originally reluctant to conform to the demands of the state, Unno eventually found a powerful ally in wartime Japanese nationalism. The presence of detective fiction elements in "Kaitō-ō," as well as Unno's long-standing skepticism toward Western science, suggests that his departure from detective fiction was gradual rather than abrupt. Nor was it so much a result of coercion as a personal and deliberate decision to search for a more suitable means of communicating his alarm over the moral ambiguities of Western science.

An analysis of the writings of the other two editors is equally indebted to detective fiction, and it lets us go back to the notion of overseas colonies as an important source of mystery in modernity. Kigi's and Oguri's works allow us to examine how imperialism affects this notion by shaping the context of the writers' encounter with the "colonial others"—non-Japanese peoples whose appearance, culture, and ways of thinking were unfamiliar to the Japanese. Paul Ricoeur describes the nature of the trauma one experiences when one discovers the relativity of one's thinking, culture, and existence:

> When we discover that there are several cultures instead of just one and consequently at the time when we acknowledge the end of a sort of cultural monopoly, be it illusory or real, we are threatened with the destruction of our own discovery. Suddenly it becomes possible that there are just *others*, that we ourselves are an "other" among others. All meaning and every goal having disappeared, it becomes possible to wander through civilizations as if through vestiges and ruins.[7]

Two of the *Shupio* editors seem to have gone through similar moments of shock during the war. The case of Kigi shows how he started out with a healthy skepticism for Japan's readiness to be the leader of Asia, but then grew increasingly nationalistic as conditions changed. His eventual shift toward right-wing ideology during the Pacific War lets us catch a glimpse of the frailty of interwar urban liberalism that Kigi supposedly operated in and helped uphold during the 1930s as a proponent of detective fiction. For him, racial and cultural ambiguities were not only the source of colonial mystery but also dangerous subversive elements that threatened the homogenization of the population based on nationalism.

The discovery of other cultures and perspectives was less traumatic and more inspiring for Oguri. It is in him that we find perhaps the most complex reaction to the emergence of Japanese nationalism and militarism. In contrast to Kigi and Unno, Oguri was a well-known antiestablishment figure *(han taiseiha)* from the years leading to the war: in 1934, he was asked, "What thing, phenomenon, and personality do you dislike the most?" to which he replied, "Thunder, new Japanese music, and Hitler."[8] His antagonism toward Japanese militarist rule grew particularly strong after a trip to Malaya, during which, though he left few written records, he supposedly witnessed firsthand the harms brought by Japanese colonialism to local populations and environments. Oguri used his fiction to express both his antimilitary sentiment and his embrace of cultural relativism; these and other political messages in his works give us a glimpse into the struggles to write in an oppressive political regime that lives off colonialism.

The diversity and the complexity of the political undertones embedded in these stories thought to have been produced under duress bring into question the prevalent view that detective fiction was decisively "banned" in Japan during 1938–45, and elucidate both the possibilities and limits of interwar Japanese detective fiction as a political and propagandistic tool. The overtly limited nature of wartime "freedom of expression" teases out the literary contrivances, manipulations, and negotiations that the writers needed to perform in order to exercise their agency.

The "Ban" on Detective Fiction: Debunking the Myth

The traditional view that the authorities suppressed detective fiction during the late 1930s to the end of the Pacific War has gone unchallenged in the postwar era. Among recent scholars, Cécile Sakai touches on the ban of the genre and its effects on authors during the war and beyond in her *Histoire de la littérature populaire japonaise,* and readily adopts this account.[9] Building on this interpretation, Mark H. Silver in his dissertation also uses 1941, the beginning of the Pacific War, as the end point of his investigation, suggesting his agreement with the view that the genre went into a hiatus following the ban.[10]

Sakai and Silver share the same view on the wartime fate of Japanese detective fiction in part because they consult the same sources: Edogawa Ranpo and Nakajima Kawatarō. Ranpo's chronology of the genre, *Tantei shōsetsu yonjūnen* (serialized from 1949 to 1961, first in *Shinseinen* and then in *Hōseki*), is regarded as the authoritative source on the activity (or lack thereof) in the genre during the difficult years of the war. In his essay "Insei wo ketsui su" (Deciding to Retire), Ranpo remembers how he felt ostracized by the publishing world. In 1939, the authorities ordered the elimination of his "Imomushi" (The Worm), a work written a decade earlier, from his new selected works series put out by the publishers Shun'yōdō and Shinchōsha.[11] In the same year, the publishers were also ordered to expunge parts of Ranpo's "Ryōki no hate" and "Kumo otoko."[12] Ranpo later lamented this period in his essay "Tantei shōsetsu yonjūnen" (Forty Years with Detective Fiction): "I thought that I could no longer write detective fiction. I thought the only option for me was to stop writing for a while, just as I did several times before. But even without my making known my intention to leave writing, the editors stopped soliciting my works anyway."[13] According to Ranpo, unless one was willing to convert *(tenkō suru)* and side with the "new regime"—or *shin taisei*, as the second Konoe cabinet (1940–41) called itself—there was no way one could get away with writing detective fiction.[14] In 1941, all of Ranpo's past works went out of print, leaving him without income. It is because of this financial difficulty, he claims, that he took the advice of his publisher and decided to write new stories under a different pseudonym.[15] In subsequent years, Ranpo published "Chie no Ichitarō" (Ichitarō the Wise; 1942) and "Idainaru yume" (Great Dream; 1943)—both nationalist and without his previous rigor—but he remained largely underproductive. Even when looking beyond the retrospective sentimentalism of later critics and fans, we see that the years 1939 to 1945 were tough indeed for Ranpo, as the state of affairs in the world prevented him from writing detective fiction, something he always loved.

The wartime fate of Ranpo and his works has long been considered representative of the fate of all detective writers. Building on Ranpo's account, Nakajima Kawatarō, his close friend, argued that it became more and more difficult for writers to publish detective fiction starting in the late 1930s, and virtually impossible after the onset of the Pacific War in 1941.[16] Such an assertion is not untrue, especially considering the changes in the tastes of publishers. For instance, *Shinseinen,* once the stronghold of the frivolous but delightfully sophisticated literatures that appealed to urban and provincial youths alike, adopted an increasingly pro-militarist tone starting in the late 1930s. In 1937, the magazine issued a special supplementary issue titled "Kagayaku kōgun" (Resplendent Imperial Army).

The theme of this issue turned out to prefigure things to come: the editorial office, headed by the fervent nationalist and savvy businessman Ōhashi Shin'ichi (1885–1956), leaned more and more toward publishing so-called *gunji shōsetsu* (military fiction) as the years went by. Inui Shin'ichirō (1906–2000), one of the editors of *Shinseinen* from 1937 to 1939, recalls that Ōhashi was willing to let the magazine become more and more pro-militarist and pro-nationalist.[17] Yokomizo Seishi (1902–81), an editor of *Shinseinen* in the late 1920s who was still close to the editorial office in the late 1930s, also recalls that Ōhashi routinely paid attention to how the authorities viewed his company and magazines.[18] The magazine kicked off 1938 with a New Year's special issue titled "Tantei sakka sōdōin kessakushū" (Masterpieces of Mobilized Detective Writers).[19] Although the stories published under this rubric did not necessarily reflect the same aggressively militaristic attitude, the nonfictional pieces in the same issue, such as "Sensō to gunryaku" (War and Strategizing) and "Hijōjika no kokumin keizai" (Domestic Economy in the Time of Crisis), pushed this agenda more forcefully. More and more pages were devoted to such essays and works of military fiction, and detective fiction was pushed to the fringes of the wartime literary world.[20]

As tensions escalated, detective fiction was seen as too frivolous for times of national crisis. Such a view is not unique to Japan: its military allies Italy and Germany also prohibited the genre on the grounds that it was "seditious" and "Anglo-Saxon."[21] As early as 1938, Kōga Saburō had already decried the harmful effects of detective fiction during crisis by arguing that its liberalism and individualism were no longer appropriate for the times. In his declaration—a veritable *tenkō* manifesto, only without the word *tenkō*—Kōga publicly denounced the endeavor of writing detective fiction altogether during the time of crisis, alluding to its frivolous nature:

> Overseas, hundreds, and at times thousands of people, are being killed. Brave and loyal soldiers are fighting for the sake of their

homeland *(sokoku)*, sacrificing their flesh and blood.... Detective fiction, it seems, is an entertainment for peaceful times.... In other countries, safety in urban areas usually declines in wartime. In our capital, order is kept with utmost care. Stories about phantom thieves, abductions of women in broad daylight, or half-human half-beasts killing people in the middle of the capital not only appear embarrassing and call for some self-imposed restraint *(enryo)*.[22]

Kōga intended not only to clarify his personal beliefs but also to encourage others to follow his lead. Moreover, since his manifesto was published in *Shupio* only months before its final issue, it is reasonable to speculate that the three editors were in agreement with Kōga, and canceled their detective fiction as a gesture of "self-imposed restraint," even though they never explicitly stated so.

Exercising "restraint," however, is different from being placed under a strict "ban." Once self-imposed inactivity and forced silence are distinguished, the arguments of Ranpo and Nakajima start to contradict other accounts put forth by other writers and their fiction. A close examination of the elements of the individual works that made it past censors during the war years, as well as testimonies from other contemporaries, reveal that detective fiction may not have been victimized as much as the two once claimed. Although conflict between Japan and the United States became more and more imminent in the late 1930s and the early 1940s, certain tidbits about everyday life in Japan inform us that elements of Western culture within Japanese life were tolerated until the last minute. For instance, English conversation lessons continued on the radio through the Sino-Japanese conflict to the day of Pearl Harbor.[23] Overtly Anglo-Saxon influence was also tolerated in the world of cinema: the Office of Information ordered film companies to produce and show the kind of films that would "inspire the national spirit and make audiences ready to tackle the national crisis with all their might."[24] Responding to this, the major cinemas in Tokyo stopped showing *Mr. Smith Goes to Washington* on December 8, 1941. Curiously, however, they continued to show movies featuring Mickey Mouse and Popeye.[25]

The examples of the radio broadcast and the film lineup imply that the authorities seized control of various facets of the media only gradually, if at all. There were many counterintuitive phenomena on the eve of and possibly during the war against America, implying that the government's control over everyday life was not "total." The censors also were keen on regulating sexual content in the movies, but even the standards for what passed as acceptable material were never clearly defined. Kanō Mikiyo points out that the standards of censorship for cinema in this period were extremely vague, and whether a movie passed as fit for screening largely depended on the subjective assessment of individual censors.[26] Tajima Tomio, who had served as the head censor *(shuseki ken'etsukan)* for several years, defined *chitai* (lewdness) in the movies as follows: "Plainly speaking, [a movie is fit for showing] if a mother and her teenage daughter see it and the mother can answer all her daughter's questions without feeling uncomfortable or having a guilty conscience."[27] However, the possible range for what contemporary mother and teenage daughter pairs would find embarrassing was, of course, left out unstated.

What got by the censors seems to have also been decided in an equally arbitrary manner in the case of detective fiction. Some of Ranpo's contemporaries appear to have interpreted the "prohibition" on his works through the symbolic elimination of "Imomushi" in 1938 as not necessarily a warning regarding the entire genre but as a check on the decadent style that Ranpo had come to represent. In 1940, fellow detective writer Ōshita Udaru (1896–1966) wrote:

> Detective fiction was greatly affected by the Manchurian Incident. The range of topics is limited, and the taste for decadence that was previously the hallmark of detective fiction to some degree was denounced. So the job of the [detective] writer is now regulated rigidly. . . . However, it is a hasty conclusion to assume that detective fiction is bound to go to ruin because of this. In reality, a considerable amount of detective fiction is published every month, though not as much as romance or period fiction. Maybe Ranpo too will start writing again. The current state of affairs does discourage decadence, but it also influences the genre in positive ways. Detective writers are asked to work with a new literary palette that can replace the flashiness of decadence.[28]

Ōshita's comments imply that it was not the genre that was being censored but rather the decadent elements in a single author's works. His contention that "a considerable amount of detective fiction is published every month" is also verified by the story lineups of none other than *Shinseinen,* which continued publishing special issues on the genre until the spring of 1940. Their spring supplementary issue, titled "Tantei shōsetsu kessakushū" (Masterpieces of Detective

Fiction), featured stories by such authors as Ellery Queen, Carter Dickson, and Agatha Christie. In terms of the lineup, *Shinseinen* was willing to be as Anglo-Saxon as it had been in previous years.

Ranpo himself seems to have originally interpreted the ban in a similar manner. The crisis that threatened to bring his literary career to an end made Ranpo reflect on his own writing and his relationship to the genre. At the height of desperation, he wrote:

> To tell you the truth, I exhausted all forms of detective fiction within the first few years of my career, and I only continued to write, without interest, because of Kōdansha's flattery and high salary. . . . From month to month I wrote whatever came to my mind, without planning the plot. . . . I could write that. However, to side with the new regime *(shin taisei)* is a totally different story. I have to completely abandon myself and become reborn. It is impossible unless I entirely commit myself to it or discover a new direction. Something inalienable I have acquired over the years, something that attracted many readers and sold many books, that same something made it impossible for me to convert *(tenkō)* to the new regime. This is why I cannot follow other detective writers.[29]

Ranpo later confessed that he wrote this brutally honest account on January 7, 1941, without thinking that it would ever be published (or that he would ever publish again): "I wrote this feeling that I would not be able to write detective fiction until the end of the war, not knowing if I would survive the war . . . so it is a truthful account."[30] According to this supposedly truthful account, Ranpo did not side with the military right (after it took an interest in having an increased voice in the publishing world) because of a firm conviction against their endeavor, but for the simpler (apolitical) reason of creative impotence.

In addition, Inui Shin'ichirō, as one of the last editors of the prewar *Shinseinen*, suggests that total and willing compliance was by no means necessary to save one's skin in the late 1930s to early 1940s. Inui recalls the relationship between the editorial office and the censors as follows: "Given the sentiment of the period, there was no way we could directly oppose the military. But there was no need to lead their invasion into the printed world either."[31] True to his word, Inui ended up leaving his enviable position at the publisher Hakubunkan in 1939.

Shinseinen, summer supplementary issue, 1939. This is one of the last supplementary issues exclusively featuring detective fiction. To the right of the image is a small stamp reading "Kokui hatsuyō" (Promoting Higher National Morale), indicating the sentiment of the time.

Contrary to the retrospectively constructed discourse on wartime detective fiction and the publishing industry, these accounts from the time inform us that it is wrong to imagine detective fiction writers enduring the kind of suppression involving physical violence, such as the brutal treatment of Kobayashi Takiji (1903–33) that led to his death. The "ban" on the genre was not carried out in the form of a strict top-down decree, but as a symbolic elimination of decade-old work by one author, and largely through self-imposed restraint and willing collaboration on the part of writers and publishers. Detective texts were solicited less frequently, but that is not to say that those who wrote them were actively persecuted. The same authorities that had banned Ranpo's works earlier also included them in care packages to soldiers on the front lines. The *Kurogane kai*, an association of men of letters with overt ties to the Japanese navy, edited a series of anthologies of stories during 1944–45. The seventeenth volume reprinted two of Ranpo's earlier works, "Nisen dōka" and "Kurote gumi" (The Black-Hand League), and the twentieth volume was a special issue on detective fiction, featuring stories by Kozakai Fuboku, Yokomizo Seishi, Ōshita Udaru, and Kōga Saburō.[32] Yokomizo, a former detective writer turned *torimonochō* author, also recalls that despite chronic shortages, the military distributed abundant supplies of paper to publishers for the specific purpose of printing detective fiction, because they were aware that the genre was extremely popular with soldiers.[33] Production of detective fiction may have slowed down, but there is evidence that demand continued and that the authorities were more than willing to accommodate that trend. Those who departed from detective fiction did so on their own initiative, and exercised considerable agency in deciding their actions beyond the genre, be it in their writing careers or in their personal lives.

The absence of a strict ban on detective fiction also brings into question the assumption that its production was frozen during the war years, the period of intense propaganda. As mentioned earlier, the Pacific War presented a new challenge for writers: for the first time they were drafted specifically as writers, not merely as Japanese citizens.[34] Faced with a government that was savvy about using literature to mobilize the population, writers needed to be able either to completely lose themselves in that ideology or to outsavvy the authorities by concealing their messages behind various literary innovations. The examples of three former editors of *Shupio* show us three different approaches to the situation, and reveal how the grim state of affairs affected each detective fiction writer differently. Even in the midst of horrendous food shortages, books and magazines continued to be produced—though many publications ended up being no more substantial than mere pamphlets: "The publishing industry did not suffer a total elimination, though [the companies and printing facilities] were burned and destroyed in air raids."[35] The works of the three authors attest that detective fiction, too, escaped total eradication.

Unno Jūza: Detective in a Rocket

As Unno Jūza was closing the door on *Shupio* in April 1938, he was also starting to serialize a long children's story called "Kaitō-ō" (The King of the Mysterious Tower) in the *Tō-nichi shōgakusei shinbun* (Eastern Japan Newspaper for Elementary School Students). It was around this time that Unno started fashioning himself as a military fiction writer. Featuring a deranged scientist engaged in aerial combat with the Japanese air force, "Kaitō-ō" appears a hybrid of military fiction *(gunji shōsetsu)* and science fiction. Some aspects of this text suggest, however, that Unno also continued to use the format and elements of his former literary passion, detective fiction, and bring into question the view that detective fiction disappeared during the war years. At the same time, the stylistic and thematic transformations Unno underwent while writing "Kaitō-ō" make clear the gradual nature of the transition he experienced.

The story's most prominent allusion to detective fiction can be found in its title. The tower is a frequently used motif in detective fiction, usually as the headquarters of the villain. One early Western text translated in the Meiji period by Kuroiwa Ruikō was *The Blue Veil/The Angel in the Belfry* (1886; Ruikō's translation 1890) by Fortuné de Boisgobey (1821–91), in which the central murder takes place in a gothic tower. Ranpo was so enamored by the setup when he first read Ruikō's translation as a child that he went on to write his own version of the same story in 1937. Other writers also used the motif of a mysterious tower in their detective texts.[36] When Unno recycles the image in "Kaitō-ō," he places his story within the already established genealogy of creepy towers filled with enigmas.

Unno also adopts setups from classic Western and Japanese detective fiction in early installments of this story. The first installment, titled "Kai rōjin" (The Mysterious Old Man), describes the first encounter on the Kujūkuri beach between an old man and two young preteen protagonists, Kazuhiko and Michiko, who are about the same age as the newspaper's target audience. The old man, who readers will later learn is the eponymous King of the Mysterious Tower, is suspicious looking with his beaklike mouth and big sack.[37] The two children are orphans who have been adopted by Homura Sōroku, the detective Unno created in the early 1930s seemingly to denounce the unethical behavior of the agents of science (as reviewed in chapter 3).[38] Although "Kaitō-ō" chronologically is his first post-*Shupio* work, the start of a new phase in his literary career, the return of an old character suggests a gradual shift rather than a complete and sudden break.

As if to justify Homura's reappearance, Unno enhances the private eye's profile by revealing more never-before-known facts about his life. When Homura makes his first appearance in the story, Unno announces to the readers: "If I mention the name Homura Sōroku, maybe some readers will recognize him. He is a famous young detective. Uncle Sōroku knows quite a bit about machines. We hear he holds a degree in science."[39] With a science degree and a newly introduced educational background, Homura becomes a more qualified hero to tackle not only the villains of detective fiction but also science fiction. In the process, he also becomes a closer literary approximation of the author, who worked as a government-employed engineer when not penning works of detective fiction.

Homura definitely needs this hastily bestowed science degree, because the story assumes much larger proportions within the first few installments. The Japanese battleship *Awaji* is stranded in the shallow waters off the coast of Kujūkuri. Since there was no neglect on the part of the ship's crew, how the vessel ran aground is anyone's guess. In addition to the mysterious mishap, the crew and the investigators are puzzled by the fact that the ship's iron mast was partially melted during the incident. It is in order to solve all these mysteries that the best detective in the country, Homura, is summoned to investigate.

Through his investigation, Homura eventually finds out that the mysterious king is none other than Dr. Ōtone, one of the leading scientists of Japan. The double identity of the most respected scientist in the country as an archvillain who seeks to take over the world is a common device in detective fiction: the possessor of knowledge, who is often believed to be on the side of the law, is actually the criminal, a plot that has enjoyed steady popularity since Gaston Leroux's *Le mystère de la chambre jaune* (1907).⁴⁰ Edogawa Ranpo used the plot repeatedly in such stories as "Kumo otoko" (1930), in which Dr. Kuroyanagi, the criminologist on the case, turns out to be the master criminal himself, who spied on his beautiful victims without their knowledge in order to ultimately kill them.

Dr. Ōtone is a much worse enemy, however: not only is he given to voyeurism, he is also equipped with the technology to invent peeping devices that allow him to observe things and people more precisely and more freely. The first verbal confrontation between Homura and Dr. Ōtone takes place while the latter is "sitting on an armchair on top of the tower" and the former is at the gate trying to break in.⁴¹ One of the walls in the room works as a high-tech screen and projects what goes on at the gate of the tower, "like a movie or a magical mirror would."⁴² The scientist's technology does not stop at giving him the power to monitor all activities on his estate. He can also gas any intruders before they enter the gate. It is later revealed that the *Awaji* wreck was Ōtone's doing, as the first step in his plot to take over Asia and eventually the entire world.

The reader also learns that the mysterious tower is actually a rocket full of fantastic but also real cutting-edge technologies. Not only can it fly across the sky, it can also drill miles into the earth and submerge under water. The mad scientists in Unno's earlier, pre-1938 stories often committed crimes as they tested the omnipotence of science, an abstract idea, to the extreme. In contrast, Ōtone in "Kaitō-ō" has a definite political and earthly goal that he wishes to achieve with his technology: he is reportedly an important member of a "secret society seeking to overturn the world order" who has been given the task of defeating the Japanese navy and destroying Asia.⁴³ In a way, the worst fears of Homura (and certainly Unno) come true in the ambition of Ōtone: the mad scientist has gone beyond the confines of his laboratory, and the current state of world affairs inspires him (and the secret society to which he belongs) to join the race for world domination.

Because of the advanced state of Ōtone's technology and the scale of his scheme, Homura is faced not only with solving the whodunit (a traditional professional duty) but also with devising a plan to stop the criminal from committing further acts of wide-scale violence and destruction. In earlier works, Homura's main task was to expose the evil deeds of mad scientists; in "Kaitō-ō," he needs to stop an especially megalomaniacal one from taking over the world by actually infiltrating enemy territory like a secret agent (in the manner of Ian Fleming's James Bond). Initially, his skills as a detective are put to use: he examines the crime scene and interviews witnesses and suspects. The pieces of evidence from his painstaking investigation lead him to the aforementioned mysterious tower on the shoreline and push him to steal his way into the tower. This act of invasion signals that the title spy has been added to his résumé: he is no longer investigating only what happened, he is also investigating what is happening and what will happen if he does not act.

The boundary between spy and detective is apparently thin, since Homura is by no means the only detective who undergoes a makeover in wartime: during World War I, Sherlock Holmes, after whom Homura is named, goes through a similar transition in "His Last Bow" (1917). In this story, set in London right after the outbreak of the Great War, Holmes pretends to be an Irish American from Chicago named Altamont in order to fight a German spy, Von Bork. To make his disguise as elaborate as possible, Holmes is supposed to have lived as Altamont for two years. Although the aging Holmes was in retirement, he returns to active duty when high-ranking government officials urge him to undertake this task: "The Foreign Minister alone I could have withstood, but when the Premier also deigned to visit my humble roof—!"[44] A former cocaine addict who once wished there were more interesting crimes and who took pleasure in defeating the law with his intellect is transformed into a fervent patriot who willingly answers the call of nationalism. Homura in "Kaitō-ō" has yet to go through a similar degree of extreme transformation, nor does he demonstrate the same degree of commitment to nationalism as Holmes. However, Homura provides one model example of what a former private eye can do if he wishes to serve his country in a time of crisis.

While various elements in "Kaitō-ō" stress the continuity between Unno in 1938 and 1939, the work also features some new components, heralding what would be the prominent characteristics of Unno's later wartime works. One such element is the long battle sequence in the middle of the story. While still in pursuit of Ōtone, Homura is chased out of the spotlight; instead, two brave soldiers, Kohama and Aoe, and their battle with the evil scientist, take center stage. The soldiers follow the flying tower in the air, and the story documents their bravery and camaraderie during the battle. The struggle results in the tragic death of one of the fighters. The intrusion of soldiers and their adventures in a story that starts out as a whodunit perhaps best reflects the tense atmosphere of the time in which Unno was writing, and how Unno as a writer tried to accommodate that trend.

As time went on, Unno departed from detective fiction—or the investigation of what happened and whodunit—and engaged himself in the pursuit of such questions as what *will* happen and who *will* do it. Judging from the stories he wrote after "Kaitō-ō," Unno's departure from the genre does not appear a response to external pressure to stop writing; rather it suggests a change of interest on Unno's part.

An engineer by training and trade, Unno was deeply troubled by the lack of ethics in science. Since early in his literary career, he had repeatedly expressed that he was disturbed by the direction in which science, and Western science in particular, was headed. A survey of Unno's works from the late 1930s to his death in 1949 suggests that he seems to have chosen nationalism only because he saw it as his most effective ally in accomplishing the goal of establishing Japanese science, a new brand of science that could both protect Japan and ultimately reorient the direction of scientific development in the world.

The more generous readers of Unno's self-titled military fiction crown him as one of the founding fathers of Japanese science fiction. Looking at the same set of Unno's wartime works, others see him as a "sell-out" and a collaborator. The success of Unno's military fiction and his high productivity have given him a certain notoriety as a possible "converted writer" *(tenkō sakka),* particularly among those who subscribe to the version of literary history put forth by Ranpo and Nakajima.[45] Unno made numerous appearances throughout the war, promoting his message of fervent militarism and nationalism. But his zeal pales in comparison to that of Kigi Takatarō.

Kigi Takatarō: From a Reserved to an Unconditional Nationalist

Following the cancellation of *Shupio* in 1938, Kigi Takatarō embraced neither Japan's expansionist policies nor its militarist ones. "Midori no nisshōki" (The Flag of the Green Rising Sun), a long adventure story serialized a year later, shows only a cautionary attitude toward contemporary Japanese politics. "Midori" includes some of the most overt and direct critiques of the Japanese government during the war years, and is one of the prime testaments of the "looseness" of wartime censorship of fiction. As the war raged on, however, Kigi's works came to assume a more zealous and troublingly unconditional devotion to Japan's nationalist and militarist causes. The story "Tōhōkō" (The Light from the East; 1941) is a particularly good example of this tendency. Kigi's earlier skepticism toward Japanese fascism implies that in the late 1930s, he and possibly other writers and intellectuals like him were still ambiguous about Japanese fascism and its overtly militarist attitude. At the same time, his later collaboration with the authorities implies the dissipation of such a critical attitude in the context of the total war.

"Midori" starts like a typical detective story with a possible case of foul play. Two boys, Keiichi and Susumu, go missing while sailing off the shore of Tokyo. Their families worry that they may have been kidnapped for ransom, as Keiichi's parents are wealthy. The mysterious disappearance of the two boys is used as a hook to hold the audience in the first half of the story. The description of the supposed scene of the crime is straight out of detective fiction:

> That night, the empty boat was found around Odaiba in Shinagawa ward. From the appearance of the inside of the boat, it was unlikely that the two boys got lost. The equipment on the boat was still there, untouched. Their elementary school hats were on board, as if the boys had taken them off to say good-bye. There was one strange, unfamiliar object on the boat. It was a flag with a green rising sun. According to an expert, it was as worn out as if it had been out in the sea for at least a few years. What indeed happened to the two boys?[46]

The return of the empty boat kicks off a full-fledged criminal investigation headed by Inspector Saitō, a police officer. The families of the two boys eventually get an answer when a strange letter arrives from Susumu addressed to his sister Chizuko:

> My dear sister. We are fine. We are working on a mysterious but important mission. We don't think we can go home any time soon, but please don't worry about us. We can't tell you exactly where we are, but it is about a hundred and twelve degrees longitude, fifty-four degrees latitude. We will tell you more details later. Ōhashi Susumu.[47]

Cover of *Kodomo no kagaku*, April 1939. "Midori no nisshōki" was serialized in this magazine.

The content of the letter suggests that the two boys are still alive and in good spirits, despite being held captive. But it also deepens the mystery of where they are and what Susumu means by "a mysterious but important mission." With the letter, the central mystery of the story shifts from the sudden disappearance of the two boys to their secret mission.

After the arrival of the letter, the police try to recover the two boys. Since Susumu only informs Chizuko that they are somewhere around "the borderline between Asia and Europe," locating them is no easy task.[48] The handwriting on the letter attests to its authenticity. However, the outlandish notion that the boys who were kidnapped in Tokyo are now in Central Asia prompts the police to seek out more information in order to determine their whereabouts. This is where old-fashioned sleuthing comes in: the police carefully examine the envelope that contained Susumu's note, and discover that it was made in and sent from Nagasaki. With this information, the entire investigation team moves to the port city.

Until the investigative forces reach Nagasaki, the story looks to the past, as the police try to find out what happened. However, the atmosphere quickly changes once Chizuko, who comes to Nagasaki with the police force in place of her ailing father, is kidnapped by two mysterious white men. Kigi was never known to be an advocate of the Van Dinean style of rigid, formal detective fiction; rather, he made a name for himself as a strong proponent of *henkaku*—roughly meaning "alternative"—detective fiction during the debate over the genre with Kōga Saburō during the mid-1930s. As such earlier works as "Jinsei no ahō" (Life's Fool; 1931) demonstrate, Kigi often let the form of his detective fiction take a backseat to the expression of more pressing issues.[49] In "Jinsei no ahō," a murder mystery in Tokyo recedes into the background as Ryōkichi, the protagonist and the prime suspect, sets out on a journey of self-discovery across the frozen fields of Russia. When Kigi leaves the current kidnapping mystery in "Midori" to focus on Chizuko's new adventure after her abduction, he is simply following a recurring pattern in his stories rather than trying to purge the story of any traces of detective fiction.

Two story lines merge once the abducted Chizuko arrives in the Land of the Green Rising Sun, a subterranean utopia filled with modern technological marvels where the two boys now live. It is also the end of the detective story: the past mystery of who kidnapped the two boys is solved, and the new question—what is this community about?—brings the mystery into the present and future. It turns out that the two men kidnapped her with the intention of reuniting Chizuko with her brother and his friend. The story after their reunion centers on Chizuko's exploration of this wondrous community ruled by advanced technology and extreme rationality. As reflected in the illustrations, her attire symbolically changes from kimono to a Western-style dress in the process. Chizuko steps into the role of the heroine, however, only to have her ignorance in science exposed: although Chizuko is Susumu's older sister, her brother's head start in this mysterious locale gives him an advantage, and Chizuko is relegated to the role of pupil while they are in the subterranean paradise. When brother and sister are first reunited on the submarine transporting them to the Land of the Green Rising Sun, the submarine comes under attack by unknown enemies, but successfully repels them with a kind of yellow gas. Chizuko is impressed, and Susumu explains the nature of the weapon:

> "Sister, have you heard of the gas helium?"
> "Helium? I suppose I've heard it before."
> "Oh, please don't say 'I suppose'—that's why people say that Japanese girls don't know anything about science."[50]

Chizuko is offended by her brother's derogatory remarks on the possible correlation between gender, nationality, and lack of scientific knowledge. She points out the ungrounded prejudice in his assertion that all Japanese girls are uniformly ignorant about science.[51] To this, Susumu responds confidently: "You still lose, sister. In our country, we have a machine that allows us to calculate how much knowledge Japanese girls do or do not have on various matters."[52] As the representative of this society's scientific enlightenment, Susumu guides his sister and ultimately the technologically backward country that she represents: Japan. The title of the installment in which Chizuko takes over as the heroine of the story is "Nihon shōjo" (Japanese Girl), implying that two entities—Japan and the female sex—are melded together in the person of Chizuko. She stands in both for a nation in need of further technological advancement in light of the volatile state of the contemporary world and for the less scientifically minded gender that possibly hinders such advancement. The story initially draws the reader with the promise of a delightful whodunit—namely, what happened to the two boys and who is responsible for their disappearance?—but it gradually evolves into an adventure story that tries to anticipate the future: what will happen to Chizuko and Japan?

Japan as embodied by Chizuko is imperfect: compared to her brother and other children in the community of the Green Rising Sun, she lacks sophistication and needs to be guided by her younger brother. To create a "mirror image of Japan" that is superior in every way was

Illustrations from the serialized version of "Midori no nisshōki." As Chizuko is shown around the Land of the Green Rising Sun by her younger brother and his friend, her attire has curiously changed from kimono to Western clothes. Courtesy of Taniguchi Yōko.

the design of the founder of the Land of the Green Rising Sun: where Manchukuo failed, the Green Rising Sun was to succeed.[53]

In the story, Japan is portrayed as a country with the potential to become the moral leader of the world. In one scene, the head of the legal department in Green Rising Sun states: "as a national body *(kokutai)*, there is no other country that supersedes Japan. It is the unshakeable, unbeatable truth for all Japanese."[54] At the same time, he denounces Japan for falling short of its potential—words that possibly reflect Kigi's view of his country.

One area in which Kigi may have been personally frustrated was Japan's policy in Asia. Although the ultimate goal of the leaders of the Green Rising Sun is to join Japan, they are hesitant to do so right away since they are critical of Japan's stance toward China. While the leaders of the Green Rising Sun commend the success of Sir Frederick Leith-Ross in his negotiations on reforming the Chinese currency system, they openly criticize Japan's role. The leaders are aware that Japanese officials underestimated the skill of the British in asserting themselves in Asia and particularly China: "Japanese politicians know much about China, but at the same time they don't understand China at all. . . . Today's Japanese politicians lack the knowledge and sensibility of the Meiji-era politicians. . . . Japanese politicians now have the vice of thinking that the best political strategy is to do nothing, commit to nothing—they think that if one observes something long enough, that something will take care of itself."[55] The concerned politicians of the Green Rising Sun make it clear that Japanese opportunism, arrogance, and ignorance about Chinese affairs influence their own policy toward Japan. They state clearly that if Japan starts a war against China (they use the term *Nitchū sensō*, or "Japan-China War") within four years—before the completion of the community of the Green Rising Sun—they will not support Japan, though doing so would betray the intention of the founder.[56]

Kigi's "Midori," with its detective fiction elements and open critique of current politics, questions the view of censors in the late 1930s as all-knowing and ever-present. The idea of omniscient censorship does not explain why such a critique of the military was published in this period. Moreover, the story is designed to mirror real history in considerable detail. At the time of the serialization of this story, the Sino-Japanese conflict was well under way: with the Marco

Polo Bridge incident in July 1937, the two countries were already engaged in what looked to be a prolonged battle. In the story, the conflict is supposed to have just gotten violent. Because of this sudden change in the political atmosphere, Chizuko decides to go home to Japan first to inform her father of her whereabouts. She intended to return to the Land of the Green Rising Sun, but the international political climate ultimately makes it impossible: while she is back in Japan, she learns that the leaders of the Green Rising Sun grew so disappointed with Japanese policy that they blew up their utopia under the Central Asian desert.

The "suicide" of the Land of the Green Rising Sun comes suddenly and shockingly, and is perhaps the most violent act to appear in the story. The two boys return to their homes in Japan and vow to apply their experience in the Green Rising Sun to their lives in Japan. Although the two boys and Chizuko sound positive in their resolve, the perfection of the Land of the Green Rising Sun, in both moral and technological terms, paints the country's decision to self-destruct in a decidedly tragic light. Seemingly contradictory messages in "Midori" suggest that Kigi was both proud and scornful of Japan at the time of writing: he is attached to his native country, but suspicious of its recent political and diplomatic decisions. Kigi's decision to cancel *Shupio* in 1938 cannot be taken as a marker of his allegiance to militarism and fascism: at that point, and still during the serialization of "Midori," Kigi could have gone either left or right, to resistance or compliance, or somewhere in between.

Kigi's commitment to nationalist causes intensified in his later works, however, particularly in those produced after the beginning of the Pacific War in 1941. As Japan drew itself more and more into continental affairs, Kigi became increasingly active in various literary circles that aimed to contribute to Japan's war effort. He became a member of the Kokubō bungei renmei (Literary Association for National Defense), along with Unno Jūza. The aim of this organization was to contribute to the war specifically through literary works.[57] He was also active in the Nihon bungei kyōkai (Association of Japanese of Letters) and played a key role in smoothing out communications between various literary associations with a pro-war, pro-Japan stance.[58] With the slogan "Don't Miss the Bus" (Basu ni noriokureruna), these circles willingly furthered various national causes in this period. While Kigi was by no means the only writer to have sided with the Japanese military and made efforts to promote pro-war nationalist rhetoric, it is fair to say that he was as active as Unno, who is often mentioned as the most famous literary collaborator from the detective writers circle, and certainly more active than people such as Edogawa Ranpo and Yokomizo Seishi, who significantly reduced output or came to write in other genres. The seeming willingness in Kigi's collaboration is particularly troubling as he was a neurologist by training, and medicine and research remained his primary occupations throughout the Pacific War years. Unlike Unno and Oguri, who did not have any other means of support, Kigi was neither under specific pressure to write nor under pressure to write propagandistic works, and that is why he appears to have collaborated with the authorities to a greater extent than he was actually required to do so as a private citizen.

The signs of Kigi's increased involvement in these nationalist literary societies were visible in his fiction. One of his works from the period, "Tōhōkō" (The Light from the East; 1941), ends with the lesson that everyone with questionable nationality and national allegiance deserves to be suspected whenever there is the possibility of foul play. "Tōhōkō" is the story of a young English spy who comes to Japan pretending to search for his half sister on the eve of World War II. In 1941, as the officials at the London branch of a Japanese shipping company get ready to leave Europe because of the increasingly volatile political climate, a well-dressed Englishman in his twenties visits their office. The young man, John Andrews, explains to the officers that he wishes to travel to Japan both to escape imminent German attacks on England and to look for his half sister. After the Japanese employees at the branch make some unsuccessful attempts at dissuading him, Andrews purchases the ticket and arrives in Japan. As soon as he steps off the ship, Andrews hires a detective to trace his half-Japanese, half-English sister. Within a page and a half, the girl, Taninaka Magako, is conveniently located.

However, the happiness of the Andrews-Taninaka family reunion is short lived, as people learn that Andrews is an English spy whose real mission is to steal some secret documents from Magako's fiancé, the government engineer Kōda. Andrews and his accomplices make a daring attempt to escape to America via Hong Kong, but they are arrested onboard a plane near Shanghai. The pilot is Oka Eiji, an American-born Japanese. When asked why he agreed to help the enemy, Oka blames his background: "I thought I'd want to go to America because I have dual citizenship. On top of that, I fell in love with a Japanese woman while in Japan, but she abandoned me. After that I felt like despising all Japanese women."[59]

The dejected Oka is "cured" of his anti-Japanism only when he sees the amazing precision and performance with which the Japanese air force stopped his plane: "I felt the great power of Japan when I was forced to land near Shanghai. From now on, even if I am found guilty and executed, I can die a true Japanese."[60] The awakening of Oka's Japanese spirit is sudden, and Kigi never elaborates exactly what sorts of emotions Oka experiences behind his shift in allegiance. Oka's abrupt transformation also emphasizes Kigi's impatience in conveying the message of nationalism: in his rush to portray Oka's ideological conversion, Kigi falls short of clearly showing the mechanism by which it occurs.

The tendency to be sketchy and at times contradictory is also seen in other scenes within the story. The story overtly and rather simplistically suggests that foreigners are untrustworthy and that so are foreign-born Japanese because of their dual citizenship. Japanese women do not fare much better, as they get weak-kneed when treated kindly by white men. When Magako meets her half brother, the factory worker girl who grew up thinking that she was an orphan is understandably elated. However, her fiancé interprets Magako's joy as an expression of her innate arrogance brought to the surface by Andrews's elegant manners and the suggestion of her white heritage. At the military police interrogation, an army officer reprimands her:

> "You are not guilty [of the espionage charges]. But why is it that you women lose sight of things so readily whenever a Westerner pays attention to you, as if he casts a spell on you? We always thought that such a weakness presents the biggest concern for espionage. There is something in that psychology that I do not wish to simply dismiss as unacceptable."[61]

To this, Magako replies by blaming the lack of respect on the part of Japanese men: "I think if Japanese men treat women [with the utmost respect], Japanese women will stop being attracted to Western men."[62] Magako's observation concerning her own weakness can potentially serve as a critique of Japanese misogyny; however, the story hardly gives Magako time to elaborate and instead makes her oblivious to her own resentment. Within moments, she expresses readiness to serve Japan as a proud citizen to build a "civilization that supersedes the West" without pursuing personal glory.[63] The story celebrates the coming together of two born-again Japanese—Magako and Oka—who were previously cultural orphans. The kind of nationalism Oka and Magako achieve is emotional—and not necessarily (easily) attainable for anyone capable of rational thinking.

The storyline of "Tōhōkō" suggests that Japanese citizenship or ethnicity is not sufficient for one to qualify as "Japanese" throughout one's lifetime: one is asked to constantly demonstrate the virtues particular to one's race. However, the virtue of selflessness, one of the most important qualities of being Japanese, according to Kigi, also creates a contradiction for marginalized Japanese who want to be accorded recognition as full Japanese: although the desire to claim an ethnic and cultural identity is personally motivated, one is also required to forsake all such individual desires. The "nationalism" Kigi asks of his readers is an extreme one, for it is not enough to be simply "Japanese." Whoever wishes to belong to the nation of Japan needs to "become Japan" in the sense that one is required to relinquish all personal desires that may or may not conflict with national interests. The scenario Kigi prescribes for his readers is not logical: his morality fails to make sense unless a reader is already unconditionally committed to nationalism. As a detective writer first and foremost, Kigi was deeply concerned with the principles of fairness and plausibility in detective fiction: "Something may be common sense, but if it does not withstand the test of the natural sciences, it has to be avoided at all cost in order not to be nonsensical *(kōtō mukei)*."[64] Patriotic devotion to one's country may have been "common sense" by the early 1940s, and it is doubtful that Kigi wrote such stories as "Tōhōkō" thinking that they were detective fiction. However, Kigi is also famous for erasing the distinction between regular fiction and detective fiction: whatever rule he established for his detective fiction, therefore, can be extended to his other, regular fictions.[65] In the attempt to promulgate the message of nationalism, Kigi sacrificed his earlier conviction: his story line no longer withstood the test of the "natural sciences"—or rationality—and anything that seemed to oppose Japanese nationalism came under suspicion.

Oguri Mushitarō: Encounter with New Rationalities

Perhaps the most complex post-*Shupio* path was traveled by Oguri Mushitarō, who followed in the footsteps of the other two editors by redirecting his literary career after 1938. He abandoned his earlier inclination for locked-room mysteries in gothic mansions—themes he explored in texts such as his debut work "Kanzen hanzai" (The Perfect Crime; 1933) and his best-known work "Kokushikan satsujin jiken" (Murders at the Black Death Mansion; 1934)—and turned to adventure stories in the wilds of the jungle. Starting in 1939, Oguri's works often entailed a hero going to the fringes of civilization to discover bizarre animals and humans. In 1939, Oguri serialized a piece called "Yūbijin" (The Tailed Tribe), and quickly followed its success with another adventure story, "Daiankoku" (The Greatest Darkness) a few months later. By the following year, Oguri's adventure stories became a fixture on the pages of the wartime, pro-militarist, pro-expansionist *Shinseinen*. Commonly grouped as the *jingai makyō* series (literally: stories from beyond the reaches of civilization), the adventure writings Oguri published in this period have been compared to some of the Martian stories of Edgar Rice Burroughs.[66] Some critics speculate that not having actually been to a real jungle may have helped Oguri to unleash his imagination and fantastically depict the world outside of civilization.[67]

However, though set in the midst of the wilderness, Oguri's adventure stories from 1939–41 are simple transplantations of the locked-room mystery from the gothic mansion to the exotic tropical jungle.[68] The true shift in Oguri's literary style and interest came in 1941–42, when he was drafted by the Japanese navy as a military writer and dispatched to the South Seas. This trip to the colonies profoundly affected Oguri's writing: he traded out-of-this-world, apolitical fantasies of the jungle for realistic accounts of the tropical forest with veiled critique of Japanese militarism and colonialism. After his return from Malaya, Oguri, just like Unno, was also invited to speak about his experiences in the colonies at military-sponsored gatherings. While Unno willingly complied, Oguri refused all such invitations. Around the same time, his friend Kigi, by this time an overt nationalist (writing stories such as "Tōhōkō"), urged Oguri to write military fiction based on his experience in Malaya.[69] However, Oguri never honored his friend's request.

Oguri's sudden change of heart is perplexing—even given his prewar antifascist sentiments—especially considering that his stay in the colonies was anything but uncomfortable. In 1942, Japan was at the height of its military success, and the sinister smell of defeat was still years away. Oguri's family and friends were initially worried about his health when he was drafted: he had a known heart condition that made his heart sag an inch lower than average, and it made him more prone to fatigue and sickness. However, to everyone's surprise, Oguri came back healthier than ever after a year in the tropical climate. His son, Oguri Senji, recalls: "In contrast to the lifeless, wax-like cheeks [he had before the trip], my father came back sporting a gaudy camel-colored jacket and rosy complexion. He had gained weight. I looked at my father in awe, as he was tanned like a completely different person. He appeared excited. He clearly looked ten years younger."[70] If his duties overseas gave him health benefits that he could not get at home, why is it that Oguri came back more antimilitarist than ever? His relative health only makes his postdraft actions appear counterintuitive.

Oguri's postdraft political shift had forced his family to face some tough consequences. About the time when Oguri finished "Kaikyō tenchikai" (Society of Heaven and Earth, henceforth "Kaikyō"; 1943), often regarded as his wartime masterpiece, his son Senji recalls that the military police paid a lengthy visit to his father. They had also been visiting Oguri whenever he submitted a false sick note to be exempted from speaking at military gatherings. Senji recalls: "A heated exchange could be heard from upstairs [where Oguri's study was]. After a few hours, the military policeman climbed down the stairs loudly and slammed the door behind him. My father ran to the bathroom, screaming 'Idiots!'"[71] Within less than two years, Oguri's style changed dramatically, and he went from being one of the most popular writers on the pages of the pro-military incarnation of *Shinseinen* to being an author carefully watched by the authorities. In addition, in Oguri's fate we can also detect the possible intensification of censorship in the early 1940s compared to the late 1930s, when Kigi's "Midori" was published.

Oguri did not leave much nonfictional, autobiographical writing that would explain his change of heart. However, judging from his post-1942 stories, it is possible to speculate. One likely factor is the arrogance and violence of the Japanese military that he came to witness during his trip. Another is Oguri's actual encounter with local peoples who possess a different culture—a different kind of logic that is neither Western nor Japanese—that had been unknown to him before. Before his actual trip to the jungle, he often used exotic locations such as the Congo, Brazil, and Greenland, and featured everything in his adventure stories from human beings with tails, bizarre animals, and sleigh-driving ghosts of *terra incognita*.[72] "Kaikyō," Oguri's work from 1943, creates a sharp contrast to these tales of wondrous creatures on the outskirts of the world: instead of "enclosed" jungles reminiscent of a "locked room," Oguri's new "jungles" expand spatially, possessing a kind of "depth of reality"—the opaque daily existence reflecting the complexity of the culture that envelops it—similar to that Japanese detective fiction once elucidated through various depictions of post-earthquake Tokyo.

In order to depict the multiple layers of reality and rationality that exist in the space described as the "jungle," Oguri also reintroduces some of the elements of detective fiction: although the text is not commonly classified as such, it adopts the genre's classic setup with a mystery, a detective, and the resolution of a case. However, the identity of the "criminal," together with Oguri's anticolonial stance, makes "Kaikyō" more than a classic detective fiction in which one universal rationality, as embodied by the detective, brings light to all dark corners of the story through scientific investigation and ratiocination. In his attack on colonialism and defense of cultural relativism, Oguri violates one of the golden rules of the genre, namely, that no cultural other should figure in the story.[73]

Oguri published "Kaikyō" twice: the first version was released in 1943, as stated earlier, as "Kaikyō tenchikai"; the second was published in 1946 as "Kaizō ni shita nakiya" (The Walrus Has No Tongue). The primary story line remained the same, but the details, particularly the depictions of the military, vary dramatically. Despite the later publication date of the second version, critics such as Ikeda Hiroshi speculate, and I agree, that what we know as the later, postwar version is actually the original text, and the first version was a modified version of it, written only after the original was rejected by the censors as unfit for publication.[74] Given the quickness with which "Kaizō" appeared in the confusion of the postwar, it is hard to imagine that Oguri came up with that version then. At the same time, only the existence of the more liberal, more critical original version explains the numerous visits paid by the military police to his home around the time of its writing and publication.

"Kaikyō" takes place at Malaya's northern border, where the Japanese army captures Chang Lun, the leader of the powerful rebel group Society of Heaven and Earth. However, as the prisoner maintains his silence throughout the interrogation, the mystery of his identity starts to develop: is he the real leader the Japanese army is looking for, or is he a double, a Chinese peasant named Kō? The military writer Kogure, who was traveling with the unit, is the self-appointed detective of this investigation. He is an obvious literary double of the author: before being drafted to Malaya, Kogure is supposed to have been a detective writer, and one of his works mentioned in the story bears the title "Kanzen hanzai," identical to Oguri's debut work.[75] Without sounding shamelessly self-serving, Oguri depicts Kogure as a likable man: "Kogure is by no means a gloomy man though his works may portray him as such. He is not a typical, stuffy bookworm. If anything, he is casual, open, likes to be mysterious, while also extremely selfish and fickle."[76] In addition, what makes him a good candidate for heroism is the presence of "something that made one believe that he was strong, and that was what allowed him to eventually crack the case."[77] The unspecified quality in Kogure that made others believe in him seems to have been a moral core that would not be influenced by external forces—a quality that many postwar intellectuals would denounce the wartime Japanese for having lacked.[78]

In contrast, Kō in the story represents a morality that remains unshakable even at the moment of utmost desperation. Kogure's strong sense of justice responds to Kō's noble attitude. Alarmed that the military will kill the prisoner without a fair investigation, Kogure launches a one-man crusade against military injustice in this outpost of the empire:

> In the military, what can a drafted writer or a medical trainee—the weakest of the hierarchy—accomplish? The fruitless outcome is fairly foreseeable. Then should Kogure not do anything? Yes, he should. Kogure held his own. Why did Émile Zola make the enemy out of the entire French army for Dreyfus? Why did he fight for Dreyfus, one Jewish man? He never heard the scream of Zola's "J'accuse" against oppression, conspiracy, and injustice as poignantly.[79]

The bravery of a man of letters in another tradition encourages Kogure to take action through an imagined bond between writers. In the face of pressure and the threat of violence, Kogure's sense of justice grows rather than shrinks:

> Here is one man. He is about to be a victim of dictatorship *(kyōken)*. He is probably no one, without birth or significant role in society.... What if we find one more corpse of a trivial insect? Kogure suffered from a moral dilemma. But he did not become a cowardly dog who turns a blind eye to [injustice] while sandwiching his tail between his legs. He chose confrontation with the military police for the pursuit of truth and ultimate accuracy.[80]

The selflessness of Kogure's act is contrasted with the greed and mercenary attitude of the officer who arrested Kō:

> Mr. Officer is in a very good mood. Because of this crowning achievement, he will probably be promoted. He may even be able to conduct an entire unit. They say "[you can accumulate] thirty million yen if you serve as the unit chief for a year," but if you are posted in the right place, you can expect to make more than four or five hundred thousand dollars. Business, business....[81]

The officer smiles to himself at the prospect of making a profit off the arrest of the hapless prisoner. The officer is everything Kogure hates about the military: "[Kogure] does not wish to see their faces. What indeed is a *kenpei* soldier? They are foot soldiers, but they are also military professionals. What do they do during peacetime? Bribe, torture, steal food, bully innocent cadets, keep prostitutes. These are the things that fill their lives."[82]

In contrast, the moral fiber of the captured Chinese Kō is depicted in the most favorable light. Toward the end of his investigation, Kogure learns that the prisoner was indeed the peasant double Kō who could have been set free if Kō had revealed his true identity. Kogure realizes that instead of saving his own skin, Kō sacrificed his life so that the real leader could have a few more days to elude the Japanese military. Kogure feels a certain dignity in Kō and urges other Japanese soldiers (and his audiences) to respect his decision: "Let's bid farewell to Kō, for we can never see him again. For the Japanese who think that telling lies and compromising morality is nothing but an everyday fact should kneel down in front of Kō in worship."[83] Pursuing the mystery surrounding the ambiguous identity of the captured Chinese man makes Kogure aware of a new, unknown, non-Western and non-Japanese system of virtue. The arrogance and egotism of the Japanese soldiers and the selfless act of Kō belong to clearly different systems of virtue, honor, and rationality, but the context of Japanese colonialism forces them into contact with each other.

The Japanese colonial enterprise often dealt with the dilemma of different rationalities or cultural differences by simply using force to subdue local cultures. Oguri indignantly describes the treatment of the local Chinese at the hands of the Japanese military: "The poor locals could not talk back to the reptiles educated to be brutes who abuse their professional power. They could not do anything to save their fellow countryman's life. Everything is decided by unilateral investigation and sentencing."[84] As Oguri's account portrays, Japanese colonialism tries to alienate what is inalienable, and attempts to suppress majority rule by the force of the minority. The successful escape of the real leader of the Society of the Heaven and Earth indicates that governing through such means is faulty and imperfect, and destined to cause unnecessary and endless suffering.

Many of Oguri's post-1942 stories include encounters with the colonial other(s) similar to Kō in "Kaikyō" who represent thought systems different from his own. In the process, the target of Oguri's criticism came to include not only Japanese colonialism but also all forms of unjustified rule over anyone. Strong anti-Western colonial sentiment, especially toward British colonial rule in Malaya, runs through "Nanpō kūrī" (Tamil Coolie; 1943). Denouncing British imperialism probably worked to appease the censors, since by this point they would have been going through Oguri's works with a fine-tooth comb.

However, Oguri denounces British colonialism without justifying the Japanese rule that replaced it: the story works as a critique of colonialism in general, rather than a justification of the new Japanese rule that exists in reality. The story, written in the form of a personal diary, chronicles the memories of brutalities committed by the English in the region as the nameless author, apparently a male Japanese writer, tours a provincial town. The presence of coolies—and their "coffee colored" skin—as they toil under the sun all day immediately catches the author's attention. The author thinks the English idea that these coolies are "inferior beings, the slaves of the twentieth century" has brainwashed the locals.[85] The prejudice against the coolies is described as one of the worst legacies of the English colonial rule. The attack against English racism dominates the first part of the story:

> [The reason why coolies are condemned even by the locals] is because the English made no bones about their inborn cruel nature in public, and ruled the coolies like butchers. The slaughterhouse is made public for the 5,000,000 Malays to see. Anyone could see it, and everyone saw it. The English publicly call the Malay coolies only slightly better than beasts, and send in more and more of them from Madras. Their ships without exception looked like slave ships. The ship owners competed to see who could stuff in as many coolies as possible. In 1939, *Rajula* [the name of a ship] won the coveted prize. During its voyage to Malay, it killed seventy-nine coolies while four killed themselves. This was the deed of a supposedly democratic society that praises justice and ethics and used deception to rule the world.[86]

At first glance, the attack solely targets British colonialism. However, the passage is also the prelude to a larger critique not only of a specific style of colonialism but of colonialism in general.

The story also mentions the brutal rape of a Malay girl named Bidā at the hands of English soldiers. Bidā was targeted because she tried to intervene when the English owners of the estate she worked for cut water and food supplies for their coolies. It is another instance in which a colonizer's rationality subdues the rationality of the colonized, as Bidā has fallen "victim to the English bestiality" in an attempt to obey her conscience.[87] Although it is English soldiers who commit this evil act, the rape of local women as a means to punish and/or control the entire local population is by no means a strategy used exclusively by the English: many Asian accounts establish that the Japanese army repeatedly indulged in such acts. As we will see in detail in the next chapter, the rumors of atrocities committed by Japanese soldiers overseas reached the Japanese people through unofficial channels. Oguri's contemporary readers in the metropole were by no means sealed off from the realities of war. With additional, extratextual information on the current social situation in the colonies, Oguri is able to get his readers to reflect on the current actions of Japanese soldiers through a critique of English colonizers of the past.

The story avoids eulogizing "humanitarian" Japanese rule to the end. The narrator is told by the local population that life for coolies improved only in one respect under Japanese rule: now they can drink their favorite alcoholic beverage, coconut liquor *(yashi shu)* more cheaply, as the governmental monopoly has been lifted after the British left. The closest thing to praise for current Japanese rule is uttered by Old Ibraham, one of the elder Malays of the town, as he narrates the change to the author: "This war surely helped the health of the coolies."[88] In reality, however, the liquor did not necessarily help the coolies or other locals but provided a temporary refuge from the harsh living conditions and gloomy future of rice paddies and rubber plantations.

A strong sense of sympathy for the oppressed runs through both "Kaikyō" and "Nanpō." What Oguri advocates through these stories is respect for the rationality of the "people in the jungle," who have their own logic by which they run their affairs. The local culture is by no means perfect—Oguri never takes steps to idealize it—but it is still better than interference from the outside world, which creates new problems on top of the homegrown ones. Oguri also depicts how multiple value systems—Malay, Chinese, and Indian—coexist within the space of a small provincial town, and shows how the narrator strives to assimilate. For example, although the narrator is not a Muslim, he observes Ramadan with the locals.[89]

In addition to the willingness to suspend one's rationality, the cultural outsider needs other aids in order to communicate verbally. Ironically, when the author and Ibraham talk, their communication is carried out in English, with the aid of an English-Malay dictionary.[90] The two cultures and two rationalities that they represent are separated by the difference in their native tongues, and they can begin to understand each other only through a mediation of another linguistic and value system. English as a common language provides not only a means for the two to express themselves but also the context in which the two have been brought together in the first place. The fact that a town elder like Ibraham, who lives in traditional Malay housing, needed to own an English dictionary is a testament to the ubiquity of colonial rule and the disappearance of *jingai makyō*—the closed jungle left untouched by civilization—that Oguri once imagined.

What Oguri wished to express with his wartime writings seems lofty: he was up against the enterprise of colonialism, what then was deemed as a rigid and unchanging world order. However, Oguri succeeded in inviting his readers—potential future colonizers—to suspend their systems of judgment and acknowledge the existence of other systems of thought besides their own. Oguri's story suggests that a Japanese detective may be able to solve the mystery of his cultural other if he understands the nonabsoluteness of his rationality. Colonial others and their cultures are inalienable components of the Japanese Empire, total war, and modernity: just as it is impossible to lock away the mob mentality of the masses, the homicidal unconscious, and other threatening forces that modernity entails, it is impossible to isolate them. If the end justifies the means, this explains why Oguri ceased to write locked-room mysteries set in gothic towers and on isolated islands and opted for ever-expanding jungles. The jungles that civilization left behind were affected by the global effects of Western and Japanese colonialism, and yet contained darkness neither an objectifying colonizer's stare nor unengaged detective's gaze could penetrate.

Total War and Detective Fiction

The wartime actions and fictions of the three former *Shupio* editors varied radically, and the multiplicity of their responses best attests to the possibilities and limits of detective fiction in the wake of the political turmoil of the late 1930s. While Unno's collaboration was deliberate, Kigi's conversion happened without his resolving to do so—a pattern of political conversion not uncommon in this period. In his examination of the advertising industry and its actions during the war, the sociologist Nanba Kōji asserts that the so-called wartime *tenkō* of advertisers occurred without the strong self-awareness that they were making an ideological transition. Kigi's siding with the fascist regime too seems to have taken place without determination or self-awareness. Nanba also speculates that such an utter lack of self-awareness is actually what enabled so many war accomplices to resume their everyday lives during the postwar era. This interpretation also explains Kigi's postwar activities: as early as 1946, Kigi resumed writing detective fiction while also editing an anthology aimed at fans long deprived of their favorite genre. Among the three former editors of *Shupio*, Kigi ended up having the longest literary career, which lasted into the 1960s. The abundance of his postwar works and his quick return to detective fiction de-emphasize his wartime writings, and allowed his seemingly comprehensive "complete works" series to be published—even though most wartime texts were omitted.

The activities and works of the three authors show that the political redirection from left to right among detective writers did not happen overnight, and in 1938–39 there were still mixed emotions, dilemmas, and hopes that if they had to go along with their government's policies, they could turn the situation to their advantage by inserting their own agendas for reform. Kigi's works attest to this view. The works and lives of Oguri and Unno indicate that it was possible to make decisions that are neither forced conversion to fascism and militarism nor outright resistance, and to continue to publish through the loopholes of power to reach an audience who quite possibly knew how to read between the lines or indulged in imaginative interpretations.

Just like Oguri, Unno was drafted to serve in the Japanese navy as a military writer and was dispatched to the South Sea colonies. Unno's views of science, nationalism, and war were profoundly affected by his sojourn in the tropics. The experiences of Oguri and Unno beg further investigation into drafted writers of this period, and put forth perspectives that see beyond the apparent support for nationalism and the expected omnipresence and omnipotence of censorship that is powerful enough to erase a genre.

As Kigi and Unno departed from detective fiction, they wrote what could be deemed propagandistic works. That fact, however, hardly justifies the neglect that many of their wartime works still suffer today. Kigi's life is a case in point. Serialized for more than a year, Kigi's "Midori" enjoyed considerable popularity among its contemporary readers. The story, however, is not included in the 1970 edition of the *Kigi Takatarō zenshū*—the only complete works series for the author to date, compiled two years after Kigi's death. The omission of "Midori," along with some other wartime works from an anthology that boasts its "completeness," is questionable to say the least. It is true that when judged by conventional standards for literary merit—such as distinction between characters, psychological depth, the strength of the premise, and the coherence of the overall plot—"Midori" might be construed to score very poorly. It is not particularly poor compared to Kigi's other works, however: if "Midori" were to be excluded for its quality, the entire project of publishing Kigi's works does not make sense. The omission of "Midori" seems to have been motivated by the editors—including the aforementioned genre historian Nakajima Kawatarō—who viewed the wartime works of Kigi and other writers as unsuitable representations of the author's literary persona.

For those who believe in the powerlessness of writers under fascist surveillance of the publishing industry, Kigi's nationalist rhetoric is nothing more than the adoption of state ideology in lieu of his more liberal, and implicitly more genuine, opinions. As Inui and other contemporaries attest, the kind of total and willing compliance Kigi demonstrated in works such as "Tōhōkō" was by no means necessary to save one's skin even at the height of war.

The wartime writings of three former editors of *Shupio* prove that there was indeed a third alternative for a writer living in total war besides overt compliance and resistance. The literary endeavors of the three former editors of *Shupio* suggest that they, and possibly other writers like them, exercised considerable agency in deciding what to write as they lived through total war. As long as they were willing to negotiate, writers could choose a third path and operate within the imposed power structure, becoming "undercover agents" of sorts. They present their works as compatible with the militarist ideology. In many cases, however, these works have multiple layers of meaning and hardly ever contain a straightforward propagandistic message. Perhaps what is needed is not to put a lid on these wartime writings but rather subject them to further scrutiny. Further study is also necessary to determine not only what it was like to write in total war but also what it was like to read in total war, in order to gauge the effectiveness and legacies of these authors' wartime writings.

In January 1946, Oguri left Nagano for a brief stay in Tokyo to see both Edogawa Ranpo and Unno Jūza, two friends who stayed in the capital throughout the air raids. He reportedly intended to discuss the future and pending revival of detective fiction in Japan. Oguri left with a backpack filled with food for the two, as provisions were hard to come by in the capital. Oguri was also carrying something else of importance: some old books of detective fiction, among which was a copy of Eden Phillpotts's *The Red Redmaynes* (1922)—a classic of Golden Age detective fiction about a draft dodger turned vengeful killer who eloquently declared the futility of war and violence in his closing monologue. The story had been popular among the detective fiction aficionados even before the war, and was selected as the third-best work of all time in 1937.[91] But the text became more important than ever after 1945: the killer may have been the closest literary avatar for Oguri and other proponents of detective fiction who survived four long years of scrutiny and decline.

Oguri died in 1946, without directly contributing to the revival of detective fiction in the postwar era. Unno, too, would succumb to illness in 1949, but until then continued to contribute to the revival of the genre. During his last years, Unno not only promoted the message of antiscientism in his fiction, but also helped close friends return to the capital. Yokomizo Seishi was one such friend. A former editor of *Shinseinen* with ever faltering health, Yokomizo had moved to Okayama to escape the air raids; he spent the war years writing *torimonochō* and reading classic Western detective fiction. In 1948, Unno lent a sizable sum to the penniless Yokomizo to help the latter build a house in the burned capital. The three-hundred-yen loan Unno made would pay tremendous dividends for him and the genre, as Yokomizo was to spearhead the movement for the triumphant restoration of the genre to the center stage of the publishing world. It was young Oguri who pinch-hit for Yokomizo when he contracted tuberculosis in 1933 and had to withdraw a planned serialization from *Shinseinen:* now it was Yokomizo's turn to take up Oguri's two major projects—a serialization in the pages of *Rokku* (Lock), a new magazine dedicated to the genre of detective fiction, and the project of rebuilding Japanese detective fiction and ultimately postwar Japan.

5. The Disfigured National Body: Unmasking Modernity in Postwar Mysteries

Detective Fiction after 1945

Having exhausted its resources on fighting an all-out war on various fronts for more than a decade, Japan surrendered to the Allied forces on August 15, 1945. Soon after, some expressed regret for not having done enough for the Emperor.[1] However, many others were elated at the news of the end of war and "hastened to remove the blackout paper from their windows, letting light back into their lives."[2] Although peace came at a high price—with territorial, material, symbolic, and emotional losses—it was a welcome change for the Japanese population, which now had the chance to reflect on "what it might mean to create a private life free from the dictates of the state."[3] This indicated, in the words of Michel Foucault, an increased interest in transitioning from a mode of existence that could be characterized as *assujettissement* (defining one's existence based upon the external forces to which one is subjugated or must submit) to one of *subjectivation* (becoming a thinking, responsible subject through self-cultivation).[4]

The early years of the American Occupation saw a "generally unpredictable efflorescence of popular sentiment and initiative" in which such a search for subjectivity figured prominently. As in decades past, the genre of detective fiction beckoned writers and readers alike as a prime site for the literary exploration of identity. Perhaps sensing the popular excitement over the prospect of new freedoms, Yokomizo Seishi issued the following call to action from his home in rural Okayama to his readers around the country in 1946:

> Our current misery stems from the fact that the Japanese do not read detective fiction as much as they should. I say this at the risk of sounding self-serving. But we all have to admit that we neglected to practice how to think and act rationally [in prewar Japan]. . . . Detective fiction has upheld rationality *(rizume na bungaku)* since its birth, so to make it as rational as possible is a duty for all those who call themselves detective writers *(tantei sakka)*. Staying faithful to that duty was discouraged during the war. However, now that the war is over, and ended in a painful defeat, we detective writers need to write rational *(gōriteki na)* and intellectual *(chiteki na)* detective fiction in order to enlighten our readers. Only when such works materialize and many supporters are willing to follow our lead, can we begin to build a [new] Japanese culture.[5]

Yokomizo's call for rationality reflects a larger societal trend to reexamine the war and Japan's defeat before facing the future. The utter destruction wreaked upon the entire country during the war made many question the wartime actions of their government and themselves: how could Japan engage in a doomed battle for so long, and why did so many educated people willingly submit to the ideals of the wartime fascist government? For Yokomizo, rationality was the tool with which to combat the irrational spiritualism, superstition, and prejudice that had led Japan into a hopeless war. This rational faculty was also synonymous with ethics and would function like a moral backbone according to which one made decisions and judgments. It was the quality that made the military writer in Oguri Mushitarō's "Kaikyō tenchi kai" pursue the truth while the soldiers looked to overpower reality with brute force.

Detective fiction's search for rationality and subjectivity resonates within the *shutai ronsō* (debates over subjectivity) between Marxist literary critics and the proponents of the journal *Gendai bungaku*. Curiously, some key players in this debate, including Hirano Ken (1907–78), Ara Masahito (1913–79), and Ōi Hirosuke (1912–76), sought refuge in detective fiction during the war. However, while they focused on how the Japanese people can assume sovereignty of their country and the function of intellectuals in that project, detective fiction authors such as Yokomizo and Sakaguchi Ango (1906–55) concentrated more on the project of possessing oneself—the quest to find one's intellectual (ideological) identity independent from externally mandated ethical constructions such as the institutions of *ie* (household), capitalism, and nationalism.[6]

The appeal for rationality was far from the *modan* urban aesthetic and cultural values that Yokomizo advocated during his days as a young *Shinseinen* editor in the late 1920s. He was adamant about contributing to the rebuilding of Japanese society and was convinced that detective fiction could most effectively drive this nationwide project of rationalization by getting readers to ratiocinate with the detective. In his view, a classic locked-room mystery fit the bill perfectly: a body with a dagger in the back is found in a sealed environment. An irrational mind accepts that it was the deed of someone with preternatural powers, or the doing of a supernatural force. A rational mind, however, will use rationality and method to find a mechanism by which an equally rational mind killed the victim and locked the room from outside.

Many other detective writers expressed support for Yokomizo's appeal especially during the decade of 1945–55, when memories of hardship, suffering, and devastation were still fresh in their minds. Edogawa Ranpo, for one, urged other writers to "create a new literature of logic" *(ronri bungaku)*,[7] while Ango sponsored a contest to guess whodunit in his first detective fiction "Furenzoku satsujin jiken" (The Nonconsecutive Murder Case; 1947). These authors sensed that their country was facing a change, from bad to good, and hoped that detective fiction would not lag behind but rather lead the movement.

The first section of this chapter focuses on the wartime reading lives of some key players for the genre's postwar resurgence: just as former detective writers such as the editors of *Shupio* continued to write mysteries under different guises, both Yokomizo and Ango spent the war years reading old copies of Japanese as well as Western classical detective fiction. Those who lament the wartime "disappearance" of the genre most often celebrate the "revival" of the genre in the postwar period. While most critics, including myself, agree that a renaissance of sorts did take place, we have not clarified the social, political, or literary factors that may have contributed to this revitalization. In the same way that it did during the 1890s to the 1910s, classical detective fiction survived by circulating through irregular means during the war, mostly thanks to the aficionados who were relentless in locating and preserving old books. Accounts by such writers as Yokomizo and Ango attest that although production of detective fiction declined, consumption of the genre continued amid supply shortages and air raids.

The second section examines what the privately circulated classical detective fiction enabled—namely, new kinds of detective fiction in the post-1945 world—through the writings of Ango and Yokomizo during the decade immediately following World War II. Ango's most important contribution to the postwar literary scene is undoubtedly the essay "Darakuron" (On Decadence; 1946), which for many contemporary readers legitimized the unleashing of personal desires after long years of oppression. A year later, Ango tried his hand at writing rational detective fiction with "Furenzoku." Despite the chronological proximity between "Darakuron" and Ango's forays into detective fiction, they have often been treated as two distinct interests existing independently of each other. However, a close examination of the figure of Professor Kose, Ango's favorite detective in his contemporary murder mysteries, reveals that the fictional sleuth practices many of the ideals articulated in "Darakuron."

Ango's attempt to use his detective fiction as a tool to instill new ways of thinking also extended beyond the physical boundaries of the text. Fashioning himself after the authors of classic Western detective fiction who challenged their readers in a friendly competition of whodunit, Ango opens his work to direct reader participation by offering a prize to those who could arrive at the correct solution. As Ango sought to construct a new system of ethics and morality that could serve as standards of judgment in the post-defeat, post–total war era, he designed his detective fiction to contribute as an exercise in logic and a way to achieve *subjectivation* and rise above the postwar intellectual and moral confusion.

Ango's effort to nurture a new system of thinking to counteract the negative forces of modernity, including total war and fascism, resonates with Yokomizo's concurrent search for rationality. Using the character of Kindaichi Kōsuke as his literary mouthpiece, Yokomizo criticizes the stubborn tradition and rigid conservatism that were still prevalent in rural Japan. Although many contemporaries considered the end of the war to be a historical breaking point, Yokomizo emphasized the continuity from past to present that still dominated postwar Japan, and warned that the inertia of that past would continue to affect the lives of people in the present if nothing was done to break free of it. The rural culture is Yokomizo's "monster"—the hidden sine qua non of Japanese modernity, as described in Gerald Figal's discussion—that has survived the waves of change.[8] Prior to 1945, Japanese detective fiction had largely, if not exclusively, been an urban genre, but it changes when Yokomizo finds fodder for new detective fiction in the anachronistic world of the Japanese countryside.

Yokomizo also draws upon the psychic pain of the injured "national body/polity" *(kokutai)* by strategically incorporating the bodies of demobilized and wounded soldiers as central parts of his plots. As a legacy of the prewar *ero-guro-nansensu* culture, Yokomizo's inclusion of grotesquely disfigured soldiers serves as both a painful reminder of the country's defeat and a new source of collective anxiety for the "injured" Japanese body. Literally bearing the scars of total war, the once familiar bodies of loved ones returned from combat as unfamiliar lumps of flesh. As these soldiers attempted to reenter a normal way of life, they brought with them their experiences in the colonies and on the battlefields: experiences that to civilians seemed mysterious and frightening.

These *shōi gunjin* (literally: injured military men) were a common sight for years after the war as they flooded the streets of the capital and provincial towns and made their living by begging. Their bodies were the most poignant evidence of the horrors of total war—bodies that were appropriated to fight the war and thrown away as though a replaceable resource for the country. When these men were drafted, their bodies became the property of the state; they only received their bodies back—through a very real feeling of suffering and pain—once they were damaged beyond repair and recognition. Although constituting a sine qua non in Yokomizo's postwar stories, these disfigured soldiers appear only to be suspected of evil intentions and ultimately annihilated at the hands of more cruel minds. They are haunting embodiments of the fragmentation of truth in modernity and serve as uneasy reminders for Kindaichi (and Yokomizo) that rationality is not a fixed formula.

Wartime Consumption of Detective Fiction

Detective fiction and writers survived the war by refashioning themselves in various different ways. However, when the time came to "punish" those responsible for Japan's wartime actions, several figures from the world of detective fiction were targeted: initially, Edogawa Ranpo, Unno Jūza, and Mizutani Jun (1904–2001) were banned from holding public office.[9] Ranpo was soon exempted from the purge. The reduction in his sentence is understandable, since Ranpo only published a couple of works during the war and was never particularly active in nationalist literary circles. Unno remained blacklisted for longer (the ban was lifted in April 1948) but continued writing under a different pseudonym, "Oka Kyūjirō," until his death in 1949. Unno's authorial disguise seems to have worked well: Yamamura Masao, a postwar detective writer and a reader in this period, confesses that he never guessed that Oka Kyūjirō and Unno Jūza were the same writer.[10] Mizutani was probably purged for his wartime activities, which included being the editor of the militarist incarnation of the formerly liberal magazine *Shinseinen*.

One of the most significant influences of the war on detective fiction, as discussed in chapter 4, was the elimination of nearly all of the small coterie magazines that had provided exclusive venues for a wide range of detective fiction. By 1945, there was no dedicated forum remaining in which returning detective writers could publish their stories. Instead of going back to their old nest *Shinseinen*, the detective writers preferred to start a new magazine under the auspices of Iwaya Mitsuru, a young businessman from a long line of successful venture capitalists and owner of Iwaya shoten. Iwaya was ready to gamble his entire fortune on a detective magazine venture headlined by Ranpo, Jō Masayuki (1904–76), and Takeda Takehiko (1919–98).

They named the new magazine *Hōseki* (Jewel) and published its inaugural issue in May 1946. *Hōseki* received immediate popular acclaim: though the official limit for circulation was eight thousand copies per issue, the publishers obtained additional paper from the black market and sold fifty thousand copies of the first issue, and sixty thousand of the second. By the fourth issue, despite the exponentially inflating price tag, the circulation reached a hundred thousand copies per issue.[11] Other magazines dedicated to the genre, such as *Rokku* (Lock) and *Purofīru* (Profile; different from the prewar magazine by the same title), found large and enthusiastic audiences.[12] This mad rush to start up detective fiction continued until 1947.[13] The enthusiastic reception *Hōseki* received as a brand-new magazine from a brand-new publisher attests to the solid fan base the genre was able to keep during the war. The new hope for democracy also fueled the consumption and production of the genre. Ango observed the high sales of detective fiction–related publications and observed: "In the past, suspects were arrested without much evidence, and prosecuted on the basis of confession alone. There was simply no ground on which detective fiction could exist. But with the new constitution [made public on November 3, 1946, and implemented on May 3, 1947], prosecution is impossible without physical evidence, and the suspect's confession alone means nothing. The new constitution guarantees revolutionary developments in detective fiction."[14]

In addition to spontaneous popular demand, the genre had the postwar censors on its side. As required, *Hōseki* delivered five copies to the censorship bureau at General Headquarters before publishing each issue.[15] Although the new Allied censors scrutinized all literatures that were nostalgic about the past, detective fiction was looked upon favorably as it was considered a Western genre.[16] Even *torimonochō* escaped scrutiny despite its period setting, supposedly because of its association with detective fiction.[17] During the Occupation, pocket editions of Anglo-American detective fiction were also made widely available to the general public, in part thanks to American soldiers who sold their collections to local libraries.[18] Conditions were optimal for detective fiction writers: the genre had readers who were hungry for new materials, publishers who were willing to give them space and opportunity, and censors who looked favorably upon their brand of literature.

The radical outburst of interest is not surprising considering how fans of the genre spent the war years. The time could be considered a rest period of sorts for both detective fiction writers and readers, as they stored up creative energy and inspiration for future rather than immediate output. As the conditions of literary production suggest, it was a luxury especially for popular authors to be able to allow their ideas to brew rather than have to produce to meet market demand.[19] While production of the genre waned during the war, consumption continued as devotees came up with creative ways to satisfy their cravings for a detective fiction fix despite the difficult material conditions of the time. Those who were already established writers and had friends with sizable libraries willingly circulated their collections among themselves. When Yokomizo visited Ranpo in Tokyo during the war, he was told to read Roger Scarlett's *Enjeruke no satsu-*

jin (*Murder among the Angells;* originally published in 1932). After mildly enjoying it, Yokomizo borrowed two more books from another friend, Inoue Eizō, a known translator of Western detective fiction. These works were by John Dickson Carr, and Yokomizo did not hesitate to say that they forever changed his life as an author.[20] Others freely engaged in critical exchanges. The one between Edogawa Ranpo and the critic-translator Inoue Yoshio (1908–45) is perhaps the most famous. Although little that was called *tantei shōsetsu* (detective fiction) was published or newly written, people were thinking about the genre.

Looking back on the war days, Ango once even suggested that he had a chance to read all detective fiction texts published in Japan thanks to the war: "During the war, we couldn't drink, we couldn't party, there were no magazines to read or write for, so the only entertainment left for us was reading."[21] He organized a reading group with fellow detective fiction aficionados in which they would cut off the last part of a work and read the rest to see who could figure out the whodunit. Ango reports that, among his peers, most of whom were former contributors to the major literary journal *Gendai bungaku* (Contemporary Literature), Hirano Ken was the most successful would-be sleuth; other participants, the future critics Ara Masahito and Ōi Hirosuke, were not as stellar.[22] Hirano's participation in this little circle suggests detective fiction's wide popularity even among those who are not commonly associated with the genre. The existence of such readers as Ango reinforces the view that while the production of detective fiction slowed down during the war, consumption of it did not. The readers made the best of what had already been published and devised ways in which these books could be widely circulated and enjoyed.

The spirit of Ango's gatherings lasted beyond defeat and gave rise to such detective fiction–themed circles as *Doyō kai* (Saturday Meetings), *Seisan kari gurūpu* (Cyanide Group), *Jūnin kai* (Circle of Ten), and *Tantei shōsetsu shinjin kai* (Circle of New Detective Fiction Writers).[23] The writers used these meetings as forums to present their works, and often held contests to see if anyone could figure out the culprit.

This friendly exercise of imagination and rationality resulted in increased respect for the Van Dinean ideal of fair play and a greater participation of readers in the genre in the postwar era. The lack of fair play—the implicit rule in detective fiction that readers and the literary detective must have equal access to clues and information in solving the crime—was already bothering Ango during the war. As he and his friends competed to figure out "whodunit," they were astonished to find that the existent Japanese works proved useless in their game; they were rarely written in the spirit of fair play and did not make all clues available to the readers as well as to the detective within the story. His wartime frustration led Ango to write "Furenzoku satsujin jiken" and "Tōshu satsujin jiken" (The Pitcher Murder Case; 1950), in which he challenged his readers to solve the crime along with the detective. He also offered a monetary prize paid out of his own pocket for those who successfully saw through his story. Just like the famous "challenge to the readers" by Ellery Queen (the joint pen name of Manfred B. Lee, 1905–71, and Frederic Dannay, 1905–82) that worked as a call to readers to solve the crime from evidence available in the story, Ango's challenge was designed to catch passive or intellectually disengaged readers off guard.

Sakaguchi Ango and the Whodunit Contest

As if to give back to the genre that helped him survive the ordeal of war, Sakaguchi Ango transitioned from reading to writing detective fiction in the postwar era. "Furenzoku," his first detective fiction, was the materialization of an "idea that I had been elaborating since the war days."[24] Adopting a setup common in the kinds of works he enjoyed during the war, the structure of "Furenzoku" resembles a Western detective work from the interwar period. In the story, the relatives and friends of Utagawa Kazuma, heir to his family's fortune, gather in the family's summer home in the country for the one-year anniversary of the death of Utagawa Kaji, the second wife of the family patriarch, Tamon. Although Kaji's death was ruled a suicide by hanging, a cloud of suspicion invades the family gathering when the invitees start receiving letters announcing that she was actually murdered, and that everything will soon come to light. When the guests finally arrive at the summer home, they are killed one by one, as if Kaji exacts revenge upon them from beyond the grave.

The setting makes "Furenzoku" a classic murder mystery: serial murders taking place in an isolated country mansion in which the victims and the killer are gathered. It most closely resembles Ellery Queen's 1932 mystery, *The Tragedy of Y*, in which the patriarch of the family, York Hutter, exacts revenge after his suicide.[25] Ango, however, gives the work a new twist by turning the story into a competition in which he, the author, engages in a friendly battle of wits with his readers. Making the whodunit a contest was by no means a new concept: Kuroiwa Ruikō held one as early as 1889 for "Makkura" (Complete Darkness), his translation of *The Leavenworth Case* (1878) by Anna Katherine Greene. The goal of readers' participation for this text was the pure honor of recognition: although the newspaper published their names, neither Ruikō nor the publisher rewarded those who reached the correct solution.[26] For more than two hundred readers this honor alone made the contest worth it.[27]

The marriage between prize competition and active reading proved to be a winning formula, however, and other writers and publishers emulated it soon after Ruikō did it. Oshikawa Shunrō (1876–1914) used it with his magazine *Bōken sekai* (World of Adventure) in 1908.[28] *Shinseinen* followed the example and had contests for everything from the whodunit in a detective fiction to who would win the battle if Japan and the United States entered a war.[29] During the mid-1930s, detective fiction coupled with such contests became a common marketing ploy for publishers (most frequently Hakubunkan, the publisher of *Shinseinen*) to entice readers to take a more active role in their reading and increase the circulation of their magazines.[30]

What Ango intended to accomplish with "Furenzoku," however, was different from other stories packaged with contests from the prewar period. It was not a marketing scheme but a purer intellectual dialogue between the author and the reader. In his first message to readers, Ango explains the setup of his competition:

> I will offer a prize for the whodunit of this story. I will give my salary for the solution part of this serialization to the most elaborate answer that solves the crime. I will give you more details about this competition later, but I intend to finish this story within nine or ten installments. Let's see who is smarter, you or me. If no one nails the killer, I will not give you the money. I am confident that I will not have to.[31]

As Ango uses the space of a supplement *(fuki)* rather than the main text to speak to readers, he is able to make the text a level playing field on which the author and the readers engage in a competition of wits (the readers do not need to worry about the possibility of a dishonest narrator, as in the case of Ranpo's "Nisen dōka" and Agatha Christie's *The Murder of Roger Ackroyd*). In addition, while in the past it was the publisher who put up the funds to hold a contest like this, Ango paid for this one on his own, indicating that the stakes were higher for him. By offering to finance the competition with his own money, Ango also challenges the view that detective writers were "in the business for the money," a prejudice that had haunted the genre since the Meiji period.

Ango issued five messages in total, using each to provide guidelines and provoke his readers. The second message emphasizes the spirit of "fair play" in his story: "I assure you that you will be told everything, be given all the clues you need to deduce the killer." Ango also explains the steps he will take to ensure that he will not cheat (or appear to be cheating): he will write the solution and submit it to the editors in a sealed envelope before he reads solutions from readers. No one will be privy to the secret, since even "one of the editors is participating in this contest." Utterly confident and ready to have maximum fun, Ango also calls on his peers to join the game: he invites such fellow detective writers as Edogawa Ranpo and Kigi Takatarō to participate.[32] A friendly game of the whodunit based on the principle of fair play, "Furenzoku" is an extension of Ango's wartime reading practice as well as the expansion of what detective fiction authors practiced among themselves.

After a year of serialization, the solution to "Furenzoku" and the winners of the competition were announced on the pages of *Nihon shōsetsu* (Japanese Novel) in 1948. The serial killings turned out to be the work of Ayaka, Kazuma's wife, and her old lover Doi, with the goal of taking over Kazuma's family fortune. Ango acknowledged that four readers figured out whodunit correctly: "Eight readers guessed right that the murders were the deeds of the Ayaka and Pikaichi (Doi's nickname in the story) team. Of these eight, the deductions of Kataoka, Akimoto, Shōji, and Sakai (the winners of first and second prizes) were identical to those of Kose (the detective in the story)." The four winners came from all around Japan, signifying the genre's widespread popularity and nationwide participation in the competition.[33] As Ango remained true to his word and paid "the price of defeat" *(haiboku ryō)* to the winners, he also expressed satisfaction in doing so: "This payment of the price of defeat is a pleasant one for the author. They accurately figured out the whodunit to the smallest detail. I am truly happy."[34] Ango reinforces the rationality of his text in the presence of the four winners: "I can probably be proud of myself that there were four readers who ratiocinated in exactly the same way as Kose. The text is written for the readers to draw that conclusion. . . . Detective fiction has to be rational *(gōriteki)*."[35] Ango gave away a total of thirty thousand yen to the eight winners, not a small price to pay, in his mind, for confirmation of one's writing and thinking ability.

"Darakuron" and Detective Fiction

As Ango serialized "Furenzoku" on the pages of *Nihon shōsetsu*, he was also gaining fame, or rather notoriety, for promoting decadence among his readers with his essays "Darakuron" and "Zoku darakuron" (On Decadence Continued; 1946). Even though the two essays (henceforth grouped together) and Ango's works of detective fiction were written virtually at the same time, critics commonly ignore the connection between these two literary endeavors. This dissociation seems to stem from the view that writing detective fiction was nothing more than a flirtation for him (as opposed to his other, more serious interests). In this regard, the only connection between the tenets of "Darakuron" and Ango's contemporary fiction seems to be that the Japanese should be decadent, and that detective fiction as an escapist puzzle offers a convenient way to be so.

Such an interpretation of "Darakuron" and Ango's fictional works fails, however, to capture the larger cultural movement for renewal and rebirth in which the genre hoped to participate. The critic Rin Shukumi offers a different reading of "Darakuron" that allows us to connect Ango's argument for decadence and his detective fiction: according to Rin, "decadence" *(daraku)* for Ango is an indispensable way to achieve social and intellectual independence that allows one to get out of not only societal obligations (that often turn out to be unreasonable and oppressive) but also all systems of thought.[36] "Darakuron" is more than a praise of the selfish pursuit of individual desires: rather, it forces the reader to accept the reality of only being able to enjoy the pleasure of realizing one's desires with the loneliness *(kodoku)* that accompanies it. Only when one accepts this loneliness can one break "the connecting points that allow the reproduction of ideologies."[37] By suggesting ways to achieve independence from ideology and other societal pressures to be "good" (i.e., an obedient subject), Ango seeks to "free" the Japanese and invites them to launch the project of *subjectivation*.

One example of the liberated subject can be found in the character of Kose. He is referred to as Professor Kose, and just like his literary counterparts, he has an incredible knack for criminal investigation. In fact, he is crowned with the title of "Professor" for his analytical skills rather than formal schooling: "Although we call him 'Professor Kose,' he is no professor. Rather, he is a young man of twenty-nine. . . . But his talent in the work of detection is nothing short of amazing. He is a genuine genius. We have witnessed many times to the point of being scared the certainty of his observations, his ability to discern the delicate nuances of human psychology."[38]

Kose's genius is in sharp contrast with his laziness: he is a "lazy ass unwilling to apply himself" who is unfamiliar with academic knowledge. He studied aesthetics at university only because "he felt too unprepared to enter any other department." Unlike other youths his age who are mentally capable of university study, and socially expected to obtain a college degree and move on to contribute to his family and society, Kose is not afraid of "falling all the way" *(ochinuku)*: "Human beings are delicate and feeble, and hence ignorant. They are too weak to fall all the way."[39] The discrepancy between Kose's genius and his unwillingness to let it take over his life makes him something of an ideal fallen hero. Kose is faithful to the mission of "Darakuron": "Humans have their individual, idiosyncratic desires, but they are too afraid to act them out as any kind of social deviation eventually results in virtual exile from society. That is why humans keep concocting systems of fake virtue such as *bushidō* [the warrior's code of conduct] and the emperor system." Ango urges: "In order to fabricate one's own *bushidō*, one's own emperor, one needs to indulge in decadence in the right way."[40] Kose too has mastered only what he wants to master: "Instead of having stuffy academic knowledge, he has a mastery over frivolous things—he reads all night, everything from silly books of *kōshaku* (storytelling), expensive collections of *rakugo* (comedic storytelling), pornography, magazines about movies, *sumō*. There is nothing frivolous that he doesn't know." In willingly indulging his whimsical interests and desires, Kose echoes an earlier literary private eye, Sherlock Holmes. Just like Holmes's, Kose's knowledge of the world is skewed, and his skill is something that is not easily transferred to occupations other than that of "consulting detective" who investigates for private clients outside official law enforcement.[41]

Kose continues to guard his autonomy from earthly and societal obligations even after successfully solving the Furenzoku case. In "Fukuin satsujin jiken" (The Demobilized Soldier Murder Case; 1949), in which Kose makes another appearance, we are told that the fame from the earlier case has allowed him to open an office in the entertainment quarter near Yūrakuchō station in Tokyo. However, he remains less interested in receiving monetary rewards from working on new cases than in womanizing. Kose's personality, perhaps along with the peculiar location of his workplace, makes his friend Yashiro suspect that his detective agency is a cover for shadier dealings. Instead of posing as a model figure of justice and being subjected to all the obligations one has to obey in order to keep up that appearance, Kose willingly projects an image of a less-than-respectable oddball.

In another story, "Shōgo no satsujin" (Murder at Midday; 1953), Kose compares nabbing a killer to winning the affections of a woman he loves: "Figuring out the whodunit and truly falling in love are similar. They involve identical processes. That's why I am busy worshipping women instead of playing a detective."[42] Having said this, Kose hurries to a rendezvous with his lover. This is not the first time he puts his romantic life before the ongoing criminal investigation: in "Furenzoku," Kose takes leave from the Utagawa mansion supposedly to see his lover during the investigation. When he fails to return by a certain time, another murder takes place. Although his conduct and statements make him appear morally flawed, it is at instances like this that Kose is the most moral. As Ango presses his readers to be decadent, he urges them to do more than finding new ethics and morality. Ango seeks to create new value systems that can function as ethics and morality.[43] In order to start all over again, humans need to go back to their true selves:

> What is the true, right state of existence for human beings? To desire the things that one desires, and reject the things that one wants to reject. That is all there is to it. To declare that one likes what one likes, love the woman one loves. Let's not pretend that we believe in pretexts, the voice that says that adultery is a taboo, and social obligation. Let's take these fake clothes off our hearts and be naked.

> To determine one's true identity and examine it is the first thing we have to do in order to come to life again. Only then can we develop selfhood *(jiga)*, humanity *(jinsei)*, and truth *(shinjitsu)*.⁴⁴

By being a free spirit and making the decision of whether to make himself available for a case each time it comes to him and by sometimes respecting his own (sexual) desire more than the ongoing investigation, Kose can practice the central teaching of "Darakuron." Even though Kose uses his talent of detection to catch criminals, he needs to stay uncommitted to the ideology that the police, the official agency of law, represents.

Rural Japan, the Hotbed of Irrationality

If the entertainment quarter near Yūrakuchō station—with its booming black market and seedy entertainments—was the center of postwar depravity, its moral antithesis may have been the peaceful, green fields of Okayama, to which Yokomizo Seishi moved during the war to escape air raids in the capital. In addition to the security, moving to Okayama had the added bonus for the former city boy of making him familiar with rural culture: "The word *'iegara'* [pedigree or social standing of a family]—an obsolete term for those in the city—is still alive and well with all its severity. They [those in the countryside] have a strong sense of clan, and demonstrate an incredibly exclusionist skepticism toward outsiders that is utterly beyond the imagination of city dwellers."⁴⁵ In his postwar detective fiction, Yokomizo shows that the green pastures of the countryside hide just as much darkness as the brothels of Yūrakuchō, and stand in the way of his quest for a new rationality.

The rural obsession with *iegara* is one of the important undertones in Yokomizo's first work of the postwar era, "Honjin satsujin jiken" (Murders at the Main Manor; 1946). Yokomizo wrote the story after Japan's surrender, but it is set a decade earlier, before the confusion of war subsumed all daily activities of rural Japan. The mystery starts when the peaceful village and the clan of Ichiyanagi are thrown into chaos when the heir, Kenzō, falls in love with Katsuko, an outsider. The tension in the village increases as Kenzō is committed to marrying her despite objections from his family. There is nothing wrong with Katsuko: she worked as a teacher at a girls' school, and her father owns a prosperous fruit farm. The family members of Ichiyanagi dislike her simply because she is an outsider, and her family's business is too new for them to evoke prestige in their minds. Yokomizo explains to the readership through the nameless narrator that the attitude of the Ichinayagis toward outsiders is illogical but typical:

> Go live in a farming village for a while. You'll know how the idea of *iegara*—an obsolete term in the city—rules everything. Because of the confusion following the defeat, the farmers in these communities no longer blindly worship social position, standing, and fortune. These things are in the process of crumbling down. But not *iegara*. The admiration, respect, and pride for good *iegara* still rules the farming community. Moreover, *iegara* for them does not necessarily mean good blood from the standpoints of eugenics and genetics. It is whether that family served as *nanushi* [Edo period village chief] or *shōya* [another term for village chief] during the Edo period. If so, even if the family has produced illnesses in every generation, it is a good *iegara*.[46]

When Katsuko and Kenzō are found dead in their "honeymoon suite" on his estate, this passage on the conservative nature of the residents of rural communities in Japan serves to incriminate almost all the characters in the story, as they subscribe to the tenet of *iegara* and deemed the union wrong. The prejudice against outsiders leads all parties involved to suspect a mysterious man with three fingers who passed through the village a day before the murders. Some evidence does point to his criminality: bloody fingerprints of three fingers are found on the wall near the bodies. However, the mystery deepens when it is determined that the honeymoon suite was locked from the inside, although the weapon, a bloody Japanese sword, was found outside, and there is no sign indicating how the killer made his entry or escape.

Kindaichi Kōsuke, the detective and another outsider to the community, is the only one who remains impervious to the indigenous prejudice and discovers the mystery of the locked chamber. In the end, Kindaichi is able to uncover that what appeared to be a double murder was actually a forced murder-suicide schemed by Kenzō himself. Having found out after the wedding is set that his fiancée, Katsuko, had a lover before him, Kenzō felt an insurmountable urge to kill her and himself in order to save his family from disgrace and himself from derision. The three-fingered man was a decoy that Kenzō used to play on the prejudice of his own people. He even took advantage of the unfortunate man's dead body to test the sharpness of the blade he planned to use to kill his bride. A man's pathological fixation on *iegara* and a community's groundless prejudice against outsiders prove lethal as they cause the death of an innocent person.

At the same time, Yokomizo informs the reader that the moral values Kenzō sought to perpetuate with his murders are on the decline. By the end of the story, Kindaichi rules with his flexible rationality, while all representatives of older, irrational exclusionism have slowly died out during the war. Saburō, Kenzō's younger brother who helped him create the "locked room" by ensuring the transport of the sword to outside the suite, is killed in a battle while awaiting trial. Ryōsuke, another family relative and the possible male heir, dies in Hiroshima's atomic blast. The youngest sister Suzuko, an innocent but ignorant girl, also dies from a chronic disease. Although the matron of the family, Kenzō's mother, Itoko, and a few other family members still live in the manor, we are told that "there are daily family quarrels," and we get the impression that the prosperous days of the Ichiyanagis are numbered.[47]

Although Yokomizo uses the setting of rural Okayama for "Honjin," he uses war and its effects on rural populations as an aspect of postwar mystery in subsequent works. Typically, Yokomizo shows how the experience of total war disrupted rural life in at least two ways. For one, the duty of military service came to all productive male residents, including even the ever-important first-born sons. As they left for the war, the villages were forced to take in former city residents, like Yokomizo himself, who sought refuge from intermittent air raids. The movement of people in these two directions made the residents extremely uncomfortable in their own familiar environment.

How a national policy of total war affected the small community of Gokumon Island, off the shore of Okayama, is part of the plot of Yokomizo's 1947 work with the same title "Gokumontō" (Gokumon Island: literally, Hell's Gate Island). The war prompts the Japanese military to construct a watchtower and fortress on the previously secluded island. The move to mobilize the village eventually brings Ukai Shōzō, a dashing young soldier, to the island. When asked about Ukai by Kindaichi Kōsuke, one of the villagers makes the connection between war and its unpleasant consequences at the everyday level: "[Ukai] is not from here. I heard he is from the country of Tajima [the present-day Hyōgo prefecture]. They say that his father is the principal of an elementary school there, but who knows?

So you ask why someone from Tajima came to such an isolated island like this one? It's all because of the war. The war brought him here."[48] After his deployment on Gokumon Island, Ukai's good looks become crucial for his regiment in smoothing out the tension between the military and the villagers: the three daughters of the most powerful family in the village, Kitō, take a particular liking to him. For those who prefer tranquil traditional life to good looks, however, the presence of an outsider represents nothing but a menace. When three daughters of the island's main clan are killed one by one, Ukai is immediately seen as one of the prime suspects.

Kindaichi Kōsuke, an outsider himself, is allowed to enter such a close-minded environment as Gokumon Island only because he is a messenger from Kitō Chimata, the oldest son of the head clan of the island (and half brother of the aforementioned three daughters). Chimata and Kindaichi were close friends during the war and were on the same ship when they returned from the battlefield. Chimata, however, contracts fever and dies on the way back to Japan. On his deathbed, he begs Kindaichi to go back to his village, because his failure to return will result in the deaths of his three sisters. Chimata also gives Kindaichi a letter of introduction, guaranteeing his good intentions in visiting the village. Theirs is a friendship occasioned only by something like total war and a universal draft system, as Chimata would never have left the island in any other circumstances.

After being in the village for ten days, Kindaichi still feels that "although the villagers behave affably, they hide and protect themselves beneath a hard layer of armor."[49] Usually, remaining objective as he wins the trust of witnesses is the hardest task of the detective; in the case of Kindaichi and the people of Gokumon Island, that task is made harder because the villagers do not trust rationality embodied by Kindaichi as the highest value and an outsider as the conveyor of justice.

The skepticism of the islanders is semijustified by an account of the island's historical background: the island was plagued by pirates until the medieval period, and under subsequent political regimes it was turned into a penal colony. For the islanders, outsiders spelled trouble: because of this, they married within their own clans for centuries. The narrator quotes a certain K, who worked as a teacher on an island similar to Gokumon: "The one I was sent to had about a thousand people. They married among themselves for two or three generations, and in some cases five and six. The entire island was like a large family. What can a police officer do when something goes wrong in a place like that? The police can't do anything, because the island is united against them."[50] Before Ukai, there was another unwanted intruder at the village: O-sayo, a traveling performer-prostitute who eventually married Yosamatsu, Chimata's father, and gave birth to the three depraved and indecent girls. Yosamatsu discovered O-sayo while she was performing in the region, and made her his mistress despite the strong objection from his late father, Kaemon, the former head of the clan. Although never explicitly stated, it is implied in the report of her eventual madness and death that O-sayo was a prostitute before becoming Yosamatsu's mistress. Yosamatsu, on the other hand, still ails in his cell within the family home as a madman. Their daughters, unscrupulous supposedly because of their parents' medical condition, live to bully their invalid father. O-sayo embodies everything the islanders fear: violent passion (Yosamatsu's obsession with O-sayo), family discord (between Yosamatsu and Kaemon), and disease (unmistakably syphilis). She threatens the society founded on the notion of *iegara* by eroding that mystique from inside with her contaminated blood. The more the islanders' prejudice is substantiated, the more difficult it becomes for them to overcome their irrational bias.

Despite the exclusionist attitude dominating the island, Kindaichi eventually uncovers the truth behind the murders of the three sisters: it was the evil design of Kaemon, the late clan head, to instruct his three confidants to kill off his granddaughters, who he thought were the shame of his family. The intellectual confrontation between Kindaichi and Kaemon is also the clash between modern rationality refined by urban culture and premodern irrationality enhanced by the insular setting. Before he died, Kaemon gathered his three confidants—Ryōnen, the Buddhist priest of the village temple; Araki, the village chief; and Murase, the village doctor—and told them what to do after his death. If Chimata, the legitimate heir to the family fortune, comes back alive from the war, he will inherit the family name as tradition commands. However, if Chimata is killed and Hajime, son of a branch family and the second one in line, survives, the three daughters would need to be killed in order to make way for Hajime. Chimata was aware of his grandfather's intentions, and that is why he urged his friend-detective to visit Gokumon Island, possibly to stop the killings.

Although Kindaichi is able to unmask the culprit, Kaemon also succeeds in eliminating his unwanted grandchildren from beyond the grave. Since Kaemon is beyond the reach of the law—he is already dead—he seems to get the longer end of the stick. The story provides another twist, however. If both Chimata and Hajime had fallen victim to the war, Kaemon intended to make the oldest daughter take a husband from outside, as contaminated blood was better than no blood ties. Knowing Kaemon's wish, the three confidants murder the daughters as soon as they hear that Hajime survived the war and is on his way to the island. The news of his pending return turns out to be nothing more than a hoax by a desperate, greedy returning soldier attempting to get as much appreciation money as possible from the families of soldiers. It is reported that he was in the habit of giving false reports of their survival, as the families willingly gave him more money in that way. Because of the rash decision by Kaemon and his confidants, Kaemon ends up wiping out the main family completely. The obsession with pedigree nearly causes the annihilation of the family line.

Brutal Deeds of Japanese Soldiers

Giving false reports of comrades in battle is an unforgivable act. It was no secret, however, that the actual and the fictional returning soldiers often committed far worse crimes and were viewed with suspicion and caution. Such skepticism at least partially has its origin in the rumors about the cruel deeds of the Japanese military that were already circulating during the war. Although officials tried to keep them to a minimum, unofficial reports about the violence and madness of drafted soldiers were reaching Japan as quickly as episodes of bravery during the war. In 1937, Nagai Kafū (1879–1959) wrote in his diary: "I heard that many soldiers in the service often suffer from mental diseases and scream obscenities questioning the meaning of war. The army secretly shoots those and announces to their families that they died all of a sudden."[51] Kafū was by no means the only one who heard suspicious rumors about the soldiers. One young barber in Osaka also confessed hearing: "In the battlefield, three to four Japanese soldiers attack Chinese houses to steal their livestock and/or rape women. They also often spear five or six Chinese prisoners at once."[52] After the Rape of Nanking, some soldiers proudly talked about how many they killed. While they are considered tales of bravery within the scheme of nationalism and militarism, these reports, often nothing more than vaguely credible rumors, coupled with the idea of killing another human being, understandably terrified the civilian population even at the height of war.[53] Although spreading such rumors was considered a prosecutable offense—as the barber later discovered—the law could not prevent people from talking about outrageous deeds of their fellow countrymen in service, and speculate the truth of their fight on the continent.

The general anxiety with regard to brave but violent soldiers quickly turned to hatred during the postwar era. One postwar police report states that "many of those who speak of pillage and rape, unsettling people's minds, are returnees from the war front."[54] The soldiers whose atrocious deeds were celebrated across the country during the war were in turn ostracized in the postwar era.[55] Even those who did not have any qualms about committing horrendous acts of brutality against other enemy nationals suffered mental breakdowns once the war was over: Kafū cites an example of a soldier who gang-raped two Chinese girls while on the continent but could not handle the news that his own mother and wife had been raped at home.[56] Incidents such as these gave rise to the rumor that there were thirty thousand to forty thousand veterans hospitalized in Ichikawa, where the Army Mental Hospital *(Rikugun seishin byōin)* for mental illness was located.[57] The point of these rumors is not whether they were genuine but that they allowed people to believe them even though they are extreme and bordering on implausible. Nevertheless, the uncanny aura emitted by the disfigured soldiers was quite real for those who stayed on the home front. Detective fiction writers worked such popular fears of demobilized soldiers into their stories.

All returning soldiers are viewed with distrust, and Kindaichi Kōsuke is no exception. When he comes back to postwar Japan as a demobilized soldier, Yokomizo encourages all the characters around Kindaichi, including readers, to observe him with curiosity and suspicion: "He is about thirty-five or thirty-six, small built. Thin, but had a suntan particular to those who have been to the South Seas. He must have just come back, as he is carrying a cloth bag slung on his shoulder."[58] From this description, it is obvious that it has only been days since Kindaichi arrived in Japan. Although written in 1951, hence chronologically after such works as "Honjin" and "Gokumontō," "Sarusuberi no shita nite" (Underneath the Indian

Lilac Tree) is supposed to be the first case Kindaichi solves immediately after returning from military service. In one scene, Kindaichi looks for his dead friend's brother-in-law to convey a message. When Kindaichi finally meets the man, he looks at Kindaichi with "an expression of concern," as he recognizes a "strange twinkling of light" in the eyes of the returning soldier.[59]

The uncanny aura of the demobilized soldier intensifies when the soldier has sustained grave injuries to his body. The body of such an unfortunate returning soldier—disfigured, amputated, and no longer familiar—exudes both the creepiness of interwar *ero-guro* and suspicion of wartime violence. On top of this generally negative social view of demobilized soldiers, injured soldiers were at a significant disadvantage in being accepted back into the community. Physical handicaps or deformities commonly provoked public aversion: such social prejudice and inadequate state support often left the injured soldiers no fate other than to be treated as "pariahs in their native land."[60] Although the returning soldiers were the town's native sons, those who stayed behind expected that the experience of war would have somewhat—even drastically—changed their loved ones. The injuries they sustained on their bodies symbolized such distance.

Yokomizo incorporates such social outcasts into the plot of his detective fiction already in "Honjin." Although the story is set in prewar Okayama, the description of the man with three fingers—his shabby clothes, unkempt hair and beard, and large surgeon's mask—is a thinly veiled depiction of a typical disfigured soldier and acts as an important "red herring" for Kenzō, who wants to mislead the investigators. At the beginning of the story, the mysterious stranger stops at a local eatery to ask for directions to the Ichiyanagi residence. The man then also asks for a glass of water. The people at the eatery willingly serve the stranger, but they are in for a shock when the man takes off his mask in order to drink the water:

> There was a large scar on his right cheek. It was the scar of a deep wound extending from the right corner of his lips to his cheek, and it made him look as if he had an unusually large mouth. The reason why this man wears a mask is neither to avoid influenza nor to keep off dust, but to hide this prominent scar. Another thing that the three [employees of the eatery] thought was strange was his right hand that was holding the glass. He only had three fingers. He only

had three complete fingers, as the pinky and the fourth finger were cut from about midway.⁶¹

As the story is set in prewar Japan, his injuries are supposed to be the result of a traffic accident that he suffered as a taxi driver while working in a city. However, the three-fingered man prefigures the long list of disfigured returning soldiers whose bodies and identities cast a sinister shadow over Yokomizo's postwar murder mysteries. His ugliness supposedly is a reflection of his inner monstrosity that is capable of murder.

The injuries a soldier sustained during the war made it impossible for anyone, even family members, to confirm his true identity. The mystery of the story "Kuruma ido wa naze kiru" (Why Does the Well Kill? 1949) centers on such an impossibility. The wife of a wealthy local family, Rie, is found dead with multiple stab wounds. The body of Daisuke, her husband who recently returned from the war, is found in a well. The scene evoked one question: what happened to the recently reunited couple? It was no secret that their marriage was in turmoil. The couple was married a year before Daisuke was drafted and went to war. Their present-day ordeal has its roots decades earlier, at Daisuke's birth. Although Daisuke was the first son of his father and therefore the heir to the family fortune, his father also had a son out of wedlock, Goichi. Goichi was actually a month older than Daisuke and bore more physical resemblance to his father than Daisuke did. Most important, it was Goichi who inherited their father's famous "double iris"—a physical idiosyncrasy that made their father special in the family's estimation. Despite these advantages, Goichi did not receive any share of his father's family wealth. This made his relationship to the family shaky, to say the least.

The difference between the physical appearances of Goichi and Daisuke started with the eyes, and diverged more and more as time went on. In their adolescence, Daisuke and Goichi looked enough alike to be considered siblings, but they were by no means identical: Daisuke, enjoying a carefree adolescence, grew up to be a healthy, attractive, and mellow young man with shiny skin. Goichi, on the other hand, was skinny, dark, and irritable because of the hard work he endured in order to survive.⁶²

The war interrupted their lives and changed the course of their bodily development completely. Although they were physically developing to be different, the war seems to have homogenized their appearance:

> More and more similarities surfaced on their bodies. Perhaps the environment of the battlefield equalized their bodies. Before the draft, Daisuke enjoyed a healthy build and complexion, but the war took fat off his body and the sunshine darkened his skin. On the other hand, Goichi put on more pounds and lost some tan. As a result, they now looked completely alike, except for the mysterious gaze of Goichi's double iris.[63]

The original physical difference between the two men is completely erased when Daisuke is blinded in battle and loses his eyes. In the meantime, Goichi is missing in action. With the last decisive mark of identity erased, the real identity of Daisuke—or the man who came back from the war claiming to be him—remains to be confirmed. Orin, Goichi's half sister, rejoices as she believes that it is actually her brother posing as the prodigal son.

Daisuke's long-ailing younger sister, Tsuruyo, also is not sure if the man who came back from the war is her brother. She writes to another brother, Shinji, a returning soldier recuperating at a nearby sanatorium:

> Things in the house have changed so much ever since Daisuke returned. They changed for the worse. Our brother Daisuke was such a cheerful, considerate person. There was laughter wherever he went, and everyone could not help but like him. But, oh, I don't know what happened. After he returned from the war, he became such a gloomy man, as if he is now a completely different person. He is not simply melancholic. I don't know exactly what, but it seems like now he casts a demonic air around him.[64]

Perhaps most surprising is that the blind returnee is indeed Daisuke: the fingerprint on an *ema* (good luck votive tablet) that he left seals his identity. This suggests the profound impact that the war had on the drafted soldiers: they used to have different, individual aspirations besides killing enemies for the good of the country. In the context of military service, however, all are trained to kill and strive for one goal. The war changed Daisuke so much that in order to establish his identity, the family has to resort to fingerprinting, a technique of criminal investigation.

Although descriptions of the grotesque appearance of the blinded Daisuke are kept to a minimum in "Kuruma ido," repulsive physical deformity takes center stage in "Inugamike no ichizoku" (The Inugami Clan; 1950). The injured demobilized soldier in "Inugamike" keeps to himself, and it is his silence that makes people around him uneasy. Inugami Sukekiyo, the oldest grandson of Inugami Sahei and the heir apparent to his family fortune, survives the hardship of war. He comes home to Okayama in one piece, but his face was horribly burned in a battle. Upon learning of Sukekiyo's injury, his mother, Matsuko, gives him a rubber mask while they are in Tokyo that is made to resemble his old face in order to spare him from humiliation.

Suspicion brews as Sukekiyo refuses to mingle with the members of his family after he returns to Okayama. Those who are vying for the family fortune suspect that the real Sukekiyo is actually dead and that Matsuko has brought a stand-in to inherit the family fortune. Inugami Sahei passed away during the war after Sukekiyo was drafted and instructed that his will be read on Sukekiyo's return. When all family members are gathered to hear the will, their suspicion boils over, and they demand that Sukekiyo take off his mask, even though it reveals his scar. Yokomizo heightens the tense moment by emphasizing the grotesqueness of Sukekiyo's face:

> For a moment, everyone fell silent. Then, Matsuko hysterically screamed, "Sukekiyo, take off your mask for those ingrates!" Sukekiyo's masked head reacted. After a moment, Sukekiyo clumsily raised his right hand and started to roll up his mask from his chin. . . . What a face! What a strange face it was. It was devoid of expression. It is a sinister thing to say, but this face had no signs of life, as if all his facial features had frozen. "Oh!" screamed Sayoko [one of Sukekiyo's cousins]. As people were at a loss for words, Matsuko again screamed hysterically: "Sukekiyo sustained a terrible injury to his face. That's why he is wearing a mask like this. That's why we stayed in Tokyo longer than expected. I made a mask that looked exactly like his old face. Sukekiyo, roll up one side and show them." Sukekiyo's trembling fingers reached his chin. He rolled up his mask as if it was his own skin. "Ah!" Sayoko flinched again. Kindaichi Kiosuke too was shaken up for the creepiness of the scene. He felt heavy in the stomach, as if he had swallowed a piece of metal. Underneath the well-crafted mask, a chin and lips that looked exactly

Illustrations from the serialized version of Yokomizo Seishi's "Inugamike no ichizoku." A menacing and mysterious demobilized soldier is literally lurking behind the drama at the Inugami household. Appeared in *Kingu*, September and November 1950. Illustrations by Tominaga Kentarō.

like the ones on the mask were revealed. No sign of abnormality. However, when Sukekiyo rolled up the mask to his nose, Sayoko flinched once again. There was no nose to speak of. Instead, there was a melted ball of dark red meat, about to let out pus. Matsuko screamed, "Sukekiyo, that's enough. Roll down the mask!" When he pulled down the mask again, everyone was relieved. If they had seen the entire face, that burned, horrible piece of meat, they could not have eaten anything for a long time to come.[65]

While the other family members are perplexed by Sukekiyo's horrible appearance, Matsuko declares the authenticity of her son's identity: "His appearance has changed, but it is indeed Sukekiyo. I guarantee it as his mother."[66]

While Matsuko is confident that her blood ties with her son can allow her to see beyond his appearance and identify him, some incidents following the unmasking of Sukekiyo suggest that such a conviction is nothing more than wishful, and irrational, thinking. Tamayo, the adopted daughter of the late Inugami Sahei and the new heiress to the fortune as specified by the will, cannot help but suspect that the masked man is not the man she grew up with. In order to inherit the clan fortune, Tamayo is required to choose a husband from Inugami Sahei's three grandsons, one of whom is Sukekiyo. Since she was closest to Sukekiyo before the war, it is natural for her to choose him as her suitor. But the catch is that he is now disfigured beyond recognition and does not seem at all to be the person he was before he was drafted. In addition, her suspicion grows stronger when she asks Sukekiyo to fix her watch, as he did once before, and he is unable to carry out the task. Tamayo fails to understand why Sukekiyo, regardless of his disfigurement and other horrible, unspoken but imaginable experiences during the war, has forgotten how to do something he used to be able to do well.

While Sukekiyo's true identity is still in question, other possible suitors, namely, Sukekiyo's two half brothers, are killed. The conniving family members now speculate that Tamayo would marry Sukekiyo, despite his appearance, as failing to do so will result in financial loss for her. Upon their marriage, Matsuko would be able to reign over the clan's fortune through Sukekiyo and Tamayo. Out of sheer jealousy, the other family members demand that Sukekiyo's identity be confirmed by a more scientific method than a mother's intuition. Although Matsuko is furious at such a demand, calling it an insult to Sukekiyo's position as the oldest son, the others insist on it. When Sukekiyo himself agrees to it, an *ema* Sukekiyo made before the war is brought in to perform this task. Just as in the story "Kuruma ido," fingerprinting, a tool of criminal investigation, is now the only way to confirm the former soldier's identity and blood ties to his family. Sukekiyo passes the test with flying colors and his identity is confirmed once and for all through an agent of science: "Mr. Fujisaki of the Criminal Identification Section nervously cleared his throat and said: 'I report to you the result of the examination. I will submit a more detailed one to the chief, but here I will avoid the professional lingo and simply tell the conclusion . . .' Mr. Fujisaki made more sound as if to clear his throat again, 'These two handprints are completely identical. Therefore, they eloquently testify that the person sitting here is none other than Sukekiyo.'"[67]

This scene does not depict the triumphant victory of science over irrational fear and suspicion, however, as science actually fails to uncover the returning soldier's disguise. As revealed later, the masked man is not Sukekiyo but Aonuma Shizuma, Sahei's long-lost son born out of wedlock. Sukekiyo and Shizuma were naturally similar in terms of physical appearance, so they switched just for the purpose of the fingerprint trial. The family members present at the announcement by the examiner also doubt the result of the fingerprinting test: "Everyone had objections to the result. But they did not know how to express them."[68] They hesitate to protest the result, even though it runs counter to their intuition: to object would be to deny science. The usually absurd Inugami clan decides to rely on science as a means to get at the truth, but instead finds that the truth it generates is in direct opposition to their "gut feeling."

In the end, the Inugami clan's intuition proves to be right, for the Sukekiyo who returned after the war is actually an impostor. At the fingerprint test, science is outmaneuvered by the general confusion of postwar Japan and the irrational but powerful bond between two hearts—the legitimate heir and the bastard—forged on the battlefield. Shizuma grew up away from the limelight and the wealth, even though he was the son of one of the richest men in the region, but the war allowed Shizuma and Sukekiyo not only to meet but also to interact on equal grounds. Their units were stationed close by in the colonies, and their striking resemblance brought the two together. The "democratic" effect of the universal draft system allowed a man who was raised without a care in the world and another who struggled through everything to become best friends who could confide intimate details of their lives to each other. When Sukekiyo learns how his mother, together with her sisters, persecuted Shizuma's hapless mother, he agrees to help Shizuma pose as himself by stepping in to pass the fingerprint test.

It is a generous but counterintuitive act, as helping Shizuma would result in Sukekiyo's loss. What is more amazing and even more illogical is that Shizuma amazingly could fool Sukekiyo's family members for a long time under the pretext that his personality changed drastically because of his experiences during the war. Sukekiyo's confusion and illogical thinking imply that there was a sizable population behind him who went through similar emotions of desperation, shock, and guilt. One of Yokomizo's favorite Western detective fiction pieces also used the stereotype of neurotic veterans.[69] In *The Red Redmaynes*, Eden Phillpotts deploys as part of the central plot the stereotype of a World War I veteran in Europe who suffers from shell shock. Even though the shell-shocked Robert Redmayne is actually the first victim, since his body is never found the police assume that all subsequent murders are his doing. One of the real killers, his niece, encourages this line of the investigation by bringing up the effects of war on its participants.[70] As Kafū's contemporary account implies, people in the early years of the postwar era were starting to have similar expectations for demobilized soldiers. In "Inugamike," the stereotype is what enables Shizuma to pull off his stunt. Even Matsuko, who once proudly confirmed the identity of the pretender as Sukekiyo, later confesses to Kindaichi that she too had doubts: "There were times when I wondered about the true identity of the man I took in as Sukekiyo. But I readily believed it when he said that he suffered a memory loss when he sustained that horrible injury to his face."[71] Just like the investigators who believed in the madness of Robert Redmayne and named him the prime suspect in Eden Phillpotts's novel, Matsuko accepts the oddness of the impostor as an unfortunate result of wartime trauma. Yokomizo depicts the disfigured soldiers as postwar Japan's cultural "others" whose true feelings and intentions are no longer reachable. When Matsuko discovers that her "son" is an impostor, she does not hesitate to kill him out of sheer hatred. Ultimately, all of Matsuko's evil doings—the murders she committed in order to secure the family fortune for her son—are exposed and she is forced to take her own life. Through this outcome, Yokomizo implies that annihilation is by no means the way to deal with one's cultural others. The disfigured soldiers have an uncanny aura, but they should not be castigated or ostracized for returning from the war as men who have undergone sometimes shocking mental and physical changes.

Rationality, Chance, and Madness

Madness as a general condition of existence poses a threat to detective fiction: but then what can a detective, a supposed purveyor of rationality, do in a world where madness exists as a reality? One strategy Kindaichi employs is not to expect everything to be rational: his solutions account for the element of chance and the illogical changes of heart in the killer's overall scheme. The awareness of (rather than mastery over) chance, and admission of (rather than denial of) illogical emotions, are the qualities that make Kindaichi an able postwar detective.

In "Honjin," Kindaichi uses his rational faculty to show how Kenzō created a locked room. He performs an "experiment" *(jikken)*, in which he proves that it is possible to move the sword, the weapon used in two murders inside the room, to the outside garden by attaching a *koto* string to a nearby waterwheel. The reproducibility of Kindaichi's experiment suggests that he is in full command of the truth. Kindaichi can even pinpoint the text from which Kenzō got the whole idea:

> This kind of trick is often used in detective fiction. The most typical example would be one of the Sherlock Holmes tales, "The Problem of the Thor Bridge." In order to make a suicide by pistol look like a murder, the criminal attaches a string and a weight to her pistol. She shoots herself on the bridge, and as soon as she releases her gun it drops into the deep end of the river. I say with utter confidence that Kenzō was inspired by this story.[72]

Kindaichi also recognizes, however, that not everything went as Kenzō planned. The passing of the three-fingered man through the village the day before the wedding offered an element of surprise: "He had nothing to do with the Ichiyanagi family until then [when he stopped at the eatery for a glass of water]. However, chance would have it that the man entered this case. Or, rather, he fell into Kenzō's scheme."⁷³ Not only did this man of suspicious appearance, a perfect red herring for Kenzō, come to the village on his own, he died of natural causes while resting on top of a cliff as Kenzō was putting the finishing touches on his demonic plan. The hapless three-fingered man died a natural death, but Kenzō did not proceed to give him proper burial. Instead, he used his corpse to test his sword for sharpness. According to Kindaichi, the sealed environment—the perfect locked room—too was a product of chance. Although Kenzō intended to make his murder-suicide appear to be a double murder by an intruder, unexpected snow on the night of the murder erased the footprints he had planted to throw off the investigation.

In order to fill in the details of what happened in a setting where not everything happens for a reason, Kindaichi also needs to be aware of the killer's quirks. This lesson is relevant in "Honjin." The means by which Kenzō pulls off his irrational designs are rational, but his motive for murder is irrational. Kindaichi reveals how Kenzō created the sealed environment with the aid of his younger brother, a length of thread, and the movement of a nearby waterwheel. In order to figure out the whodunit and howdunit, Kindaichi has to be able to understand both the rationality and irrationality in Kenzō's thinking. The former allows him to unravel the mechanism of the *koto* string, wheel, and the sword, and the latter lets him figure out the peculiar reasons for which Kenzō killed his bride in the way he did. If he lacked either of these qualities, Kindaichi would be unable to completely explain what transpired.

In the solution to "Inugamike," Kindaichi willingly admits that there were details of the case that escaped his comprehension: "I have told you that the real Sukekiyo returned on November twelfth as Yamada Sanpei, but I don't know exactly why he used a pseudonym [to return to his native village]."⁷⁴ Although in the end Kindaichi is able to uncover Shizuma and Matsuko's crimes, he was unable to exactly tell with rationality alone what happened on the day of the first murder. In order for what he sees as truth to be true, he has "to take into account so many coincidences." Kindaichi attains the truth only when he admits how "scary coincidences took place one after the other."⁷⁵ His investigation concludes that whoever is in possession of Tamayo's broken watch, the key piece of evidence, is the killer. The watch did fall into the possession of Matsuko, the killer, but only by chance. After killing Suketake, Matsuko found the watch near his body: "I didn't know why Suketake had the watch Tamayo asked Sukekiyo to fix, but I vaguely felt that it was better to keep it, so I brought it back and hid it." The narrator comments: "It was another coincidence. Matsuko did not hide the watch knowing its true meaning. Truth must be something like this."[76] After everything becomes clear through Sukekiyo's confession, Kindaichi turns to the inspector: "You see, Mr. Tachibana [the inspector], in this case the real killer did not deliberate anything. It was the doing of the two other accomplices who complicated matters. Therein lay the charm and difficulty of this case."[77] As the narrator summarizes the incident, he emphasizes this point: "What a strange tale. All was coincidence. All was a series of coincidences."[78]

By pointing out the fortuitous, uncontrolled elements in the killer's designs, as well as the elaborateness of his plans, Kindaichi reminds readers of the existence of "chance"—an element that we cannot control—and that not everything happens for a reason. The so-called red draft notice *(akagami)* does not discriminate between the silver-spoon heir and the family outcast. The selection, at least partially, depends on chance. The confusion of defeat further reshuffles their lives and enhances the element of chance, ultimately making possible a sinister changeling and several murders. To solve a case in this complex—and post–total war—world, Kindaichi has to comprehend various forces besides rationality.

Being a Thinking Subject in Postwar Japan

The kind of morality proposed by Ango through the figure of Kose and by Yokomizo through Kindaichi is different from the values that excited people during the Enlightenment but eventually disappointed them. The ideal of universal rationality and faith in progress did not prevent the moderns from being drawn by the grandeur of fascism, and a stronger system of ethics would be needed to combat it in the future.

Kindaichi allows an element of chance to affect his ratiocination, acknowledging that there are elements of truth one can never know, or cannot make sense of. Although he strives to be rational in figuring out whodunit, he does not expect the killer to always be rational and consistent in planning and carrying out his or her designs. The series of historical events in Japan—from urbanization to total war—showed Kindaichi and everyone else who lived through them that in modernity cause-and-effect relationships are never straightforward, and things are neither entirely deliberate nor completely accidental. It is only by accepting such a precarious worldview that one can escape the *assujettissement* brought about by the realization of truth: the unexpected (and ultimately misguided) reliance on science of the Inugami clan at Sukekiyo's fingerprinting test reinforces this view.

However, outsmarting the truth does not entail neglecting self-cultivation through its pursuit. Although Ango and Yokomizo never coordinated their writings, Ango's challenge to the readers—in which author and readers compete in the game of whodunit on an equal playing field—contributes to Yokomizo's desire to encourage the intellectual and emotional participation of his audience.[79] It is an exercise in *subjectivation* in which the mediation of the publishing industry is kept at a minimum.

Both Kose and Kindaichi possess great detective skills, but they refuse to belong to the official institution of investigation and do not allow their expertise—and consequently their reason for being—to be subject to external control. They remain partially uncommitted to their cases in order to preserve their privileged position as disinterested bystanders and pursue their professional activities without compromising their personal values. Such an attitude may be construed as immoral or selfish, but it certainly helps them realize the moral code of *subjectivation* as proposed by Ango in "Darakuron."

Epilogue
Beyond the Whodunit

By the late 1940s, detective fiction once again was alive and well in Japan: the genre had rebounded from the war and enjoyed a renaissance in popularity. But the term *tantei shōsetsu* was not so fortunate. This moniker, which had served the reading public well for decades, eventually gave way to the name *suiri shōsetsu* (fiction of detection) in the postwar period. It could be argued, though, that this change of label is arbitrary and perhaps even misleading.

The term was first used when Yūkeisha published *Suiri shōsetsu sōsho* (Selected Works of Fiction of Detection) in 1946 as part of the postwar detective fiction craze. As the editor, Kigi Takatarō opted for a fresh term to announce a "new beginning" for the genre. The adoption of the new term was part of Kigi's project to include more kinds of works under the rubric.[1] On the other hand, Edogawa Ranpo hoped to use the term to elevate works of *tantei shōsetsu* that focused primarily on detection and logic, as *tantei shōsetsu* as a classification had become too inclusive in his eyes. Later that year, the government issued a revised list of standard characters in common use *(tōyō kanji hyō)*, and the character *tei* in *tantei* was not included. This happenstance, though it had little to do with the attitudes of authors, editors, and readers toward the term *tantei shōsetsu*, helped *suiri shōsetsu* supplant its predecessor as the accepted name of the genre.

Critics such as Nakajima Kawatarō defined the difference between *tantei shōsetsu* and *suiri shōsetsu* in terms of their varying degrees of social consciousness, arguing that the latter is more socially minded.[2] Retrospectively speaking, Nakajima's theory is reasonable: the styles of Matsumoto Seichō (1909–92) and Kuroiwa Jūgo (1924–2003) suggest that the proponents of *suiri shōsetsu* more readily engaged contemporary social issues than the former. However, some authors whose works were not considered *suiri shōsetsu,* such as Yokomizo Seishi, recognized that their own works were not devoid of social critique: such a justification is not always satisfactory.[3] The warnings that such writers as Kozakai Fuboku, Yumeno Kyūsaku, and Unno Jūza issued through their tales of murderous mad scientists also refute Nakajima's implicit assumption about the apolitical nature of *tantei shōsetsu.*

In truth, *suiri shōsetsu* never completely replaced *tantei shōsetsu,* in much the same way that *postmodernity* never replaced *modernity:* the terms overlap more than they exclude. In describing the state of the modern world, Anthony Giddens envisions the present as the continuity of the past: "Rather than entering a period of post-modernity, we are moving into one in which the consequences of modernity are becoming more and more radicalized and universalized than before."[4] In much the same way, Japan has not been able to rise above modernity despite some poignant historical lessons: the concerns, phenomena, and realities that motivated *tantei shōsetsu* in the early twentieth century continue to exist today. H. D. Harootunian argues: "While the war and defeat brought an end to this particular experience [various forms of fascist totalizing], it would be wrong to say that they terminated either modernism or fascism, which would reappear in different forms and registers in Japan and elsewhere in the years after the war."[5] *Tantei shōsetsu,* too, has not played itself out. As long as detective fiction—be it *tantei shōsetsu* or *suiri shōsetsu*—remains a cumulative genre that wishes to keep certain connections with its predecessors, detective fiction as it was known in the first half of the twentieth century never completely disappeared.

The undercover agents of modernity described in the previous chapters have shown us how detective fiction as a genre explored the ways in which modern subjects can deal with undesirable but also unalienable elements of modern life. The enemies of peace that the genre single out—such as scientists, soldiers, sexuality, and the unconscious—are often impossible to simply isolate and imprison. Evil is never clearly separated from good, and moments of transgression, in which people go from well-meaning, simpleminded common people to menacing criminals, are always blurred by the ambiguity of their identity and motive as well as eternal, uncontrollable forces such as chance. As a collective genre, detective fiction does not pretend to "restore" order as conventionally believed; rather, it encourages us to take comfort in knowing that the only order we can identify is disorder. Japanese diphtheria is now a chronic condition, and its patients grew accustomed to treating it, rather than trying to find a complete cure.

On the other hand, the same undercover agents of modernity show that the genre does not paint an entirely grim picture of human existence in modernity or life with cultural diphtheria. Detective fiction always offers a glimpse of hope for maintaining control over one's existence and hints for ways in which modern subjects can pursue their individual goals in life. As the agents serve as guides to the shady side of modernity, they also elucidate for themselves and readers the parameters of their freedom within which to stylize their existence. Some of the most able detectives and fascinating criminals emerged following an unprecedented economic depression, the devastation of total war, and the prospect and actual experience of the atomic bomb. Detective fiction decodes the general anxiety of such modern perils and repackages them in digestible, consumable form; this would seem to explain why the genre always enjoyed a certain surge in popularity after each disastrous historical event. As the individual agents spearhead the symbolic transformation of indescribable fear into a comprehensible problem, they also end up reinventing themselves in their relationship to the present; rather than accepting themselves as caught "in flux of the passing moments," they take themselves as "object(s) of a complex and difficult elaboration."[6]

Such skills of self-manipulation are close to what Michel Foucault describes as the "arts of existence"—techniques of mastering the self.[7] For Foucault, "taking care of the self" or cultivating oneself in every possible way in the face of insurmountable odds is the ethical goal for a thinking subject who lives in the post-Enlightenment age. It is an amalgam of actions that permits individuals "to effect by their own means or with the help of others a certain number of operations on their own bodies and souls, thoughts, conduct, and way of being, so as to transform themselves in order to attain a certain state of happiness, purity, wisdom, perfection, or immortality."[8]

The undercover agents of modernity in this project embody this virtue. What is found in a character who transforms himself into a woman or tails another person out of boredom is the urge to both satisfy his personal desires and test the limits of his self-forming ability. Other, more extreme characters reveal that the obsession to achieve one's personal desire at times leads one to forget more conventional morality, as in the case of the mad scientists bent on world domination and self-fashioned artists who prey on *moga*. However, the desire to remain faithful to one's desires could motivate the creators of detective fiction to take a stance against one of the most comprehensive fascist regimes in modern history.

It is here that we can glimpse the reason for comparing detective fiction to diphtheria, and the allure of morbid tales of murder and deception—something that may have been elusive to us at the onset of this literary investigation. Readers who enjoyed such stories may have felt the desire to learn from other people's "intentional and voluntary actions by which men not only set themselves rules of conduct, but also seek to transform themselves, to change themselves in their singular being, and to make their life into *an oeuvre* that carries certain aesthetic values and meets certain stylistic criteria."[9] Political, social, and economic institutions try to suppress and intrude upon individuals and their desires, and persuade modern subjects that morality lies within the strict observance of prescribed rules. Foucault's "technologies of the self," on the other hand, encourage the individual to find a certain aesthetic value in his or her existence and take an active role in fashioning and refashioning it throughout one's life: "In this form of morality, the individual [does] not make himself into an ethical subject by universalizing the principles that informed his action; on the contrary, he [does] so by means of an attitude and a quest that individualize his action, modulate it, and perhaps even give him a special brilliance by virtue of the rational and deliberate structure his action manifested."[10] The ardent quest for this special brilliance—the quality that makes a human being an individual different from the rest—quite possibly fuels the fervor for fiction about ratiocination, imagination, and action.

Despite several negative effects, the radicalization of modernity brought about other collateral benefits. One such phenomenon may be cultural globalization, in which "the intensification of worldwide social relations links distant localities in such a way that local happenings are shaped by events occurring many miles away and vice versa."[11] As if to reflect this ongoing cultural trend, intragenre communication reached a new level of activity in the second half of the twentieth century. For the first time, some works of Japanese detective fiction were translated into Western languages. For instance, a collection of Edogawa Ranpo's short stories from the 1920s was translated into English by James B. Harris, and published in 1956 as *Japanese Tales of Mystery and Imagination*. As a result, some giants of Western detective fiction were aware of works by Ranpo and others. Ellery Queen consulted this volume to create the anthology *Ellery Queen's Japanese Golden Dozen: The Detective Story World in Japan* in 1978. The introduction states:

> Only a few Japanese detective stories, perhaps less than a dozen, have been translated into English and published in the United States; and probably no more than that in Europe. The Japanese mystery is therefore unknown to almost all American readers, and Western critics have had little or no opportunity to judge its qualities. As a result, the influence of the Japanese mystery has been negligible, if not nonexistent. It is hoped that the publication of the *Japanese Golden Dozen* will prove to be a breakthrough in the current history of the Eastern detective-crime story.[12]

The former "imagined guild" no longer exists solely in the fantasy of Japanese writers. In a way, the intertwined nature of the modern world makes direct communication between two parties unnecessary for them to influence each other. At the same time, the increasingly interconnected nature of modernity also occasions moments of direct communication, in which the pursuit of self-identity through fiction in one locale can have an effect on the other side of the globe.

The genre's latent presence in modern everyday life is reflected in the fact that it enjoys a steady following and constantly enjoys cross-gender, cross-class attention. The major publishers in Tokyo such as Kōbunsha, Sōgensha, and Hayakawa routinely print detective fiction by native as well as foreign authors. The guild of detective writers continues to promote self-cultivation as a way to navigate the twists and turns of modernity. By sponsoring various literary prizes dedicated to the genre, such as *Tantei sakka kurabu shō* (Prize from the Association of Detective Writers' Club) and *Edogawa Ranpo shō* (the Edogawa Ranpo Prize), the circle of Japanese detective writers has made conscious efforts to both encourage new talent and reward established authors.[13] Many "classic" works from the first half of the twentieth century still fascinate readers of today: works by S. S. Van Dine, Agatha Christie, and Ellery Queen are still widely available in mass-market paperback *(bunko)* editions. Throughout 2002, the publisher Kadokawa shoten hosted various events to celebrate the one hundredth anniversary of the birth of Yokomizo Seishi. During the same year, three new TV adaptations of Kindaichi mysteries were produced: "Gokumontō" (discussed in chapter 5), "Jinmenso" (A Face-Shaped Scar; 1949), and "Meirōsō no sangeki" (Murders at the Meiro Manor; 1975). In addition, two new anthologies about Yokomizo Seishi were published: one a collection of autobiographical essays and the other an ensemble of essays by contemporary authors on Yokomizo.[14] As if to commemorate this on an international scale, the English translation of "Inugamike no ichizoku" was published in 2003.[15] The continuing interest in Yokomizo's works attests to the keen ability of the genre to sustain popular fascination, suggesting that even if the solution to a whodunit has been available to readers for decades, the work can still have considerable staying power for other reasons. Various translation projects of the works by Ranpo and other authors are also under way.

Vincent Starrett has said that Sherlock Holmes never lived, so he shall never die.[16] It seems that the same can be said about detective fiction: the genre is a site in which the idea of progress, the existence of definite historical beginnings and endings, and the possibility for qualitative improvement and decline, have little currency. It seems that cultural diphtheria to detective fiction is not a terminal condition but a productive challenge to heighten one's self-awareness. As long as someone somewhere is haunted by the past, uncertain about the present, and anxious about the future, detective fiction will plumb the murky depths of the modern experience.

Notes

Introduction

1. Yumeno, "Tantei shōsetsu no shōtai," in *Yumeno Kyūsaku zenshū*, vol. 11, 47. Originally published in *Purofuiru* (January 1935).
2. Ishikawa, *Tōkyōgaku*, 1–31.
3. Hasegawa, *Tōkyō no kaibō*, 2.
4. Mentioned in Matsuyama, *Ranpo to Tōkyō*, 27.
5. Giddens, *The Consequences of Modernity*, 1.
6. Fukuzawa, *An Encouragement of Learning (Gakumon no susume)*, 16.
7. Hashizume, *Modan toshi no tanjō*, 3.
8. Tipton and Clark, *Being Modern in Japan*, 7.
9. Harootunian and Najita, "Japanese Revolt against the West," 714.
10. Figal, "Prologue," 4–5.
11. Harootunian, *Overcome by Modernity*, xvi.
12. Yoshimi, "'Sōsetsu,'" 55.
13. Tipton and Clark, *Being Modern in Japan*, 13.
14. In the current project, I assign different meanings to the terms modern and *modan*: I use the adjective *modan* to mean "unique to" or "has origins in" the period between the end of World War I and the gradual shift toward total war in the late 1930s. *Bunka jūtaku*, for instance—Taishō architecture known for its addition (inclusion) of a Western-style reception lounge off the entrance of a Japanese-style home whose famous fictional residents include Naomi and Jōji in Tanizaki Jun'ichirō's *Chijin no ai*—is, in the scheme of this book, *modan*.
15. Washburn, *The Dilemma of the Modern in Japanese Fiction*, 5.
16. Tipton and Clark, *Being Modern in Japan*, 13.
17. Seaman, *Bodies of Evidence*, 7.

18. Lippit, *Topographies of Japanese Modernism*, 3–36.

19. Kuroiwa Ruikō, "Yo ga shinbun ni kokorozashita dōki" (Why I Aspired to a Career in Journalism), 10.

20. For instance, Walter Benjamin connects the gaze of the *flâneur*, the poster child of modernity, and the detective in *Charles Baudelaire;* Jacques Dubois bases his study on the close connection between the genre and modernity as historical phenomenon in his *Le roman policier ou la modernité*.

21. Kuroiwa Ruikō, *Muzan*.

22. According to Ronald R. Thomas, the tendency to use science to embellish their intellect is often seen among Western literary detectives from the nineteenth century. The detectives often use "practical forensic devices that extended the power of the human senses to render visible and measurable what had previously been undetectable." Twentieth-century detectives, on the other hand, tend to "reevaluate their usefulness." See Thomas, "Devices of Truth."

23. Foucault, "What Is Enlightenment?" 41. Foucault cites Baudelaire, "On the Heroism of Modern Life," 12.

24. "Generally associated with the late 1920s and early 1930s, this formula refers to the conspicuous fascination with the 'erotic,' the 'grotesque,' and the 'nonsensical' that pervades the popular culture of that era. Each of the three elements implied a perversion, as it were, of conventional values. The celebration of the 'erotic' *(ero)* in its myriad forms constituted a rejection of the Meiji dictum that sexuality was unsuited for public display or representation unless it conformed to the narrow standards of 'civilized morality.' The elevation of the 'grotesque' *(guro)* betrayed a similar disregard for prevailing esthetic codes, with their focus on traditional canons of beauty and concealment of the seamier sides of existence. Finally, the valorization of the 'nonsensical' *(nansensu)* signaled a discontent with the constraining nature of received moral and epistemological certitudes." Pflugfelder, *Cartographies of Desire*, 290.

25. Siegfried Kracauer's theory of film was particularly useful for me in thinking about tools of reflection that bear the labels of distraction. See Kracauer, "The Cult of Distraction," 323–28.

26. Uchida, *Tantei shōsetsu no shakaigaku*, 48.

27. The most telling case of a reader carefully preserving periodicals intended for ephemeral consumption might be that of a middle-aged day laborer in the early 1920s. When the man suddenly passed away, his landlord unwrapped a cloth that contained all of the dead man's prized possessions. Among them were a poetry anthology and two issues of *Chūō kōron*. The worker had read the two issues so many times, often aloud, that he could recite the articles in them. See Nagamine, *Modan toshi no dokusho kūkan*, 195–96.

28. Yokomizo Seishi discusses the less-than-perfect and at times down-

right disgusting condition of these books from lending bookstores. See Yokomizo, "Kuroiwa Ruikō wo yomu."

29. See Benjamin, *Charles Baudelaire*.

30. Mikuriya, *Tōkyō*, 13–74.

31. A good example of two very distinct neighborhoods developing next to each other may be Marunouchi and the Ginza: the former is a business district, and the latter an entertainment quarter. For more information on these two areas of Tokyo, see Yoshimi, *Toshi no doramaturugī*, 193–261.

32. Kawamoto Saburō contrasts the idea of *tokai* (metropolis, urbanity) with the idea of *nōson* (rural village), and the idea of *toshi* (city) with the idea of *ie* (the institution of the family). See Kawamoto, "1920 nendai, henbō suru Tōkyō," 114.

33. Yoshimi, *Toshi no doramaturugī*, 265.

34. Harootunian, *Overcome by Modernity*, 13.

35. Ikeda, "Joshō," 10.

36. Ibid.

37. Ricoeur, "Civilization and National Cultures," 278.

38. In much the same way that the post-Renaissance poets are supposed to have operated in the English tradition. More recently, Miriam Sas has suggested a new model based on the Freudian notions of "trauma" and "shock," and conceptualized the kind of intercultural (or any kind of) influence that enters the realm of the unconscious as the most powerful one. See Sas, *Fault Lines*.

39. Hasebe, "Ōbei tantei shōsetsu hon'yakushi."

40. The idea of *sekai dōjisei* also runs through Unno Hiroshi's seminal work on the culture of interwar Japan; see Unno, *Modan toshi Tōkyō*.

41. I thank Gerald Prince for bringing these examples to my attention.

42. The work in question here is the aforementioned *Muzan* (Merciless; 1889).

43. Ruikō's self-labeling, however, should not be taken at face value. For instance, as Ruikō reduced his own role as the translator, he also erased the contribution of the original author by often omitting his or her name completely from the translation (because of this, it is often hard for today's Ruikō scholars to pinpoint the original texts). Despite his own insistence, it is more appropriate to describe his translations as *hon'an*, literally "translating ideas," as the term better alludes to the liberal manner in which Ruikō transformed the texts. As Ruikō translates the original text, he converts it by giving the characters and places Japanese names and infusing the story line with his own social agenda. One example of this is "Hito ka oni ka" (Human or Beast? 1888), Ruikō's translation of Gaboriau's *L'affaire Lerouge* (1867). In the preface, Ruikō declares that he translates in order to "inform people of the difficulty involved in the profession of detective *(tantei)* and enlighten them of the sacredness of judicial ruling" and "illustrate the

preciousness of human rights *(jinken)* and the importance of not slighting *(keiyō subekaran)* the law." This is an odd statement to make, especially because the changes he makes to the original text suggest anything but the acceptance of the law as just and perfect. It is his deliberate strategy to escape the censors by minimizing his involvement in and responsibility for the final product; the importance of realizing this goal outweighed the right to any claim of creativity and/or originality.

44. The commercial success of Ruikō's translations encouraged many others to translate Western detective fiction, especially after he slowed down his production of translations in the mid-1890s; however, none of these translations enjoyed the kind of wild popularity that his did. Even though Ruikō never acknowledged his "creativity," his readers seem to have known that the translator's choices could directly affect their enjoyment of the text.

45. Kinkley, *Chinese Justice*, 181.

46. See Simpson, *Detective Fiction from Latin America;* Tani, *The Doomed Detective*.

47. Kinkley, *Chinese Justice*, 171.

48. For instance, when Japanese translations of new Western works were slow in coming, some writers took the initiative to make them available to the Japanese audience. Hirabayashi Hatsunosuke translated several Van Dine works, and Inoue Yoshio translated stories by Freeman Willis Crofts and Ellery Queen. For more information on the translation of Western detective texts into Japanese, see Hasebe, *Ōbei suiri shōsetsu hon'yakushi*.

49. Eliot, "Tradition and Individual Talent," 4.

50. Lippit, "The Literature of Dislocation," 5.

51. Ibid., 3.

52. Yokomizo, "Honjin satsujin jiken," 7–8.

53. Ibid., 198–99.

54. Hardt and Negri, *Empire*, 45. Emphasis in the original.

1. Tailing the Tail

1. Natsume Sōseki, *Higansugi made*, 95.

2. For the best account of the introduction of Freudian psychoanalysis to Japan, see Blowers and Yang Hsueh Chi, "Freud's *Deshi*."

3. Nagai, *Bikōshatachi no machikado*, 239.

4. See Ginzburg, *Myths, Emblems, Clues*.

5. Uchida, *Tantei shōsetsu no shakaigaku*, 82.

6. Foucault, *Discipline and Punish*.

7. Uno Kōji, in "Yumemiru heya" (Dreamy Room), describes the experience of tailing as "the feeling of being the thief and the detective at the same time." Uno, *Uno Kōji zenshū*, 290. For an in-depth study of the *flâneur*, see Tester, *The Flâneur*.

8. Screech, *The Western Scientific Gaze and Popular Imagery in Later Edo Japan*.

9. Miyake, "Himitsu to kaihō," 1.

10. The scrutiny of the lives of public figures and sensationalized reports of them by the media as we know it today developed in Japan in the mid- to late Meiji period under the influence of Kuroiwa Ruikō. See Kōno, "Sukyandaru jānarizumu to 'hō' no shihai."

11. Abe, "Himitsu naki katei no kōfuku," 73.

12. Yamamoto, "Himitsu wo saguru kiken to kyōmi," 12.

13. Even when unfaithful spouses confessed their dalliances, their partners also often turned back to this medium for advice. In the October 24 issue of *Yomiuri Shinbun*, one man confides his torment after his wife confessed to him that he was not her first husband. Society may promote honesty as a virtue, but such a gesture only creates conflict if it is not made in the context of a value system that rewards those who choose to adopt that virtue. See letter from "Ibaragi no hitori" (literally: One in Ibaragi Prefecture).

14. For various twists and turns the municipal government went through during mid-Meiji, see Suzuki, *Toshi e*, 156–68.

15. See Hatsuda, *Toshi no Meiji*. Chapter 2, "Yōfūka e no tamerai," is especially relevant.

16. Nagai, *Bikōshatachi no machikado*, 168.

17. The works of Satō Haruo (1892–1964) best attest to this phenomenon. His writings from the 1910s often feature spaces that exist within the realm of the everyday but also function as gates to a parallel universe. For an analysis of Satō's treatment of urban space and utopian alternative to reality, see Dodd, "Fantasies, Fairies, and Electric Dreams."

18. The first private investigative agency in Tokyo was started by Iwai Saburō, a former police officer, around the mid-1890s. The 1910s through the 1930s saw a steady increase in the number of investigative agencies that studied various aspects of city life. For more information, see Nagai, "Kōshinjo to tantei jimusho," in *Bikōshatachi no machikado*, 193–233.

19. This method was regularly used by the interwar *chian keisatsu* (Police for Public Order) to keep extreme leftists, particularly socialists, in check. For more information, see Nagai, *Bikōshatachi no machikado*, 127–28.

20. Kōga, "Kohaku no paipu," 203.

21. Ibid.

22. Ibid., 226.

23. Tanizaki, "Himitsu," 249–50.

24. Ibid., 251.

25. Edogawa Ranpo, "Akai heya," in vol. 1 of *Edogawa Ranpo zenshū*, 161.

26. Ibid.

27. Simmel, "The Metropolis and Mental Life," 413–14.
28. In Tanizaki's "Himitsu," the story ends before the protagonist's inclination for the unknown takes its final bloody turn. The last sentence of the story reads: "My heart grew tired of the lukewarm sensation derived from 'secrets,' and became more and more hungry for gaudy, bloody pleasures" (270).
29. Edogawa Ranpo, "Yaneura no sanposha," in vol. 1 of *Edogawa Ranpo zenshū*, 253.
30. Ibid.
31. Matsuyama, *Ranpo to Tōkyō*, 57–58.
32. Edogawa Ranpo, "Yaneura no sanposha," 256–57.
33. Ibid., 255.
34. Gunning, "Tracing the Individual Body," 32.
35. Matsuyama, *Ranpo to Tōkyō*, 64.
36. See Foucault, "Panopticism," in *Discipline and Punish*.
37. Edogawa Ranpo, "Yaneura no sanposha," 255–56.
38. "Before the Earthquake, it seemed so formidable a task to gather data in a large city, but as Tokyo went back to its primitive state *(genshiteki na jōtai)*, I thought it would be easier." Kon, "Kōgengaku towa nanika," 362.
39. Kon and Yoshida, "Tōkyō Ginzagai fūzoku kiroku," 87.
40. Silverberg, "Constructing the Japanese Ethnography of Modernity," 33.
41. Iwata, "Shinjuku Mitsukoshi madamu bikōki," 36.
42. Ibid., 39.
43. Ibid.
44. Ibid., 42.
45. Doyle's Sherlock Holmes stories were translated into Japanese as early as the mid-Meiji period (late 1880s). For a taste of these translations, see Kawato and Sakakibara, *Meiji no hon'yaku misuterī*, vol. 3.
46. "A Study in Scarlet," in Doyle, *Sherlock Holmes*, 1:16. Emphasis in the original.
47. Poe, "The Man of the Crowd," 91. Emphasis in the original.
48. Iwata, "Shinjuku Mitsukoshi madamu bikōki," 40–43.
49. Kon and Yoshida, "Tōkyō Ginzagai fūzoku kiroku," 93.
50. Ibid., 99.
51. Silverberg, "Constructing the Japanese Ethnography of Modernity," 39.
52. Ōba, *Kojin shikibetsu hō* (1908) and the second and expanded edition (1910). His mug shot appears on page 207.
53. "The Five Orange Pips," in Doyle, *Sherlock Holmes*, 1:300.
54. Gunning, "Tracing the Individual Body," 32–33.
55. Nagai, *Bikōshatachi no machikado*, 138. This law was a direct re-

sult of the infamous Debagame Incident of 1908 and the public outcry over the lack of legal recourse for stalking. *Debagame* (literally: Turtle with Buckteeth) was the nickname the public chose for Ikeda Kametarō, the supposed culprit in a rape and murder case. On March 22 of the same year, Ikeda peeped into a bathhouse in his neighborhood, spotted a young woman, tailed her after she left the bathhouse, and then raped and murdered her in a nearby field. Immediately following the case, with influence from Western criminology and Freudian psychoanalysis, previously tolerated acts such as peeping started to be seen as a pathological symptom of (incurable) criminality and were outlawed.

56. Iwata, "Shinjuku Mitsukoshi madamu bikōki," 37.
57. Kon, "Kōgengaku sōron," 396.
58. Unno, "Kaidan," 39.
59. Iwata, "Shinjuku Mitsukoshi madamu bikōki," 37.
60. Yoshida, "Ren'ai kōgengaku," 57.
61. Ibid.
62. For a thorough account of this cultural trend, see Takahashi, *Ranpo no jidai*.
63. Kon and Yoshida, "Tōkyō Ginzagai fūzoku kiroku," 118.
64. Ibid., 87–88.
65. Edogawa Ranpo, "Hitori futayaku," in vol. 1 of *Edogawa Ranpo zenshū*, 289.
66. Ibid., 292.
67. Ibid.
68. Girard, *Deceit, Desire, and the Novel*, 101.
69. Edogawa Ranpo, "Hitori futayaku," 294.
70. Edogawa Ranpo, "Ryōki no hate," 70.
71. Ibid., 79.
72. See Ōba, *Kojin shikibetsu hō* (1908) and the second and expanded edition (1910). Satō Haruo's "Shimon" was originally published in 1917, in the aforementioned summer supplement issue of *Chūō kōron*.
73. Edogawa Ranpo, "Ryōki no hate," 83.
74. Ibid., 86.
75. Edogawa Ranpo, "Tantei shōsetsu to katarushisu," 116. For an articulation of Sayers's theory, see Sayers, "Aristotle on Detective Fiction."
76. Edogawa Ranpo, "Ryōki no hate," 103.
77. Ibid., 110.
78. Ranpo admits that it became nonsensical in the course of serialization. His comment is cited in Nakajima, "Sakuhin kaidai," 409–10.
79. Edogawa Ranpo, "Ryōki no hate," 116.
80. From the midpoint on, the curious tale of urban fantasy is reshaped to adopt a structure that is more overtly detective fiction. The private eye Akechi Kogorō, one of Ranpo's most popular recurring characters,

is brought in at the request of Yokomizo Seishi, a fellow detective fiction writer and the editor in chief of the magazine *Shinseinen*, in which this story was serialized. Ranpo himself was surprised to see the story he wrote "so irresponsibly" sell so well even when it was turned into a book after serialization. For more information, see Nakajima, "Sakuhin kaidai," 409–10. Also see Edogawa Ranpo, "Tantei shōsetsu yonjūnen."

81. See Van Dine, "Twenty Rules for Writing Detective Stories," and Knox, "Detective Story Decalogue."

82. Uchida, *Tantei shōsetsu no shakaigaku*, 83.

83. Ibid., 30.

2. Eyeing the Privates

1. Edogawa Ranpo, "Majutsushi," in vol. 4 of *Edogawa Ranpo zenshū*, 241.

2. For information on the infamous *Tamanoi Barabara Jiken* (Tamanoi dismemberment case), see Kata, *Shōwa jiken shi*, 44–48. For the case in Nagoya, see "Ryōki hanzai jikenbo," 112–14.

3. Ranpo expressed disgust for some themes in his own works: for instance, cannibalism in "Mōjū" (1931) and exaggerated eroticism in "Issun bōshi" (1926). Disappointment at having written the latter story resulted in his taking a leave from writing and the genre altogether in 1927.

4. For instance, "Issun bōshi" (Tom Thumb) was made into a movie first in 1927 and again in 1948. See Suzuki, *Edogawa Ranpo*, 104–8.

5. Vera Mackie discusses a new concern for the female body in public space in her "Modern Selves and Modern Spaces: An Overview."

6. Edogawa Ranpo, "Kumo otoko," in vol. 3 of *Edogawa Ranpo zenshū*, 286.

7. Ibid., 317. See also De Quincey, "On Murder as One of the Fine Arts."

8. I would like to thank my friend and colleague Bruce Baird for this fine insight.

9. For a more detailed account of Oden's crime and analysis on fabrication of her life at the hands of Kanagaki Robun, see Hirata, "Monogatari no onna, onna no monogatari," and Marran, *Poison Woman*.

10. Figal, *Civilization and Monsters*, 1–17.

11. The most in-depth study on contemporary views of *moga* can be found in Silverberg, "The Modern Girl as Militant."

12. According to the national census *(Kokusei zue)* taken in 1920, the percentage of salaried women in the city of Tokyo was 14. Of this number, more than 85 percent received less than thirty yen per month, significantly less than the average living cost in Tokyo. It cost approximately forty yen to pay room and board in this period. The salary was sufficient to support

neither independent nor consumerist life for most women. Figures quoted in Kurosawa, "Shukkyō suru shōjo tachi," 91.

13. My use of the term "male gaze" is very much influenced by Laura Mulvey's seminal article "Visual Pleasure and Narrative Cinema," though here I would like to downplay the psychoanalytical aspect of this concept. See Mulvey, *Visual and Other Pleasures.*

14. Benjamin, *The Arcades Project,* 389.

15. Kitada, *Kōkoku no tanjō,* 11–13.

16. Ibid., 9.

17. Hartman, "Benjamin in Hope," 344. Kitada translates the term as *kisanji* in his argument.

18. Kataoka, "Akadama pōto wain" (1922), poster. Reproduced in Tahashi, *Danpatsu suru onna tachi,* 94.

19. The model was later disowned by her family for posing nude in this poster. Kataoka's career, on the other hand, took off with the success of this particular work, which went on to win the first prize in an international competition in Germany.

20. Machida, "Union Beer" (1924–25), poster.

21. Machida, "Kabuto Beer" (1924–25), poster.

22. Edogawa Ranpo, "Yōchū," in vol. 6 of *Edogawa Ranpo zenshū,* 279.

23. Ibid., 280.

24. Robertson, "Gender-Bending in Paradise," 56.

25. Treat, "Yoshimoto Banana's *Kitchen,*" 281.

26. Edogawa Ranpo, "Yōchū," 324.

27. Ibid., 322.

28. Ibid., 374.

29. The Blind Beast can be described as Rodinian, as Rodin was known to subtract and add limbs from and to his statues. For a discussion of the relationship between his style of sculpture and literature, see Scholz, "Rilke, Rodin, and the Fragmented Man."

30. In grounding their own brand of criminology, interwar Japanese criminologists often consulted Western texts such as Cesare Lombroso's *Criminal Man* (originally published in 1876), *Man of Genius* (1891), *Female Offender* (1895), and Richard von Krafft-Ebing's *Psychopathia Sexualis* (1886), as well as works by Ali Coffignon, Havelock Ellis, and Leo Taxil. For more information, see Nagai, *Bikōshatachi no machikado,* 55–94.

31. Nagai, *Bikōshatachi no machikado,* 94.

32. For an elaboration of this idea, see Akita, "Hentai shinri to josei."

33. On average, *Shinseinen* sold about 30,000 copies per issue. While "Injū" was being serialized, however, the publisher (Hakubunkan) had to print extra copies. Nakajima, "Sakuhin kaidai," 428.

34. Matsuyama, *Uwasa no enkin hō,* 69–70. For more detailed information on the topic of *zōkaki ron,* see Akagawa, "Kaika sekusorojī no episutēme."

35. Cited in Asakura, *Dokufu no tanjō*, 44.

36. Cited in ibid., 58–59. Originally appeared in the magazine *Hanashi* in January 1937.

37. Asakura, *Dokufu no tanjō*, 45–46.

38. Oden's genitalia, along with the brains of Natsume Sōseki and other notables of the era reportedly preserved at the University of Tokyo hospital, were lost during the confusion of World War II (Asakura, *Dokufu no tanjō*, 23). See Akita, "Takahashi Oden no joseiki hyōhon."

39. Nozoe, *Josei to hanzai*, 32.

40. Ibid., 3.

41. Ibid., 19–22.

42. Ibid., 24.

43. Ibid., 32, 43.

44. Ibid., 23.

45. Ibid., 39.

46. Ibid., 348.

47. Ranpo conceded to the editors' demand and emphasized Shizuko's guilt when "Injū" was incorporated into an anthology. However, when another anthology was edited, Ranpo insisted that the ending be restored to its original open-endedness.

48. Edogawa Ranpo, "Injū," in vol. 3 of *Edogawa Ranpo zenshū*, 32.

49. Ibid., 31.

50. On another level, Ranpo seems to use Shizuko as a vehicle through which he plays with the principles of naturalism, the literary school that dominated the world of literature during Ranpo's adolescence and detective fiction's formative years. The naturalistic conflation of a writer's life and his "fiction" in the name of an accurate portrayal of life and, subsequently, truth is Ranpo's target. His question: what if crime is the aspect of life he wishes to portray? I discuss the oppositional stance of detective fiction vis-à-vis naturalism more broadly in the introduction.

51. Ranpo, "Injū," 37.

52. A great example of such a postmodern reading elevated to the level of a serious academic study is Pierre Bayard's *Who Killed Roger Ackroyd?* Using psychoanalysis, the patterns in Agatha Christie's other works, and conventions of the genre, Bayard pinpoints the *real* killer in Christie's 1923 mystery *The Murder of Roger Ackroyd* more than seventy years later.

53. Edogawa Ranpo, "Injū," 62.

54. Ibid., 62–63.

55. Kashida, *Hanzai sōsa hen*, 10.

56. Edogawa Ranpo, "Injū," 23.

57. Ibid., 51.

58. Ibid., 65

59. Terada, *Fujin to hanzai*, 263.

60. Edogawa Ranpo, "Injū," 65.
61. Ibid., 77.
62. Ibid., 78.
63. Ibid., 77.
64. Hasebe, "Ōbei tantei shōsetsu hon'yakushi."
65. Edogawa Ranpo, "Injū," 74.
66. Ibid., 73.
67. Ibid., 74.
68. Ibid.
69. Ibid., 75.
70. Ibid., 78.
71. Hammett, *The Maltese Falcon*, 211.
72. Ibid., 212.
73. Žižek, "Two Ways to Avoid the Real of Desire," 63. Emphasis in the original.
74. Edogawa Ranpo, "Injū," 81.
75. Žižek, "Two Ways to Avoid the Real of Desire," 65.
76. One telling example of this story's popularity is the competition the *Nagoya Shinbun* put up for readers to guess the right killer, a contest reserved for popular works. The prizes in this competition *(kenshō)* ranged from the first prize of a chromium watch to the fifth-place prize, a special fan. Itō, *Shōwa no tantei shōsetsu*, 83.
77. Hamao, "Satsujinki," in *Hamao Shirō shū*, 290–91.
78. Ibid., 305.
79. Ibid., 313.
80. Ibid., 351.
81. Ibid., 368.
82. Ibid., 370.
83. Ibid., 393–94.
84. Ibid., 508–9.
85. Ibid., 514–15.
86. In the end, the killer in this story turns out to be the detective Sadako hires to counter Hiroko and Fujieda's suspicion of her.
87. The ninth rule of Van Dine's "Twenty Rules for Writing Detective Stories" states: "There must be but one detective—that is, but one protagonist of deduction—one *deus ex machina*." The first rule Ronald A. Knox lists in his "A Detective Story Decalogue" is: "The criminal must be someone mentioned in the early part of the story, but must not be anyone whose thoughts the reader has been allowed to follow." Both essays appear in Haycraft (ed.), *The Art of the Mystery Story*, 189–93, 194–96.
88. Grella, "The Hard-Boiled Detective Novel," 116.
89. Sakai, *Nihon no taishū bungaku*, 120.
90. Although I treat Sada as the last *modan* heroine in this chapter, and

she certainly enjoyed popularity among her contemporaries, her popularity has not waned even in postwar years. However, as Christine Marran analyzes, postwar adaptations of Sada's life and relationship with Kichizō are highly romanticized. See Marran, "So Bad She's Good."

91. See "Yoshin chōsho," 136.

92. *Yomiuri Shinbun*, 20 May 1936. Reproduced in Maesaka, *Abe Sada shuki*, 16. Kaneko's analysis appears again on 21 May.

93. *Yomiuri Shinbun*, 21 May 1936. Reprinted in *Abe Sada densetsu*, 9.

94. Maesaka, *Abe Sada shuki*, 151.

95. Asakura, *Dokufu no tanjō*, 286.

96. Hiratsuka was one of the panelists who participated in the special discussion hosted by *Fujin kōron* in the July 1936 issue. She locates Sada's unruly behavior in her upbringing. Hiratsuka, "Katei kyōiku no tachiba kara" (From the Standpoint of Children's Education at Home).

97. Maesaka, *Abe Sada shuki*, 28.

98. Ibid., 142.

99. For instance, the *Kokumin Shinbun* asks in its 9 December edition: "How normal is Takeuchi going to portray O-sada?" (2).

100. In the trial, Judge Hosoya also demonstrated the tendency to assume Sada a pervert. His probing questions included: "When did you first recognize that you became a woman?" (insinuating first menstruation), and "When did you become a woman in a different sense?" (insinuating the loss of her virginity). When he found that Sada had had a sexual encounter (she was raped) before menstruation, Hosoya commented, "Oh, so it was before menstruation" (*Kokumin Shinbun*, 26 November 1936, 2). Hosoya also assumed that Sada was a self-recognized nymphomaniac, though she denied it. It could be argued that Takeuchi built on to the expectation of Sada as a pervert who could not control her sexual desire rather than constructing such an image from the ground up.

101. Although Takeuchi appeared capable only of usurping contemporary criminologists' pseudoscientific discourse on women in his defense of Sada, he was by no means a third-rate lawyer: after the end of this case, his name would resurface again in 1941, when he took up the task of defending Ozaki Hotsumi, the famous Japanese activist and Soviet secret agent who was accused of conspiring against the state with the famous German-born Soviet spy Richard Sorge.

102. *Kokumin Shinbun*, 9 December 1936, evening edition, 2.

103. Maesaka, *Abe Sada shuki*, 98.

104. Takeuchi's defense, reproduced in *Kokumin Shinbun*, evening edition, 9 December 1936, 2.

105. Edogawa Ranpo, "D-zaka no satsujin jiken," in vol. 1 of *Edogawa Ranpo zenshū*, 113–14.

106. Knox, "A Detective Story Decalogue," 195.

107. Mentioned in *Yomiuri Shinbun*, 21 March 1932. Ranpo, too, has a cutout of his article in his *Harimaze nenpu* (271).

3. Mad Scientists and Their Prey

1. Although the circle of writers gathered under the rubric of detective fiction dealt with the issue of ambiguous ethicality in science in the most consistent, concerted, and cumulative manner, certainly other writers were disturbed by the prospect of science preceding morality and expressed it in their literary production. Arishima Takeo wrote of the sadistic pleasure of a surgeon dissecting his own wife in the 1917 work *Jikkenshitsu* (Laboratory); the poet Hagiwara Sakutarō repeatedly warned of science's dark power to deprive people of their capacity for imagination. For an example of the latter, see Hagiwara, "Kagaku e no fushin."

2. Unlike the contemporary Western (French) Marxists who chose technology over religion, interwar Japanese Marxists expressed a certain skepticism toward technology. J. Victor Koschmann discusses this attitude and points out that Miki Kiyoshi and other contemporary Marxists understood technology as a process that represents certain ways of thinking, acting, existence, rationale, creativity, and ethics in human life. Similar to Marx's initial concern about the replacement of "tools" (which help humans achieve things) with "machines" (which only alienate humans from their achievements and themselves), as expressed in *Das Kapital*, Koschmann argues that the interwar technocracy and its effects should be examined on the micro level, in terms of how they affected the everyday, private lives of people. See Koschmann, "Tekunorojī no shihai/shihai no tekunorojī."

3. Students of science were exempt from conscription until the last stages of World War II. See Morris-Suzuki, *The Technological Transformation of Japan*, 155.

4. Aizu Shingo, a widely renowned and published critic on Japanese science fiction, offers the best chronology of translations of key Western science fiction works on his Web site: see "Nenpyō," http://www.kaibido.jp/nenpyo/nenpyo.html (accessed 30 September 2006). In the absence of genre-specific periodicals in the Meiji period, translations of such works were often undertaken by the same group of translators, published side by side with Western detective fiction in general-interest magazines, and consequently shared a similar readership. These omnivorous translators include Kuroiwa Ruikō (1862–1920), Inoue Tsutomu (dates unknown), and Morita Shiken (1890–1965). See also Aizu's chronology in Nagayama, *Natsukashii mirai*, 342–53.

5. Hiroshige, *Kagaku no shakaishi*, 14.

6. See ibid., 21–22.

7. The account of how Japan came to look to Germany for medical matters can be found in Ogawa, *Igaku no rekishi*. See also Bartholomew, *The Formation of Science in Japan*, 49–88.

8. Hiroshige, *Kagaku no shakaishi*, 24, 37.

9. The government was not the only entity striving to bring technological advancement to Japan. As Tessa Morris-Suzuki shows in her discussion of Meiji industrialization, Japanese entrepreneurs and artisans, the key players in the budding modern capitalism and ebbing feudal mercantilism, also played a crucial role in the industrialization of modern Japan. See Morris-Suzuki, *The Technological Transformation of Japan*, 71–142.

10. Letter from Natsume Sōseki to Terada Torahiko, 12 September 1901. Sōseki expresses to Terada his excitement at hearing a lecture on atomic theory and confesses, "I now really want to do something to do with science" (boku mo nanika kagaku ga yaritakunatta). See *Sōseki zenshū*, 188. For a good discussion in Japanese of how Ōgai and Sōseki viewed science, see Nagayama, *Ōgai no okaruto, Sōseki no kagaku*.

11. See Nagai, *Bikōshatachi no machikado*, 109.

12. Interested in making Thorndyke the poster child for forensic science, Freeman has his fictional detective apply the technology of fingerprinting in his 1907 work *The Red Thumb Mark*, 263–64. With its emphasis on Thorndyke's "handsomeness" and "attractiveness," the narrative is reminiscent of the moment of sexual epiphany often found in gay awakening literature. Thorndyke becomes the Adonis of science—and readers were set up to watch him in awe.

13. Freeman's popularity continued into the early 1920s: in 1920, the editors of the new magazine *Shinseinen* chose his *The Eye of Osiris* as the first Western detective fiction to be serialized.

14. Nagayama, *Kindai Nihon no monshōgaku*, 121–22.

15. See Sakai, *Nihon no iryōshi*, 371–72.

16. In many of the early versions of the episode, the object of the experiment is said to have been Jenner's own son, rather than his gardener's son. While this reassignment is no less problematic, this switch may have been an intentional manipulation on the part of the textbook writers in order to make Jenner's action a little less shocking, as it could be construed as the exploitation of a social inferior.

17. The statue was completed in 1897 and was placed in the Tokyo National Museum in 1904. *Tōkyō Geijutsu Daigaku hyakunenshi*, 1:343.

18. Although Kōun was commissioned to create the sculpture, the actual execution was done by his disciple Yonehara Unkai (1869–1925). Ibid.

19. Quotation attributed to Jenner. Lesson 8, "Hatsumei," in vol. 4 of *Jinjō shōgaku shūshinsho* (4th edition, in use from 1934 to 1940), 32–33. Reprinted in *Fukkoku kokutei shūshin kyōkasho*.

20. Kaneko, *Ainshutain shokku*, 2:230.
21. For a detailed discussion of these two magazines and *Kodomo no kagaku*, founded in 1924, see Mizuno, "Science, Ideology, Empire," 254–71.
22. Ogawa Mimei, cited in Kaneko, *Ainshutain shokku*, 2:113.
23. Miyake Yasuko, cited in ibid.
24. Ibid., 2:117–19 and 1:107.
25. Abe Norinari, cited in ibid., 2:121.
26. Ibid., 1:143.
27. Shikanogi Masanobu, cited in ibid., 2:188. Originally appeared in "Kōdō ni okeru Ainshutain," *Kaizō*, January 1923.
28. Matsuyama, *Gunshū: kikai no naka no nanmin*, 226.
29. See Hanzawa, *"Kōbō" no jokyoku*.
30. Kozakai attended the University of Tokyo, the most respected institution of higher education in Japan since its establishment in 1877. It was also a hotbed of controversy: despite its elite status, it was often criticized for being "a bastion of sloth and complacency" (Bartholomew, *Formation of Science*, 273). The characteristics of educational institutions often influenced the writers who attended them, as in the case of Unno Jūza, who was a Waseda University graduate. For the history of the University of Tokyo during its early years and its contribution to the study of science in Japan, see Bartholomew, ibid., 90–98.
31. Kozakai, "Kagaku hatsumei no kyōi," 311. Originally published in *Fujin kōron*, October 1925.
32. Kozakai, "Jennā den," 435–43. Originally appeared in *Shōnen kurabu*, May 1928.
33. Ibid., 441.
34. Ibid., 442.
35. Ibid., 437 and 443.
36. Kozakai, "Tōsō," 195.
37. It is hard to decide whether Kozakai actually agreed with his character Mōri regarding the exemption of scientists from morality. The story reports at the end that both Kario and Mōri died shortly after the conclusion of the Kitazawa incident, and the author Kozakai also passed away from acute pneumonia soon after completion of the story. Perhaps Kozakai's last opinion had been close to that of Mōri, who dies without resolving the dilemma between science and ethics.
38. For an in-depth study of the figure of the scientist in Western literature, see Haynes, *From Faust to Strangelove*. Her chapter "Scientia Gratia Scientiae: The Amoral Scientist" is particularly pertinent.
39. Wells, *The Island of Dr. Moreau*, 47, 48, 49.
40. Ibid., 51–52.
41. Kozakai, "Tōsō," 197.
42. Hiroshige discusses the content of "Gakumon jiritsu no jidai," the

last chapter of *Nihon no kagakukai* (Dainihon bunmei kyōkai, 1917), to illustrate this point. See Hiroshige, *Kagaku no shakaishi*, 39.

43. Matsuyama, *Gunshū*, 228.

44. See ibid., 219–39.

45. The idea of innate or hereditary criminality also convinced some contemporary Western authors. See Van Dine, *The Greene Murder Case*.

46. In a similar vein, Sébastien Japrisot also experiments with the plot of lost memory and culpability in *Piège pour Cendrillon* (1962), with a heroine suffering from amnesia. Jacques Dubois analyzes the unique setup of this story in *Le roman policier ou la modernité*.

47. Nakamura, "Horror and Machines in Prewar Japan," 374.

48. Yumeno, *Dogura magura*, 707.

49. *Karigari hakase* (Dr. Caligari) was first released in Tokyo at Asakusa Kinema Kurabu on 13 May 1921, following the original release at the Odeon in Yokohama on 23 April with the title *Nemuri otoko* (The Sleeping Man/The Somnambulist). See "Karigari hakase to sono jidai" at http://www.shokoku.ac.jp/~nakazawa/caligari.html (accessed 30 September 2006).

50. In the film, Caligari is described as a historical figure from eighteenth-century Italy, but Siegfried Kracauer explains that the name actually came from a figure in little-known correspondence by Stendhal (Marie-Henri Beyle). See Kracauer, "Caligari."

51. Wiene, *Das Kabinett des Doktor Caligari* (1919).

52. See Tanizaki, "Saikin no kesshutsu eiga, 'Karigari hakase' o miru," and Satō, "'Karigari hakase' o mite."

53. Kracauer, "Caligari," 65.

54. Yumeno, *Dogura magura*, 399–411. Yumeno may have also drawn inspiration from the 1926 film *Kurutta ichipeiji* (A Page Gone Mad; directed by Kinugasa Teinosuke) in depicting the various behaviors of patients in the mental hospital.

55. Matsuyama, *Gunshū*, 239.

56. See Kracauer, "Caligari." Kracauer detests the change Wiene made so much that he almost says that both kinds of director—not only of the psychiatric institution (the nameless psychiatrist) but also of the film (Wiene)—are crazy.

57. Yumeno, *Dogura magura*, 729.

58. Oguri, "Kanzen hanzai," 86.

59. Ibid.

60. Robertson, "Japan's First Cyborg?" 16.

61. Ibid., 3.

62. For a detailed account of the status of eugenics in Germany during the first half of the twentieth century, see Weiss, "The Race Hygiene Movement in Germany, 1904–1945." According to Weiss, with the ascen-

sion of the Nazis to power in 1933, the racial hygiene aspect of the German eugenics movement, although it was not one of the main tenets prior to it, came to be emphasized. The call for eugenics in Germany started with the onset of the Depression in 1929, when the need for the more efficient use of the country's dwindling resources (rather than spending money on detaining criminals) became important.

63. See Fujino, *Nihon fashizumu to yūsei shisō*.

64. See, for instance, Ōishi, *"Shinseinen" no kyōwakoku*.

65. Oguri, "Senja fuda kigen no kōyaku," 392, 393.

66. See Adams, "Eugenics in the History of Science" and "Towards a Comparative History of Eugenics," in *The Wellborn Science*.

67. Unno, "Fushū," 253.

68. Ibid., 274–75.

69. Unno, "Ningen kai," 304.

70. Nagayama, "Kaidai," in vol. 2 of *Unno Jūza zenshū*, 565.

71. Poe, "The Murders in the Rue Morgue," 115.

72. Unno, "Hae otoko," in vol. 2 of *Unno Jūza zenshū*, 470.

73. Ibid., 465–66.

74. Ibid., 542.

75. Here is where Frankenstein, another mad scientist turned failed father figure from Mary Shelley's 1818 gothic masterpiece, scores better than Shiota, as the experience of "fatherhood" finally makes him realize "what the duties of a creator toward his creature were, and that I ought to render him happy before I complained of his wickedness." Although Unno does not refer to the text specifically, the Japanese translation of Shelley's *Frankenstein; or, The Modern Prometheus* was certainly available from the late nineteenth century on. It first appeared as "Shinzō monogatari" (New Creation Story) in 1889 in the magazine *Kuni no motowi*.

76. Gunn, *Alternate Worlds*, 116.

77. See Matsuyama, *Gunshū*, 304–18.

78. What allowed the gruesome medical experiments on and ultimate execution of the American GIs is the central theme of Endō Shūsaku's book *Umi to dokuyaku* (serialized in *Bungakukai*, June–October 1957).

79. Yuasa Ken, cited in Tsuneichi, *Nana san ichi butai*, 92, 100.

80. Morris-Suzuki, *The Technological Transformation of Japan*, 156.

4. Drafted Detectives and Total War

1. Giddens, *The Consequences of Modernity*, 58.

2. Nakajima, "Tantei shōsetsu tsūshi," 181.

3. See Oguri, Kigi, and Unno, "Sengen," 116–17.

4. The editors cited economic difficulties in running an unprofitable magazine. This explanation is reasonable only in light of the fact that many magazines were started and cancelled within three issues, most often for

financial reasons. This tendency created the expression *sangō zasshi* (three-issues magazine) to denote a magazine that got canceled within three issues. (See Sakuramoto, *Hon ga dangan datta koro*, 175.) However, there is little evidence to suggest that it applied to *Shupio* in this period.

5. Oguri suggested that the magazine enjoyed a steady following up to its cancellation: "Those who are loved die young . . . flowers fall in full bloom . . . and *Shupio* lowers its curtains at the peak of its sales." See Oguri, "Shishi wa shiseru ni hizu," 464.

6. Nakajima, "Suiri shōsetsu tsūshi," 181.

7. Ricoeur, "Civilisations and National Cultures," 278.

8. "Sanjūyonen mondōroku," excerpt in Shinseinen Kenkyūkai, ed., *Shinseinen yomihon*, 93.

9. Sakai, *Nihon no taishū bungaku*, 171–72.

10. Silver, "Purloined Letters," 25.

11. Yamamae, *Nihon misuterī no hyakunen*, 106.

12. Edogawa Ranpo, "Tantei shōsetsu yonjūnen," 20.

13. Ibid., 22.

14. *Tenkō* is a term originally used to describe the recanting of jailed Communist leaders in 1933. By the postwar era, when Ranpo writes this essay, it came to mean a general ideological shift from left to right. One place where Ranpo explicitly uses the term is in "Tantei shōsetsu yonjūnen," 21.

15. Ranpo serialized "Chie no Ichitarō" starting in the January 1942 issue of *Shōnen kurabu,* under the pen name Komatsu Ryūnosuke. The following year, he tried a new genre, science/spy fiction, with "Idainaru yume." This story was printed in *Hinode*, starting in November 1943.

16. Nakajima, "Suiri shōsetsu tsūshi," 181–82.

17. Inui, *"Shinseinen" no koro*, 189.

18. Yokomizo, "Todoroku ashioto no koto," 227.

19. *Shinseinen*, 19, no. 1 (1938).

20. Inui Shin'ichirō recalls that the new owner of Hakubunkan, the publishing house that owned *Shinseinen,* had played a key role in giving the magazine a pro-militarist facelift in this period. See Shimonaka, *Meisaku sashie zenshū,* 135.

21. Some news from the outside world also enhanced this anti–detective fiction trend in the publishing industry. In 1939, a few months before the outbreak of World War II, the Italian fascist government announced to the outside world that it was banning the works of Agatha Christie and Edgar Wallace, the two English detective writers most popular among Italian readers. The persecution of detective fiction among the Axis continued during the early stages of war; the Third Reich banned all foreign detective fiction in Germany, giving a more explicit reason: they claimed that the genre was an "illegitimate offspring of English literature" and was noth-

ing but "pure liberalism" designed to stuff German heads with the wrong ideas. See Haycraft, "Dictators, Democrats, and Detectives," 312–13.

22. Kōga, "Tantei shōsetsu kyūgyō sengen."

23. Yamaguchi, *Eigo kōza no tanjō*, 1–2.

24. Cited in Sakuramoto, *Daitōa sensō to Nihon eiga*, 52.

25. Ibid., 53.

26. Kanō, *Onnatachi no "jūgo,"* 47.

27. Tajima Tarō, *Ken'etsushitsu no yami ni tsubuyaku* (1938). Cited in Kanō, *Onnatachi no "jūgo,"* 47.

28. Ōshita, "Tantei shōsetsu kai."

29. Edogawa Ranpo, "Gen'eijō," in vol. 15 of *Edogawa Ranpo zenshū*, 20–21.

30. Ibid., 21.

31. Shimonaka, *Meisaku sashie zenshū*, 135.

32. I would like to thank Aizu Shingo for sharing the information on this rare anthology with me. Volume 20, published on 30 July 1944, included Kozakai Fuboku's "Chokusetsu shōko," Hoshino Tatsuo's "Shin'ya no kyaku," Edogawa Ranpo's "Haijinraku," Yokomizo Seishi's "Sanbon no mōhatsu," Ōshita Udaru's "Satsujin eiga," and Kōga Saburō's "Kogeta seisho."

33. Yokomizo, "Todoroku ashioto no koto," 228.

34. Sakuramoto, *Bunkajintachi no daitōa sensō*, 12.

35. Shimizu, *Hon wa nagareru;* cited in Sakuramoto, *Hon ga dangan datta koro*, 125.

36. See, for example, Yokomizo Seishi's "Noroi no tō" (The Cursed Tower; 1932).

37. Unno, "Kaitō-ō," in vol. 6 of *Unno Jūza zenshū*, 25.

38. Homura Sōroku first appears as a private eye in "Mājan satsujin jiken" (Mahjong Murders) published in the September 1931 *Shinseinen*. Homura also appears as a spy in Unno's 1932 work "Kūshū sōsō kyoku," but this transformation was short-lived, as he goes back to being a conventional private investigator in subsequent works until "Kaitō-ō."

39. Unno, "Kaitō-ō," 24.

40. In "Le mystère de la chambre jaune," one of the two detectives, Larsan, turns out to be the attacker who chased the victim into the yellow chamber.

41. Unno, "Kaitō-ō," 31.

42. Ibid.

43. Ibid., 227.

44. "His Last Bow," in Doyle, *Sherlock Holmes*, 2:453–54.

45. Without taking an accusatory tone, Ranpo mentions in places that Unno was extremely cooperative with the military during the war years. See, for example, Edogawa Ranpo, "Tantei shōsetsu yonjūnen," 39.

46. Kigi, "Midori no nisshōki," 344.
47. Ibid., 347.
48. Ibid.
49. For a detailed discussion of Kigi's "Jinsei no ahō," see Ikeda, "Ryōkichi wa kyōkai wo dō koetaka—saigo no chōsen."
50. Kigi, "Midori no nisshōki," 381.
51. Ibid.
52. Ibid.
53. Ibid., 404.
54. Ibid., 405.
55. Ibid., 401–2.
56. Ibid., 402.
57. Sakuramoto, *Nihon bungaku hōkokukai*, 10.
58. Ibid., 15–19.
59. Kigi, "Tōhōkō," in *Kigi Takatarō zenshū*, 3:371.
60. Ibid.
61. Ibid., 372.
62. Ibid.
63. Ibid.
64. Kigi, "Tantei shōsetsu ni okeru fēa ni tsuite," in *Kigi Takatarō zenshū*, 6:185.
65. In his debate with Kōga Saburō, Kigi argued that good detective fiction is composed of two parts: the detective element and the novelistic element. See Kigi, "Iyoiyo Kōga shi ni chōsen," in *Kigi Takatarō zenshū*, 6:176.
66. Tsuduki, "Kaisetsu," 320.
67. Nagayama, "Oguri Mushitarō to fuzai no nan'yō," 22.
68. Nagayama Yasuo analyzes Oguri's works in this way. Nagayama describes the "enclosed space" in Oguri's works, detective fiction and adventure stories alike, using the term *kekkai*, a Buddhist concept indicating a sealed space for clergy and the temple's central icon. See Nagayama, "Kekkai no hō e."
69. Oguri, "Shōden Oguri Mushitarō," 45.
70. Ibid.
71. Ibid.
72. Oguri's *jingai makyō* series can be found in volume 6 of *Oguri Mushitarō zensakuhin*.
73. Ronald A. Knox did not put it mildly when he said, "No Chinaman must figure in the story," because of their supposed immoral nature and different way of thinking. See Knox, "A Detective Story Decalogue," 194–96.
74. See Ikeda, "Ikyō, nazo no gensen."

75. Oguri, "Kaikyō tenchikai," in vol. 2 of *Oguri Mushitarō zensakuhin*, 284.
76. Ibid., 277.
77. Ibid.
78. For instance, in a series of essays, Maruyama Masao discusses the lack of any sense of personal responsibility on the part of wartime politicians. See Maruyama, *Gendai seiji no shisō to kōzō: zōhoban*.
79. Oguri, "Kaikyō tenchikai," 282.
80. Ibid.
81. Ibid., 275.
82. Ibid., 268.
83. Ibid., 302.
84. Ibid., 281.
85. Oguri, "Nanpō kūrī," in vol. 9 of *Oguri Mushitarō zensakuhin*, 103.
86. Ibid.
87. Ibid., 112–13.
88. Ibid., 115–16.
89. Ibid., 114.
90. Ibid.
91. *Shinseinen*, spring supplementary issue, 1937.

5. The Disfigured National Body

1. Iokibe, *Sensō, senryō, kōwa*, 222.
2. Dower, *Embracing Defeat*, 121.
3. Ibid.
4. See Foucault, "Morality and Practice of the Self," 25–37.
5. Yokomizo Seishi, "Tantei shōsetsu to sensō," cited in Itō, *Shōwa no tantei shōsetsu*, 335.
6. For a detailed account of the debate among Marxist critics, proponents of *Kindai Bungaku,* and other individual thinkers, see Koschmann, "Literature and the Bourgeois Subject."
7. Edogawa Ranpo, "Eibei tantei shōetsu no tenbō," in "Gen'eijō," vol. 15 of *Edogawa Ranpo zenshū*, 68. Originally published in *Ondori tsūshin*, November–December 1947.
8. Figal, *Civilization and Monsters*.
9. Yamamura, *Suiri bundan sengoshi*, 34.
10. Ibid., 21.
11. Ibid., 25–26.
12. Yamamae, *Nihon misuterī no hyakunen*, 124–25.
13. *Toppu* (Top) was inaugurated in April 1946; *Tantei yomimono* (Detective Readings) in November 1946; *Kuroneko* (The Black Cat), *Shinju* (Pearl), and *Tantei shōsetsu* (Detective Fiction) in April; *Yōki* (Mysterious

Aura) in July; *G-men* (G-men) and *Uindo miru* (Windmill) in October; and *Fūdanitto* (Whodunit) in November 1947. See Yamamae, *Nihon misuterī no hyakunen*, 122–31.

14. Sakaguchi Ango, "Suiri shōsetsu ni tsuite," in vol. 15 of *Sakaguchi Ango zenshū*.

15. Yamamura, *Suiri bundan sengoshi*, 23.

16. Manabe, *Taishū bungaku jiten*, 400.

17. Sakai, *Nihon no taishū bungaku*, 179. *Hōseki* featured this subgenre in one of its early issues without being aware of the ban by the Occupation Forces. When Jō Masayuki, one of the editors of the magazine, received praise for his brave decision to feature *torimonochō* despite the potential for conflict with the censors, he confessed that he acted out of ignorance: "It's no brave decision. I simply didn't know. If I was told about the warnings in detail, considering what a coward I am, I wouldn't have planned a special issue on *torimonochō*." Cited in Manabe, *Taishū bungaku jiten*, 401.

18. Sakai, *Nihon no taishū bungaku*, 173.

19. See Kawana, "The Price of Pulp."

20. Yokomizo, "Katasumi no rakuen," 233.

21. Sakaguchi Ango, "Watashi no tantei shōsetsu," in vol. 5 of *Sakaguchi Ango zenshū*.

22. Ibid.

23. Yamamura, *Suiri shōsetsu sengoshi*, 54–60. Among these groups, the *Seisankari gurūpu* (Cyanide Group) consisted of detective fiction critics rather than writers. The name "Cyanide Group" has a unique origin: it comes from the anecdote that one young detective writer cursed the members for their harsh criticisms against his works, wishing that he could poison them with cyanide. See Yamamura, *Suiri shōsetsu sengoshi*, 58.

24. Sakaguchi Ango, "Watashi no tantei shōsetsu," 45.

25. It was translated into Japanese in 1937 by Inoue Yoshio.

26. Itō, *Shōwa no tantei shōsetsu*, 261–62.

27. Ibid., 262.

28. The inaugural issue of *Bōken sekai* sold out on the first day. However, the publisher Hakubunkan made a mistake and the issue was published without the question for the readers, and some readers eager to participate wrote to the publisher to complain about the error. See Aizu and Yokota, *Kaidanji Oshikawa Shunrō*, 195–96.

29. Itō, *Shōwa no tantei shōsetsu*, 262.

30. Ōshita Udaru (1896–1966) is perhaps the author who is most commonly associated with this group of writing. He published works in both *Kingu* and *Kōdan kurabu* in this period. See Itō, *Shōwa no tantei shōsetsu*, 263–80.

31. Sakaguchi Ango, "Furenzoku satsujin jiken," in vol. 11 of *Sakaguchi Ango zenshū*, 41.

32. Ibid., 78-79.

33. Kataoka, the winner of the coveted first prize, was from Tokyo, while the others were from Nagano, Kōchi, and Osaka. Murata Motoko was the only woman who won one of the eight prizes. See Sakaguchi Ango, "Furenzoku satsujin jiken," in vol. 11 of *Sakaguchi Ango zenshū*, 274.

34. Ibid., 275.

35. Ibid., 277.

36. Rin, roundtable discussion, in *"Sengo" to iu seido*, 12.

37. Ibid., 8.

38. Sakaguchi Ango, "Furenzoku satsujin jiken," in vol. 11 of *Sakaguchi Ango zenshū*, 26.

39. Ibid., 59.

40. Sakaguchi Ango, "Darakuron," in vol. 4 of *Sakaguchi Ango zenshū*, 59.

41. A "consulting detective" is how Sherlock Holmes first describes himself to Watson. Kose's specialized knowledge also echoes Holmes's self-training. According to Watson, Holmes's talents are also as skewed and specific as Kose's. See Doyle, "A Study in Scarlet," 12–13 and 15.

42. Sakaguchi Ango, "Furenzoku satsujin jiken," in vol. 11 of *Sakaguchi Ango zenshū*, 712.

43. Rin, roundtable discussion, in *"Sengo" to iu seido*, 8. What Ango seeks to achieve is similar to what pragmatic philosophers aim to accomplish with notions such as "human nature": rather than seeking its true nature, they attempt to define it artificially but in terms that benefit us all. See Rorty, "Human Rights, Rationality, and Sentimentality."

44. Sakaguchi Ango, "Furenzoku satsujin jiken," in vol. 11 of *Sakaguchi Ango zenshū*, 274.

45. Yokomizo, "Honkaku tantei shōsetsu e no tenki," 245.

46. Yokomizo, "Honjin satsujin jiken," 18.

47. Ibid., 198–99.

48. Yokomizo, "Gokumontō," 51.

49. Ibid., 33.

50. Ibid., 7–8.

51. Nagai Kafū, diary entry from 4 October 1937. Cited in Matsuyama, *Uwasa no enkin hō*, 352.

52. Cited in Matsuyama, ibid., 356.

53. Ibid., 357.

54. Cited in Dower, *Embracing Defeat*, 124. See Awaya, *Haisen chokugo no seiji to shakai*, 219–20. Dower points to a similar example in Hachiya, *Hiroshima Diary*, 194.

55. Matsuyama, *Uwasa no enkin hō*, 410. Also see Dower, *Embracing Defeat*, 60.

56. Nagai Kafū, diary entry from 18 June 1946. Cited in Matsuyama, *Usawa no enkin hō*, 368.
57. Ibid.
58. Yokomizo, "Sarusuberi no shita nite," in *Yokomizo Seishi shū*, 328.
59. Ibid.
60. Some of them chose to defy the taboo and flaunted their disabilities on the street in the hope of arousing sympathy. See Dower, *Embracing Defeat*, 60–61.
61. Yokomizo, "Honjin satsujin jiken," 14.
62. Yokomizo, "Sarusuberi no shita nite," 677.
63. Ibid., 679.
64. Ibid., 703.
65. Yokomizo, "Honjin satsujin jiken," 63–64.
66. Ibid., 65
67. Ibid., 186.
68. Ibid., 188.
69. Yokomizo chose *The Red Redmaynes* in 1938 as one of his ten favorite Western detective fictions of all time. Other authors, such as Edogawa Ranpo, Ōshita Udaru, Tsunoda Kikuo, Oguri Mushitarō, Ōsaka Keigo, and Kigi Takatarō, also selected the story as one of the ten best of all time. These lists were published as "Kaigai tantai shōsetsu jukketsu" (Best Ten Works of Foreign Detective Fiction) in 1937.
70. To mislead the detective Mark Brendon, the niece, Jenny Pendean, implicates her uncle Robert Redmayne by alluding to his unstable mental health after the First World War: "The war had given him wide, new interests; he was a captain and intended, if he could, to stop in the army. He had escaped marvelously on many fields and seen much service. During the last few weeks before the armistice, he succumbed to gassing and was invalided; though, before that, he had also been out of action from shell shock for two months. He made light of this; but I felt there was really something different about him and suspected that the shell shock accounted for the change." Eden Phillpotts, *The Red Redmaynes*, 35.
71. Yokomizo, "Honjin satsujin jiken," 399.
72. Ibid., 169.
73. Ibid., 178.
74. Yokomizo, "Inugamike no ichizoku," 372.
75. Ibid.
76. Ibid., 388.
77. Ibid., 401–2.
78. Ibid., 384.
79. Ango does, however, mention his impressions of some of Yokomizo's works in his essays. For instance, in "Watashi no tantei shōsetsu" (1947), Ango expresses a liking for Yokomizo's "Gokumontō" (1947), which was

being serialized in *Hōseki* at that time. In contrast to the favorable view of this work, Ango offers some heavy-handed criticism of Yokomizo's "Chōchō satsujin jiken" (The Butterfly Murder Case; 1946) in "Suiri shōsetsu ni tsuite" (1947–51).

Epilogue

1. Kigi articulated his theory of *suiri shōsetsu* in various essays, but the most accessible one may be "Suiri shōsetsu no han'i" in *Kigi Takatarō zenshū*, 220–23. Among the works he recognized as *suiri shōsetsu* are Akutagawa Ryūnosuke's *Haguruma*, Mori Ōgai's *Takasebune*, Ōshio Heihachirō. See Nakajima Kawatarō, "Suiri shōsetsu tsūshi," 185.

2. Yokomizo discusses an incident in which he directly asked Nakajima what the difference between *tantei shōsetsu* and *suiri shōsetsu* was in "Tantei shakka no nageki." Although being labeled a non–*suiri shōsetsu sakka* does not bother him, he finds Nakajima's distinction unsatisfactory. See Yokomizo, "Tantei sakka no nageki," in vol. 18 of *Yokomizo Seishi zenshū*, 148–50.

3. Ibid.

4. Giddens, *The Consequences of Modernity*, 3.

5. Harootunian, *Overcome by Modernity*, xxxii.

6. Foucault, "What Is Enlightenment?" 41.

7. Foucault, *The Use of Pleasure*, 10.

8. Foucault, "Technologies of the Self," in Martin, Gutman, and Hutton, *Technologies of the Self*, 18.

9. Foucault, *The Use of Pleasure*, 10–11.

10. Ibid., 62.

11. Giddens, *The Consequences of Modernity*, 64.

12. Ellery Queen, "Introduction," *Ellery Queen's Japanese Golden Dozen*, 11–12.

13. *Tantei sakka kurabu shō* (later renamed *Nihon suiri sakka kyōkai shō*) started in 1948. *Edogawa Ranpo shō* was established in 1955. *Nihon suiri sakka kyōkai* (Association of Mystery Writers of Japan; their own translation) is what *Doyōkai* evolved into in the late 1940s.

14. The two titles are Shinpo, *Yokomizo Seishi jidenteki zuihitsushū*, and Kadokawa Sho-ten, *Yokomizo Seishi ni tsugu shinseikikara no tegami*.

15. Yokomizo, *The Inugami Clan*.

16. Starrett, *221b*. See also Blackbeard, *Sherlock Holmes in America*, 152.

Bibliography

Abe Isoo. "Himitsu naki katei no kōfuku." *Chūō kōron* 33, no. 8 (Summer supplement 1918), Kōron section: 73.
Adams, Mark B., ed. *The Wellborn Science: Eugenics in Germany, France, Brazil, and Russia.* New York: Oxford University Press, 1990.
Aizu Shingo. http://www.kaibido.co.jp.
Aizu Shingo and Yokota Jun'ya. *Kaidanji Oshikawa Shunrō.* Tokuma shoten, 1991.
Akagawa Manabu. "Kaika sekusorojī no episutēme." In *Sekushuaritii no rekishi shakai gaku,* 81–108. Keisō shobō, 1999.
Akita Masami. "Hentai shinri to josei." In *Sei no ryōki modan,* 165–84. Seikyūsha, 1994.
———. "Takahashi Oden no joseiki Hyōho." *Nyōin kō: seigaku koten yori.* Ōtō shobō, 1999.
Altick, Richard D. *Victorian Studies in Scarlet: Murders and Manners in the Age of Victoria.* New York: W. W. Norton, 1970.
Asakura Kyōji. *Dokufu no tanjō: warui onna to seiyoku no yurai.* Yōsensha, 2002.
Awaya Kentarō, ed. *Haisen chokugo no seiji to shakai.* Vol. 2 of *Shirō: Nihon gendai shi.* Ōtsuki shoten, 1980.
Bartholomew, James R. *The Formation of Science in Japan: Building a Research Tradition.* New Haven, Conn.: Yale University Press, 1989.
Baudelaire, Charles. "On the Heroism of Modern Life." In *The Mirror of Art: Critical Studies by Charles Baudelaire,* translated by Jonathan Mayne, 127–32. London: Phaidon, 1955.
Baudrillard, Jean. *The Perfect Crime.* Translated by Chris Turner. New York: Verso, 1996.
Bayard, Pierre. *Who Killed Roger Ackroyd? The Mystery behind the Agatha*

Christie Mystery. Translated by Carol Cosman. New York: New Press, 2000.

Benjamin, Walter. *The Arcades Project*. Translated by Howard Eiland and Kevin McLaughlin. Cambridge, Mass.: Harvard University Press, 1999.

———. *Charles Baudelaire: A Lyrical Poet in the Era of High Capitalism*. Translated by Harry Zohn. London: Verso, 1973.

Blackbeard, Bill. *Sherlock Holmes in America*. New York: Abrams, 1981.

Blowers, Geoffrey H., and Serena Yang Hsueh Chi. "Freud's *Deshi*: The Coming of Psychoanalysis to Japan." *Journal of Behavioral Sciences* 33, no. 2 (1997): 115–26.

"Bungaku shakai no genjō." *Kokumin no tomo*, 3 May 1893. Quoted in Itō Hideo, *Meiji no tantei shōsetsu*. Futabasha, 2002.

Chance, Linda H. *Formless in Form: Kenkō, "Tsurezuregusa," and the Rhetoric of Japanese Fragmentary Prose*. Stanford, Calif.: Stanford University Press, 1997.

Chesterton, G. K. "A Defence of Detective Stories." In *The Art of the Mystery Story: A Collection of Critical Essays*, edited by Howard Haycraft, 3–6. New York: Universal Library, 1946.

Dainihon bunmei kyōkai, ed. *Nihon no kagakukai*. Dainihon bunmei kyōkai, 1917.

De Quincey, Thomas. "On Murder as One of the Fine Arts." In *The Collected Writings of Thomas de Quincey: New and Enlarged Edition*, edited by David Masson, 9–124. Edinburgh: Adam and Charles Black, 1890.

Dodd, Stephen. "Fantasies, Fairies, and Electric Dreams: Satō Haruo's Critique of Taishō." *Monumenta Nipponica* 49, no. 3 (Autumn 1994): 287–314.

Dower, John W. *Embracing Defeat: Japan in the Wake of World War II*. New York: W. W. Norton, 1999.

Doyle, Arthur Conan. *Sherlock Holmes: The Complete Novels and Stories*. 2 vols. New York: Bantam, 1986.

Dubois, Jacques. *Le roman policier ou la modernité*. Paris: Éditions Nathan, 1992.

Edogawa Ranpo. *Edogawa Ranpo zenshū*. 15 vols. Kōdansha, 1970.

———. *Harimaze nenpu*. Kōdansha, 1989.

———. "Hitori futayaku." In vol. 1 of *Edogawa Ranpo zenshū*.

———. "Injū." In vol. 3 of *Edogwa Ranpo zenshū*.

———. *Japanese Tales of Mystery and Imagination*, trans. James B. Harris. Rutland, Vt.: Tuttle, 1956.

———. "Kumo otoko." In vol. 5 of *Edogawa Ranpo zenshū*.

———. "Maedakō Kōichirō shi ni." *Shinseinen*, May 1925.

———. "Ruikō shinsui." In *Ranpo uchiake banashi*. Kawade shobō, 1994.

———. "Ryōki no hate." In vol. 4 of *Edogawa Ranpo zenshū*.

———. "Tantei shōsetsu to katarushisu." In *Edogawa Ranpo zuihitsusen*, edited by Kida Jun'ichirō, 114–18. Chikuma shobō, 1994.
———. "Tantei shōsetsu yonjūnen." In vols. 13 and 14 of *Edogawa Ranpo zenshū*.
———. "Yōchū." In vol. 8 of *Edogawa Ranpo zenshū*.
Eliot, T. S. "Tradition and the Individual Talent." In *Selected Essays*, 13–22. London: Faber and Faber, 1951.
Figal, Gerald. *Civilization and Monsters: Spirits of Modernity in Meiji Japan*. Durham, N.C.: Duke University Press, 1999.
Foucault, Michel. *Discipline and Punish: The Birth of the Prison*. Translated by Alan Sheridan. New York: Vintage Books, 1995.
———. "Morality and Practice of the Self." In *The Use of Pleasure*. Vol. 2 of *The History of Sexuality*, translated by Robert Hurley, 25–32. New York: Pantheon Books, 1985.
———. *The Use of Pleasure*. Vol. 2 of *The History of Sexuality*. Translated by Robert Hurley. New York: Pantheon Books, 1985
———. "What Is Enlightenment?" In *The Foucault Reader*, edited by Paul Rabinow, 32–50. New York: Pantheon Books, 1984.
Freeman, R. Austin. *The Red Thumb Mark*. New York: A. L. Burt, 1924.
———. *Sōndaiku hakase no jikenbo*. Translated by Ōkubo Yasuo. Sōgen suiri bunko, 2002.
Fujino Yutaka. *Nihon fashizumu to yūsei shisō*. Kyoto: Kamogawa shuppan, 1998.
Fukkoku kokutei shūshin kyōkasho. Ōzorasha, 1990.
Fukuzawa Yukichi. *An Encouragement of Learning* [Gakumon no susume]. Translated by David A. Dilworth and Umeyo Hirano. Yotsuya, Japan: Sophia University Press, 1969.
Giddens, Anthony. *The Consequences of Modernity*. Stanford, Calif.: Stanford University Press, 1990.
Ginzburg, Carlo. *Myths, Emblems, Clues*. Translated by John Tedeschi and Anne Tedeschi. London: Hutchinson Radius, 1990.
Girard, René. *Deceit, Desire, and the Novel: Self and Other in Literary Structure*. Baltimore: The Johns Hopkins University Press, 1976.
Grella, George. "The Hard-Boiled Detective Novel." In *Detective Fiction: A Collection of Critical Essays*, edited by Robin W. Winks, 84–102. Woodstock, Vt.: Countryman Press, 1980.
Gunn, James. *Alternate Worlds: The Illustrated History of Science Fiction*. Englewood Cliffs, N.J.: Prentice-Hall, 1975.
Gunning, Tom. "Tracing the Individual Body: Photography, Detectives, and Early Cinema." In *Cinema and the Invention of Modern Life*, edited by Leo Charney and Vanessa R. Schwartz, 15–45. Berkeley and Los Angeles: University of California Press, 1995.
Hachiya Michihiko. *Hiroshima Diary: The Journal of a Japanese Physician,*

August 6–September 30, 1945. Translated by Warner Wells. Chapel Hill: University of North Carolina Press, 1955.
Hagiwara Sakutarō. "Kagaku e no fushin." In *Hagiwara Sakutarō zenshū.* 4:605–7. Shinchōsha, 1960.
Hamada Yūsuke. "Taishū bungaku no kindai." In *Nijusseiki no bungaku.* Vol. 13 of *Iwanami kōza: Nihon bungakushi.* Iwanami shoten, 1996.
Hamao Shirō. *Hamao Shirō shū.* Vol. 5 of *Nihon tantei shōsetsu zenshū.* Tōkyō sōgensha, 1997.
———. "Satsujinki." Vol. 4 of *Hamao Shirō zenshū.* Chūsekisha, 2004.
Hammett, Dashiell. *The Maltese Falcon.* 1930. New York: First Vintage Crime, 1992.
Hanzawa Shūzō. *"Kōbō" no jokyoku: Sakaki Yasuzaburō to Kyūdai Firu.* Ashi shobō, 2001.
Hardt, Michael, and Antonio Negri. *Empire.* Cambridge, Mass.: Harvard University Press, 2000.
Harootunian, Harry. *Overcome by Modernity.* Princeton, N.J.: Princeton University Press, 2000.
Harootunian, Harry, and Tetsuo Najita. "Japanese Revolt against the West: Political and Cultural Criticism in the Twentieth Century." In *The Twentieth Century.* Vol. 6 of *The Cambridge Encyclopedia of Japan,* edited by Peter Duus. Cambridge: Cambridge University Press, 1988.
Hartman, Geoffrey. "Benjamin in Hope." *Critical Inquiry* 25, no. 2 (winter 1999): 344–52.
Hasebe Fumichika. *Ōbei suiri shōsetsu hon'yakushi.* Hon no zasshisha, 1992.
———. "Ōbei tantei shōsetsu hon'yakushi: Dashīru Hametto." *Ellery Queen* (September 1995): 206–11.
Hasegawa Tōgai. *Tōkyō no kaibō.* Kenbundō, 1917.
Hashizume Shin'ya. *Modan toshi no tanjō: Ōsaka no machi, Tōkyō no machi.* Yoshikawa kōbunkan, 2003.
Hatsuda Tōru. *Toshi no Meiji: Rojō kara no kenchikushi.* Chikuma shobō, 1981.
Haycraft, Howard, ed. *The Art of the Mystery Story.* New York: Universal Library, 1946.
———. "Dictators, Democrats, and Detectives." In *Murder for Pleasure: The Life and Times of the Detective Story,* 316–17. New York: Appleton-Century, 1941.
Haynes, Roslynn D. *From Faust to Strangelove: Representations of the Scientist in Western Literature.* Baltimore: The Johns Hopkins University Press, 1994.
Hirata Yumi. "Monogatari no onna, onna no monogatari." In *Jendā no Nihonshi: Shutai to hyōgen, shigoto to seikatsu.* Tokyo Daigaku shuppan-kai, 1995.

Hiratsuka Raichō. "Katei kyōiku no tachiba kara." Reprinted in *Abe Sada shuki*, edited by Maesaka Toshiyuki, 56–60. Chūō kōronsha, 1998.
Hiroshige Tetsu. *Kagaku no shakaishi*. Chūō kōronsha, 1973.
"Ibaragi no hitori [One in Ibaragi Prefecture]." *Yomiuri Shimbun*, 24 October 1916. Quoted in *Taishō jidai no minoue sōdan*, edited by Katarogu Hausu, 16. Chikuma shobō, 2002.
Ikeda Hiroshi. "Ikyō, nazo no gensen." In *"Kaigai shinshutsu bungaku" ron josetsu*, 32–45. Impakuto shuppankai, 1997.
———. "Joshō: Ikyō, nazo no gensen." In *"Kaigai shinshutsu bungaku" ron josetsu*. Inpakuto shuppankai, 1997.
———. "Ryōkichi wa kyōkai wo dō koetaka—saigo no chosen." In *Tenkō no meian: "Shōwa jūnen zengo" no bungaku*. Vol. 3 of *Bungakushi wo yomikaeru*, 234–79. Impakuto shuppankai, 1999.
Inui Shin'ichi. *"Shinseinen" no koro*. Hayakawa shobō, 1991.
Iokibe Makoto. *Sensō, senryō, kōwa*. Vol. 6 of *Nihon no kindai*. Chūō kōronsha, 2001.
Ishikawa Tengai. *Tōkyōgaku*. Ikuseisha, 1909.
Itō Hideo. *Shōwa no tantei shōsetsu*. San'ichi shobō, 1993.
Iwata Yoshiyuki. "Shinjuku Mitsukoshi madamu bikōki." In *Kōgengaku saishū*. Edited by Kon Wajirō and Yoshida Kenkichi. Kensetsusha, 1931.
Japrisot, Sébastien. *Piège pour Cendrillon*. Paris: Éditions Densël, 1962.
Kadokawa Shoten, ed. *Yokomizo Seishi ni sasagu shinseiki kara no tegami*. Kadokawa shoten, 2002.
"Kaigai tantei shōsetsu jukketsu." *Shinseinen*, spring supplement, 1937. Reprinted in *Meisakushū*, supplement to vol. 12 of *Nihon tantei shōsetsu zenshū*, 1–7. Tōkyō sōgensha, 1999.
Kaneko Tsutomu. *Ainshutain shokku*. 2 vols. Kawade shobō, 1981.
Kanō Mikiyo. *Onnatachi no "jūgo."* Inpakuto shuppankai, 1995.
Kasai Kiyoshi. *Tantei shōsetsuron josetsu*. Kōbunsha, 2002.
Kashida Tadami. *Hanzai sōsa hen*. Vol. 3 of *Bōhan kagaku zenshū*. Chūō kōronsha, 1936.
Kata Kōji. *Shōwa jiken shi*. Isseisha, 1985.
Kataoka Toshirō. "Akadama pōto wain" (1922), poster. Reproduced in Tahashi Yasuo, *Danpatsu suru onna tachi: Modan gāru no fūkei*. Kyōikushuppan kabushikigaisha, 1999.
Kawamoto Saburō. "1920 nendai, henbō suru Tōkyō." In *Kindai nihon e no shikaku*. Vol. 1 of *Kindai Nihon bunka ron*, 104–31. Iwanami shoten, 1999.
Kawana, Sari. "The Price of Pulp: Women, Detective Fiction, and the Profession of Writing in Interwar Japan." *Japan Forum* 16:2 (July 2004): 207–29.

Kawato Michiaki and Sakakibara Takanori, eds. *Meiji no hon'yaku misuterī*. 3 vols. Satsuki shoten, 2001.

Kigi Takatarō. *Kigi Takatarō zenshū*. 6 vols. Asahi shimbunsha, 1970–71.

———. "Midori no nisshōki." In *Kūsō kagaku shōsetsu shū*. Vol. 8 of *Shōnen shōsetsu taikei*. San'ichi shobō, 1986.

Kinkley, Jeffrey C. *Chinese Justice, the Fiction: Law and Literature in Modern China*. Stanford, Calif.: Stanford University Press, 2000.

Kitada Akihiro. *Kōkoku no tanjō: Kindai media bunka no rekishi shakai gaku*. Iwanami shoten, 2000.

Knight, Stephen T. *Jack the Ripper: The Final Solution*. New York: HarperCollins, 1979.

Knox, Ronald A. "A Detective Story Decalogue." In *The Art of the Mystery Story*, edited by Howard Haycraft, 194–96. 1929. New York: Universal Library, 1946.

Kōga Saburō. "Kohaku no paipu." In *Kuroiwa Ruikō, Kozakai Fuboku, Kōga Saburō shū*. Vol. 1 of *Nihon tantei shōsetsu zenshū*. Tōkyō sōgensha, 1984.

———. "Tantei shōsetsu kyūgyō sengen." *Shupio* (January 1938): 19.

Kon Wajirō. "Kōgengaku sōron." In *Kōgengaku nyūmon*, edited by Fujimori Terunobu, 371–402. Chikuma shobō, 1987.

———. "Kōgengaku towa nanika." In *Kōgengaku nyūmon*, edited by Fujimori Terunobu, 358–70. Chikuma shobō, 1987.

Kon Wajirō and Yoshida Kenkichi. "Tōkyō Ginzagai fūzoku kiroku." In *Kōgengaku nyūmon*, edited by Fujimori Terunobu, 86–153. Chikuma shobō, 1987.

Kōno Kensuke. "Sukyandaru jānarizumu to 'hō' no shihai: 'Yorozu chōhō' no aru 'kantsū jiken' kiji ni tsuite." In *Media, hyōshō, ideorogī: Meiji sanjūnendai no bunka kenkyū*, edited by Komori Yōichi, Kōno Kensuke, and Takahashi Osamu, 21–49. Ozawa shoten, 1997.

Koschmann, J. Victor. "Literature and the Bourgeois Subject." In *Revolution and Subjectivity in Postwar Japan*, 41–87. Chicago: University of Chicago Press, 1996.

———. "Tekunorojī no shihai/shihai no tekunorogī [The Rule of Technology/ Technology of Rule]." In *Sōryokusenka no chi to seido*. Vol. 6 of *Iwanami kōza: Kindai nihon no bunka shi*, 139–72. Iwanami shoten, 2002.

Kozakai Fuboku. "Jennā den." In *Shōnen kurabu meisakusen*, edited by Katō Ken'ichi, vol. 3, 435–43. Kōdansha, 1966.

———. "Kagaku hatsumei no kyōi." In *Kozakai Fuboku zenshū*. Vol. 18. Kaizōsha, 1930.

———. "Kagakuteki kenkyū to tantei shōsetsu." In *Hanzai bungaku kenkyū*. Kokusho kankō kai, 1991.

———. "Tōsō." In *Kuroiwa Ruikō, Kozakai Fuboku, Kōga Saburō shū*. Vol. 1 of *Nihon tantei shōsetsu zenshū*. Tōkyō sōgensha, 1984.
Kracauer, Siegfried. "Caligari." In *From Caligari to Hitler: A Psychological History of the German Film*, 61–76. Princeton, N.J.: Princeton University Press, 1947.
———. "The Cult of Distraction: On Berlin's Picture Palaces." In *The Mass Ornament: Weimar Essays*, translated by Thomas Y. Levin, 323–30. Cambridge, Mass.: Harvard University Press, 1995.
Kuroiwa Ruikō. "Jingaikyō." In *Gendai suiri shōsetsu taikei*, supplement 2, edited by Nakajima Kawatarō. Kōdansha, 1980.
———. "Muzan." In *Kuroiwa Ruikō, Kozakai Fuboku, Kōga Saburō shū*. Vol. 1 of *Nihon tantei shōsetsu zenshū*, 44–49. Tōkyō sōgensha, 1984.
———. "Yo ga shinbun ni kokorozashita dōki." In *Kuroiwa Ruikō: kindai sakka kenkyū gyōshō*, ed. Ruikō Kai, 111. Nihon tosho sentā, 1992.
Kurosawa Ariko. "Shukkyō suru shōjo tachi: 1910-20 nendai, Yoshiya Nobuko, Kaneko Misuzu, Ozaki Midori, Hirabayashi Taiko, Hayashi Fumiko, hoka." In *Taishū no jidai: hīrō to dokusha no 20-30 nendai*, edited by Ikeda Kōji, 78–97. Izara shobō, 1998.
Lippit, Seiji M. "Introduction: Fissures of Japanese Modernity." In *Topographies of Japanese Modernism*. New York: Columbia University Press, 2002.
Lo, Ming-Cheng M. *Doctors within Borders: Profession, Ethnicity, and Modernity in Colonial Taiwan*. Berkeley and Los Angeles: University of California Press, 2002.
Lougherty, John. *Alias S. S. Van Dine*. New York: Scribner's, 1992.
Machida Ryūyō. "Kabuto Beer" (1924–25), poster. Reproduced in Jackie Menzies, ed., *Modern Boy Modern Girl: Modernity in Japanese Art 1910–1935*. Sydney, Australia: Art Gallery of New South Wales, 1998.
———. "Union Beer" (1924–25), poster. Reproduced in Jackie Menzies, ed., *Modern Boy Modern Girl: Modernity in Japanese Art 1910–1935*. Sydney, Australia: Art Gallery of New South Wales, 1998.
"Machikado no kindaishoku: Hard to Please Occidental Sisters—The Modern Girls of Japan," *Asahi Graph*, 8 June 1927.
Mackie, Vera. "Modern Selves and Modern Spaces: An Overview." In *Being Modern in Japan: Culture and Society from the 1910s to the 1930s*, edited by Elise K. Lipton and John Clark, 185–99. Honolulu: University of Hawai'i Press, 2000.
Maesaka Toshiyuki, ed. *Abe Sada shuki*. Chūō kōronsha, 1998.
Manabe Motoyuki. *Taishū bungaku jiten*. Seikei shobō, 1967.
Marran, Christine L. *Poison Woman: Figuring Female Transgression in Modern Japanese Culture*. Minneapolis: University of Minnesota Press, 2007.

———. "'Poison Woman' Takahashi Oden and the Spectacle of Female Deviance in Early Meiji." *U.S. Japan Women's Journal* English Supplement, no. 9 (1995): 93–110.

———. "So Bad She's Good: The Masochist's Heroine in Postwar Japan, Abe Sada." In *Bad Girls of Japan*, edited by Laura Miller and Jan Bardsley, 80–95. London: Palgrave Macmillan, 2005.

Martin, Luther H., Huck Gutman, and Patrick H. Hutton, eds. *Technologies of the Self: A Seminar with Michel Foucault*. Amherst: University of Massachusetts Press, 1988.

Maruyama Masao. *Gendai seiji no shisō to kōzō: zōhoban*. Miraisha, 2000. Originally published in 1956–57.

Matsuyama Iwao. *Gunshū: Kikai no naka no nanmin*. Vol. 12 of *Nijusseiki no Nihon*. Yomiuri shinbunsha, 1996.

———. *Ranpo to Tōkyō*. Chikuma shobō, 1994.

———. *Uwasa no enkin hō*. Kōdansha, 1997.

Mikuriya Takashi. *Tōkyō: Shuto wa kokka wo koeruka*. Vol. 10 of *Nijusseiki no nihon*. Yomiuri shimbunsha, 1996.

Miyake Setsurei. "Himitsu to kaihō." *Chūō kōron* 33, no. 8 (summer supplement 1918), Kōron section: 1.

Mizuno Hiromi. "Science, Ideology, Empire: A History of the 'Scientific' in Japan from the 1920s to 1940s." PhD diss., University of California, Los Angeles, 2001.

Morris-Suzuki, Tessa. *The Technological Transformation of Japan: From the Seventeenth to the Twenty-first Century*. Cambridge: Cambridge University Press, 1994.

Mulvey, Laura. "Visual Pleasure and Narrative Cinema." In *Visual and Other Pleasures*, 14–26. Bloomington: Indiana University Press, 1989.

Nagai Yoshikazu. *Bikōshatachi no machikado*. Yokohama: Seori shobō, 2000.

Nagamine Shigetoshi. *Modan toshi no dokusho kūkan*. Nihon editā sukūru shuppanbu, 2001.

Nagayama Yasuo. "Kekkai no hō e: Oguri Mushitarō teki tachiba wo megutte." In *Kindai Nihon no monshōgaku*, 124–38. Seikyūsha, 1992.

———. *Kindai Nihon no monshōgaku*. Seikyūsha, 1992.

———. *Ōgai no okaruto, Sōseki no kagaku*. Shinchōsha, 1999.

———. "Oguri Mushitarō to fuzai no nan'yō." *Shuka: bunka tankyūshi*, no. 13 (Fall 1999): 18–26.

Nagayama Yasuo, ed. *Natsukashii mirai: Yomigaeru Meiji, Taishō, Shōwa no mirai shōsetsu*. Chūō kōron shinsha, 2001.

Nakajima Kawatarō. "Maedakō-Ranpo ronsō." In *Nihon suiri shōsetsushi*. Vol. 2. Tōkyō sōgensha, 1994.

———. *Nihon suiri shōsetsushi*. 3 vols. Tōkyō sōgensha, 1993.

———. "Sakuhin kaidai." In *Edogawa Ranpo zenshū*. Vol. 4. Kōdansha, 1970.

———. "Tantei shōsetsu tsūshi." In *Gendai suiri shōsetsu taikei*. Supplement 2. Kōdansha, 1980.

Nakajima Kawatarō, ed. *Gendai suiri shōsetsu taikei*. Kōdansha, 1980.

Nakamura Kikuji. *Fukkoku kokutei shūshin kyōkasho*. Ōzorasha, 1994.

Nakamura, Miri. "Horror and Machines in Prewar Japan: The Mechanical Uncanny in Yumeno Kyūsaku's 'Dogura magura.'" *Science Fiction Studies* 29 (2002): 374.

Nakazawa Wataru. "Karigari hakase to sono jidai." http://www.shokoku.ac.jp/~nakazawa/caligari.html [Accessed 4 November 2001].

Nanakita Kazuto. *Abe Sada densetsu*. Chikuma shobō, 1998.

Nanba Kōji. *Uchiteshi yaman: Taiheiyō sensō to kōkoku no gijutsusha tachi*. Kōdansha, 1998.

Natsume Sōseki to Terada Torahiko. 12 September 1901. In vol. 14 of *Sōseki zenshū*. Iwanami shoten, 1976.

Natsume Sōseki. *Higansugi made*. In vol. 5. of *Sōseki zenshū*. Iwanami shoten, 1966.

Nozoe Atsuyoshi. *Josei to hanzai*. Bukyōsha, 1930.

Ōba Shigema. *Kojin shikibetsu hō*. Chūjōsha, 1908; second and expanded edition, Chūō Daigaku, 1910.

Ogawa Teizō. *Igaku no rekishi*. Chūō kōronsha, 1964.

Ogura Kōsei. *Suiri shōsetsu no genryū: Gaborio kara Ruburan e*. Kyoto: Tankōsha, 2002.

Oguri Mushitarō. "Kanzen hanzai." In *Oguri Mushitarō shū*. Vol. 6 of *Nihon tantei shōsetsu zenshū*. Tōkyō sōgensha, 1999.

———. *Oguri Mushitarō shū*. Vol. 6 of *Nihon tantei shōsetsu zenshū*. Tōkyō sōgensha, 1998.

———. *Oguri Mushitarō zensakuhin*. 9 vols. Chūsekisha, 1997.

———. "Senja fuda kigen no kōyaku." In *Shitsurakuen satsujin jiken*, 392–95. Fusōsha, 2002.

———. "Shishi wa shiseru ni hizu." In *Shupio kessakusen*. Vol. 3 of *Maboroshi no tantei zasshi*. Kōbunsha, 2000. Originally published in *Shupio*, April 1938.

Oguri Mushitarō, Kigi Takatarō, and Unno Jūza. "Sengen." In *Shupio kessakusen*. Vol. 3 of *Maboroshi no tantei zasshi*. Kōbunsha, 2000. Originally published in *Shupio*, January 1937.

Oguri Senji. "Shōden Oguri Mushitarō." In *Oguri Mushitarō Wandārando*, edited by Kida Jun'ichirō, 36–48. Chūsekisha, 1990.

Ōishi Masahiko. *"Shinseinen" no kyōwakoku*. Suiseisha, 1992.

Ōshita Udaru. "Tantei shōsetsu kai." *Nihon dokusho shinbun*, 1 March 1940.

Pflugfelder, Gregory M. *Cartographies of Desire: Male-Male Sexuality in Japanese Discourse, 1600–1950*. Berkeley and Los Angeles: University of California Press, 1999.
Phillpotts, Eden. *The Red Redmaynes*. New York: Macmillan, 1922.
Poe, Edgar Allan. "The Man of the Crowd." In *Edgar Allan Poe: Selected Tales*, 84–91. New York: Oxford University Press, 1998.
———. "The Murders in the Rue Morgue." In *Edgar Allan Poe: Selected Tales*, 92–122. New York: Oxford University Press, 1998.
Queen, Ellery, ed. *Ellery Queen's Japanese Golden Dozen: The Detective Story World in Japan*. Rutland, Vt: Tuttle, 1978.
Ricoeur, Paul. "Civilization and National Cultures." In *History and Truth*, translated by Charles A. Kelbley, 271–84. Evanston, Ill.: Northwestern University Press, 1965.
Rin Shukumi. Roundtable discussion. In *"Sengo" to iu seido*. Impakuto shuppankai, 2002.
Robertson, Jennifer. "Gender-Bending in Paradise: Doing 'Female' and 'Male' in Japan." *Genders* 5 (1989): 50–69.
———. "Japan's First Cyborg? Miss Nippon, Eugenics and Wartime Technologies of Beauty, Body and Blood." *Body and Society* 7, no. 1 (2001): 1–34.
Rorty, Richard. "Human Rights, Rationality, and Sentimentality." In *Truth And Progress*. Vol. 3 of *Philosophical Papers*, 167–85. Cambridge: Cambridge University Press, 1998.
"Ryōki hanzai jikenbo." In *Ranpo no jidai: Shōwa ero guro nansensu*, 112–14. Vol. 88 of *Bessatsu Taiyō*. Heibonsha, 1995.
Sakaguchi Ango. *Sakaguchi Ango zenshū*. 18 vols. Chikuma shobō, 1998; paperback edition, 1990.
Sakai Shizu. *Nihon no iryōshi*. Tōkyō shoseki kabushikigaisha, 1982.
Sakai, Cécile. *Nihon no taishū bungaku* [Histoire de la littérature populaire japonaise]. Heibonsha, 1997. Originally published in Paris: L'Harmattan, 1987.
Sakuramoto Tomio. *Bunkajin tachi no daitōa sensō: PK butai ga iku*. Aoki shoten, 1993.
———. *Daitōa sensō to Nihon eiga*. Aoki shoten, 1993.
———. *Hon ga dangan datta koro*. Aoki shoten, 1996.
———. *Nihon bungaku hōkokukai: Daitōa sensō ka no bungakusha tachi*. Aoki shoten, 1995.
Sas, Miriam. *Fault Lines: Cultural Memory and Japanese Surrealism*. Stanford, Calif.: Stanford University Press, 1999.
Satō Haruo. "'Karigari hakase' wo mite." *Shinchō*, August 1921.
Sayers, Dorothy E. "Aristotle on Detective Fiction." In *Detective Fiction: A Collection of Critical Essays*, edited by Robin W. Winks, 25–34. Woodstock, Vt.: Countryman Press, 1980.

Scholz, F. M. "Rilke, Rodin, and the Fragmented Man." *Symposium* 30 (1974): 61–74.
Screech, Timon. *The Western Scientific Gaze and Popular Imagery in Later Edo Japan: The Lens within the Heart.* Cambridge: Cambridge University Press, 1996.
Seaman, Amanda C. *Bodies of Evidence: Women, Society, and Detective Fiction in 1990s Japan.* Honolulu: University of Hawai'i Press, 2004.
Shimamura Hōgetsu. "Tantei shōsetsu." In *Gendai suiri shōsetsu taikei*, supplement 2, edited by Nakajima Kawatarō.
Shimizu Bunkichi. *Hon wa nagareru.* Quoted in *Hon ga dangan datta koro*, by Sakuramoto Tomio. Aoki shoten, 1996.
Shimonaka Kunihiko, ed. *Meisaku sashie zenshū.* Vol. 8. Heibonsha, 1980.
Shinpo Hirohisa, ed. *Yokomizo Seishi jidenteki zuihitsushū.* Kadokawa shoten, 2002.
Shinseinen Kenkyūkai, ed. *Shinseinen yomihon.* Sakuhinsha, 1988.
Silver, Mark H. "Purloined Letters: Cultural Borrowing and Japanese Crime Literature, 1868-1941." Ph.D. diss., Yale University, 1999.
Silverberg, Miriam. "Constructing the Japanese Ethnography of Modernity." *Journal of Asian Studies* 51, no. 1 (February 1992): 30–54.
———. "The Modern Girl as Militant." In *Recreating Japanese Women, 1600–1945*, edited by Gail Lee Bernstein, 239–66. Berkeley and Los Angeles: University of California Press, 1991.
Simmel, Georg. "The Metropolis and Mental Life." In *The Sociology of Georg Simmel*, translated by Kurt H. Wolff. New York: Free Press, 1950. Originally published in 1903.
Simpson, Amelia S. *Detective Fiction from Latin America.* Madison, N.J.: Fairleigh Dickinson University Press, 1990.
Snow, Charles Percy. *Two Cultures and the Scientific Revolution.* Cambridge: Cambridge University Press, 1959.
Starrett, Vincent, ed. *221b: Studies in Sherlock Holmes.* New York: Macmillan, 1940.
Suzuki Hiroyuki. *Toshi e.* Vol. 10 of *Nihon no kindai.* Chūō kōronsha, 1999.
Suzuki Sadami. *Nihon no "bungaku" gainen.* Sakuhinsha, 1998.
———. *Nihon no bungaku wo kangaeru.* Kadokawa sensho, 1994.
———, ed. *Edogawa Rampo.* Vol. 41 of *Shinchō Nihon bungaku arubamu.* Shinchōsha, 1993.
Tahashi Yasuo. *Danpatsu suru onna tachi: Modan gāru no fūkei.* Kyōiku shuppan kabushikigaisha, 1999
Takahashi Yōji, ed. *Ranpo no jidai.* Vol. 88 of *Bessatsu Taiyō.* Heibonsha, 1995.
Tani, Stefano. *The Doomed Detective: The Contribution of the Detective*

Novel to Postmodern American and Italian Fiction. Carbondale: Southern Illinois University Press, 1984.

Tanizaki Jun'ichirō. "Himitsu [Secrets]." In *Tanizaki Jun'ichirō zenshū*, vol. 1, 247–71. Chūō kōronsha, 1966.

———. "Saikin no kesshutsu eiga, 'Karigari hakase' wo miru [Seeing 'Dr. Caligari,' the best recent film]." *Jiji shinpō*, 25–27 May 1921.

Terada Seiichi. *Fujin to hanzai*. Dai Nippon bunmei kyōkai, 1916.

Tester, Kevin, ed. *The Flâneur*. New York: Routledge, 1994.

Thomas, Ronald R. "Devices of Truth." In *Detective Fiction and the Rise of Forensic Science*, 1–18. Cambridge: Cambridge University Press, 1999.

Thomson, Jon. *Crime, Fiction, Empire: Clues to Modernity and Postmodernism*. Urbana: University of Illinois Press, 1993.

Tipton, Elise K., and John Clark. *Being Modern in Japan: Culture and Society in the 1910s to 1930s*. Honolulu: University of Hawai'i Press, 2000.

Tōkyō Geijutsu Daigaku hyakunenshi kankō iinkai, ed. *Tōkyō Geijutsu Daigaku hyakunenshi*. 2 vols. Gyōsei, 1987–91.

Treat, John Whittier. "Yoshimoto Banana's *Kitchen*, or the Cultural Logic of Japanese Consumerism." In *Women, Media and Consumption in Japan*, edited by Lise Skov and Brian Moeran, 274–99. Honolulu: University of Hawai'i Press, 1995.

Tsubouchi Shōyō. *Shōsetsu shinzui*. Vol. 9 of *Meicho fukkoku zenshū*. Kindai bungakukan, 1968.

Tsuduki Michio. "Kaisetsu." In *Jingai makyō*. Vol. 6 of *Oguri Mushitarō zensakuhin*. Chūsekisha, 1997.

Tsuneishi Keiichi. *Nana san ichi butai: Seibutsu heiki hanzai no shinjitsu*. Kōdansha, 1995.

Uchida Ryūzō. *Tantei shōsetsu no shakaigaku*. Iwanami shoten, 2001.

Unno Hiroshi. *Modan toshi Tōkyō: Nihon no 1920 nendai*. Chūō kōronsha, 1988.

———. "Toshi to bungaku." In *Modan toshi Tōkyō*. Chūō kōronsha, 1983.

Unno Jūza. "Fushū." In *Unno Jūza shū: Sannin no sōseiji*. Vol. 5 of *Kaiki tantei shōsetsu kessakusen*. Chikuma shobō, 2001.

———. "Kaidan." In *Unno Jūza shū: Sannin no sōseiji*. Vol. 5 of *Kaiki tantei shōsetsu kessakusen*. Chikuma shobō, 2001.

———. "Ningen kai." In *Unno Jūza shū: Sannin no sōseiji*. Vol. 5 of *Kaiki tantei shōsetsu kessakusen*. Chikuma shobō, 2001.

———. "Tantei shōsetsu nōto." *Purofīru*, January 1936. Quoted in Nakajima Kawatarō, *Nihon suiri shōsetsushi*.

———. *Unno Jūza zenshū*. 15 vols. San'ichi shobō, 1988–93.

———. "Yumemiru heya [Dreamy Room]." In vol. 3 of *Uno Kōji zenshū*. Chūō kōronsha, 1968.

Uno Kōji. *Uno Kōji zenshū*, vol. 3. Chūō kōronsha, 1968.

Van Dine, S. S. *The Greene Murder Case*. New York: Scribner's Sons, 1928.
———. "Twenty Rules for Writing Detective Stories." In *The Art of the Mystery Story: A Collection of Critical Essays*, edited by Howard Haycraft. New York: The Universal Library, 1946.
Washburn, Dennis C. *The Dilemma of the Modern in Japanese Fiction*. New Haven, Conn.: Yale University Press, 1995.
Weiss, Sheila Faith. "The Race Hygiene Movement in Germany, 1904–1945." In *The Wellborn Science: Eugenics in Germany, France, Brazil, and Russia*, edited by Mark B. Adams, 8–68. New York: Oxford University Press, 1990.
Wells, H. G. *The Island of Dr. Moreau*. Edited by Robert M. Philmus. Athens: University of Georgia Press, 1993.
Wilson, Edmund. "Who Cares Who Killed Roger Ackroyd?" In *Detective Fiction: A Collection of Critical Essays*, edited by Robin W. Winks, 35–40. Woodstock, Vt.: Countrymen Press, 1980.
Yamaguchi Makoto. *Eigo kōza no tanjō: Media to kyōyō ga deau kindai Nihon*. Kōdansha, 2001.
Yamamae Yuzuru. *Nihon misuterī no hyakunen: Osusumehon gaidobukku*. Kōbunsha, 2001.
Yamamoto Seikichi. "Himitsu wo saguru kiken to kyōmi." *Chūō kōron* 33, no. 8 (summer supplement 1918), Zei'en section: 12.
Yamamura Masao. *Suiri bundan sengoshi*. Futabasha, 1973.
Yokomizo Seishi. "Gokumontō." In vol. 3 of *Kindaichi Kōsuke fairu shirīzu*. Kadokawa shoten, 2002.
———. "Honjin satsujin jiken." In vol. 2 of *Kindaichi Kōsuke fairu shirīzu*. Kadokawa shoten, 2002.
———. "Honkaku tantei shōsetsu e no tenki: *Honjin satsujin jiken* no zengo." In *Yokomizo Seishi jidenteki zuihitsushū*. 1973. Kadokawa shoten, 2002.
———. *The Inugami Clan*. Translated by Yumiko Yamazaki. ICG Muse, 2003.
———. "Inugamike no ichizoku." In vol. 5 of *Kindaichi Kōsuke fairu shirīzu*. Kadokawa shoten, 2002.
———. "Katasumi no rakuen." In *Yokomizo Seishi jidenteki zuihitsushū*. 1959. Kadokawa shoten, 2002.
———. *Kindaichi Kōsuke fairu shirīzu*. Kadokawa shoten, 2002.
———. "Kuroiwa Ruikō wo yomu." In *Yokomizo Seishi zenshū*, 18:150–68. Kōdansha, 1975.
———. "Sorekara no koto domo." In *Yokomizo Seishi jidenteki zuihitsushū*. Kadokawa shoten, 2002.
———. "Tantei shōsetsu ankoku jidai," in *Yokomizo Seishi zenshū*, 18:43–46. Kōdansha, 1975.

———. "Tantei shōsetsu to sensō." Cited in Itō Hideo, *Shōwa no tantei shōsetsu*. 1946. San'ichi shobō, 1993.

———. "Todoroku ashioto no koto." In *Yokomizo Seishi jidenteki zuihitsushū*. 1971. Kadokawa shoten, 2002.

———. *Yokomizo Seishi shū*. Vol. 9 of *Nihon tantei shōsetsu zenshū*. Tōkyō sōgensha, 1996.

———. *Yokomizo Seishi zenshū*. Kōdansha, 1975.

Yoshida Kenkichi. "Ren'ai moderunorojio: gendai seikatsu ni okeru ren'aiteki bamen no saishū hōkoku." In *Kōgengaku saishū*, edited by Kon Wajirō and Yoshida Kenkichi. Kensetsusha, 1931.

Yoshimi Shun'ya. "'Sōsetsu': Teito Tōkyō to modaniti no bunkaseiji." In *Kakudai suru modaniti*. Vol. 6 of *Iwanami kōza: Nihon no kindai bunkashi*. Iwanami shoten: 2002.

———. *Toshi no doramaturugī*. Kōbundō, 1987.

"Yoshin chōsho." In *Abe Sada shuki*, edited by Maesaka Toshiyuki. Chūō kōronsha, 1998.

Yumeno Kyūsaku. *Yumeno Kyūsaku shū*. Vol. 4 of *Nihon tantei shōsetsu zenshū*. Tōkyō sōgensha, 1999.

———. *Yumeno Kyūsaku zenshū*. Chikuma shobō, 1991–92.

Žižek, Slavoj. "Two Ways to Avoid the Real of Desire." In *Looking Awry: An Introduction to Jacques Lacan through Popular Culture*, 48–66. Cambridge, Mass.: The MIT Press, 1991.

Index

Created by David Prout

Note: Page numbers with an *f* indicate figures.

Abe Isoo, 33, 43
Abe Sada, 17, 72–73, 101–8, 102f
advertisements, 77–78, 79f
aging: research on, 123–24, 145
Aizu Shingo, 237n4
Akimoto Sueo, 146
Akutagawa Ryūnosuke, 126
Anderson, Benedict, 24
Ara Masahito, 187, 193
Arishima Takeo, 237n1
assujettissement, 186, 218
autopsies, 83–85

Bartholomew, James, 113
Baudelaire, Charles, 10, 12, 226n20
Bayard, Pierre, 234n52
Benjamin, Walter, 5, 12, 77, 226n20
Bentham, Jeremy, 43
Bertillon, Amphonse, 52f
blood-type analysis, 111
Boisgobey, Fortuné de, 23
Bolyai, János, 22
boredom: urbanization and, 39–42, 59, 61
Burroughs, Edgar Rice, 174
bushidō (warrior's code), 198

Cabinet of Dr. Caligari (film), 113–14, 130, 132–35
Carr, John Dickson, 25, 193
cathartic effect, 65
censorship: during World War II, 148–59, 169–70, 182–85, 246n17
Cheng Xiaoqing, 24
China, 23–24; Japanese wars of, 4, 34, 155, 169–70, 205–6
Christie, Agatha, 20–21, 156, 224; censorship of, 242n21; *Murder of Roger Ackroyd*, 20–21, 27, 196, 234n52
Clark, John, 4
colonialism, 4, 14–15, 150, 151, 174–82
Columbo (TV series), 116
copyright issues, 24
Crofts, Freeman Willis, 25
cultural relativism. *See* multiculturalism

Dannay, Frederic, 194
De Quincey, Thomas, 75
Dickson, Carter, 156

265

Dine, S. S. Van, 26
"diphtheria," cultural, 1–3, 7, 11, 221
Disney cartoons, 154
dokufu (poison women), 76, 82
Doyle, Arthur Conan, 14, 20, 21, 90–91, 116, 224; "His Last Bow," 162; "Problem of the Thor Bridge," 215; "Scandal in Bohemia," 58; "Study in Scarlet," 48; translations of, 24, 230n45
dress, 56f, 70, 71f
Dubois, Jacques, 226n20, 240n46

Edogawa Ranpo, 5, 16, 74, 78, 101, 188, 192–93, 232n3; "Akai heya" (Red Chamber), 40, 41; blacklisting of, 191; "Chie no Ichitarō" (Ichitarō the Wise), 152; Christie and, 20–21; "D-zaka no satsujin jiken" (Murder on D-Hill), 106; English translations of, 223; Freeman and, 116; Hammett and, 21–22; *Harimaze nenpu* (Cut-and-Paste Chronology of My Life), 148; "Hitori futayaku" (Playing Two Roles), 59–62; "Idainaru yume" (Great Dream), 152; "Imomushi" (Worm), 152; "Injū" (Beast in the Shadow), 21, 72, 82–83, 88–97, 100, 107; "Insei wo ketsui su" (Deciding to Retire), 152; "Kumo otoko" (Spider Man), 74–75, 80, 152, 161; "Kurote gumi" (Black-Hand League), 158; "Majutsushi" (Magician), 69–70; nationalism of, 152, 154, 156, 171; "Nisen dōka" (Two-Sen Copper Coin), 20–21, 90, 158, 196; "Ryōki no hate" (Beyond the Bizarre), 61–63, 152; "Shinri shiken" (Psychological Test), 116; Tamanoi murder case and, 108; "Tantei shōsetsu yonjūnen" (Forty Years with Detective Fiction), 152, 243n45; urban ennui and, 40–42; "Yaneura no sanposha" (Wanderer in the Attic), 40–44, 79, 90, 116; "Yōchū" (Mysterious Worm), 78–81
Einstein, Albert, 119–23, 122f
Eliot, T. S., 24–25
elixir vitae, 123–24, 145
ennui: urbanization and, 39–42, 59, 61
ero-guro-nansensu culture, 10, 55–56, 72, 103, 190, 207
ethics: military and, 145–46, 177–79; science and, 117–19, 120f, 125–28, 145–46, 150, 163
ethnology, urban, 44–45. See also modernology
eugenics movement, 112–13, 137–39, 240n62

fashions, 56f, 70, 71f
femmes fatales, 94, 95
Figal, Gerald, 5, 76, 190
films: *In the Realm of the Senses*, 101; *Kabinett des Doktor Caligari*, 113–14, 130, 132–35; *Mr. Smith Goes to Washington*, 154. See also specific directors, e.g., Kracauer, Siegfried
fingerprinting, 50, 51f, 62–63, 111, 115, 209, 213
flâneur, 32, 226n20
Fleming, Ian, 162
forensic science, 51, 83, 90, 111, 115, 143

Foucault, Michel, 10; on discipline, 75–76; on subjectivation, 186, 189; on surveillance, 31, 43; on technologies of the self, 221, 222
Freeman, Richard Austin, 116
Fukuzawa Yukichi, 3, 5
Furuhata Tanamoto, 86

Gaboriau, Émile, 9, 23
Gauss, Carl, 22
gaze, 2, 15; male, 77. *See also* voyeurism
genre, 25–27, 219–20; as imagined guild, 24–25, 223
Germany: detective fiction in, 153, 242n21
Giddens, Anthony, 3, 147, 220
Ginzburg, Carlo, 31
Girard, René, 60
globalization, 27–28, 182
Great Kantō Earthquake (1923), 30, 35–36, 44–45
Greene, Anna Katherine, 195
guild, imagined, 24–25, 223
gunji shōsetsu (military fiction), 153, 159

Hamao Shirō, 16, 101; "Satsujinki" (Murderous Devil), 72, 82, 83, 95–100, 107–8
Hammett, Dashiell, 21–22, 93, 94
Hardt, Michael, 27
Harootunian, Harry D., 5, 22, 220
Harris, James B., 223
Hasegawa Tōgai, 2
Hearn, Lafcadio, 121
Hirano Ken, 187, 193
Hiratsuka Raichō, 103
Hiroshige Tetsu, 114
Holmes, Sherlock. *See* Doyle, Arthur Conan
homosexuality, 80

human experimentation: during World War II, 145–46
hysteria, 92

identity theft, 63
Ikeda Hiroshi, 14, 176
Inoue Eizō, 193
Inoue Tsutomu, 237n4
Inoue Yoshio, 193, 228n48, 246n25
In the Realm of the Senses (film), 101
Inui Shin'ichirō, 156
Ishida Kichizō, 101, 105–6
Ishiwara Jun, 103, 121
Italy: detective fiction in, 23–24, 153, 242n21
Itō Hideo, 148, 149
Iwata Yoshiyuki, 45–50, 47f, 54–55, 58
Iwaya Mitsuru, 191

Janowitz, Hans, 132
Japrisot, Sébastien, 240n46
Jenner, Edward, 117–19, 119f, 120f, 124–25
jikeidan (self-policing unit), 36–38
Jō Masayuki, 191, 246n17
jungle stories, 174–76, 181–82

Kabinett des Doktor Caligari (film), 113–14, 130, 132–35
Kamiyama Sōjin, 2
Kanagaki Robun, 104
Kanō Mikiyo, 155
Kantō Earthquake (1923), 30, 35–36, 44–45
Kashida Tadami, 90–91
Kataoka Toshirō, 78, 79f
Kawamoto Saburō, 13
Kawatake Mokuami, 104
Kigi Takatarō, 17–18, 219; "Jinsei no ahō" (Life's Fool), 166;

"Midori no nisshōki" (Flag of the Green Rising Sun), 163–70, 165f, 168f, 183; nationalism of, 150–51, 163–73, 182–83; Oguri and, 174; *Shupio* magazine and, 148–49, 163; "Tōhōkō" (Light from the East), 164, 171–73, 184
Kinkley, Jeffrey, 24
Kitada Akihiro, 77
Knox, Ronald A., 66, 100, 107
Kobayashi Takiji, 158
Kōga Saburō, 16, 158, 166; "Kohaku no paipu" (Amber Pipe), 36–39, 58, 67; on wartime fiction, 153–54
kōgengaku. See modernology
Kominami Mataichirō, 86
Kon Wajirō, 44–45, 49–50, 56–58; "Kōgengaku sōron" (On Modernology), 54–55
Kozakai Fuboku, 17, 20, 112, 121, 158, 220; Freeman and, 116; scientific writings of, 124–25, 146; "Tōsō" (Conflict), 125–30
Kracauer, Siegfried, 226n25, 240n50, 240n56
Krafft-Ebing, Richard von, 81
Kure Shūzō, 133
Kuroiwa Jūgo, 220
Kuroiwa Ruikō, 8–12, 22–23; *Hito ka oni ka* (Human or Beast), 9; "Makkura" (Complete Darkness), 195; *Muzan* (Merciless), 9; translations of, 159, 237n4

Leblanc, Maurice, 24, 26
Lee, Manfred B., 194
Leibniz, Gottfried, 22
Leroux, Gaston, 26, 161
Lindbergh kidnapping, 108
Lombroso, Cesare, 81

mad scientists, 111–46, 161–62, 220
Manchukuo, 169
Manchurian Incident, 155
Marco Polo Bridge incident (1937), 169–70
Marxism, 112, 187, 237n2
masochism. *See* sadomasochism
Matsumoto Seichō, 220
Matsuyama Iwao, 43, 130
Mayer, Carl, 132
Meiji Enlightenment, 3–6, 86, 217
Mitsuki Harukage, 116
Miyake Setsurei, 33
Miyake Yasuko, 121
Mizuno Hiromi, 113
Mizutani Jun, 191
mobo (modern boys), 82
modernity, 2, 5–12, 17, 77, 142, 150, 182, 189–90, 218–23, 226n20
modernology, 32, 44–58, 67–68
moga (modern girls), 70–82, 71f, 222
Mori Ōgai, 84, 114–15
Morishita Uson, 20
Morita Shiken, 237n4
Morris-Suzuki, Tessa, 146, 238n9
Mr. Smith Goes to Washington (film), 154
muishiki. *See* unconscious
multiculturalism, 15, 150, 151, 174–82
Mulvey, Laura, 233n13

Nagai Kafū, 205
Nakajima Kawatarō, 148, 149, 183, 219–20; on wartime censorship, 152–54
Nanba Kōji, 182
Nanba Mokusaburō, 90
Nanking atrocities, 205–6

narcissism, 80
Natsume Sōseki, 29, 114–15
Negri, Antonio, 27
Newton, Isaac, 22
Nihon bungei kyōkai (Association of Japanese of Letters), 170
Nozoe Atsuyoshi, 85–86, 87f, 110

Ōba Shigema, 50, 62
Oden. *See* Takahashi Oden
Ogawa Mimei, 121
Oguri Mushitarō, 18, 112; "Daiankoku" (Greatest Darkness), 171; death of, 184–85; "Kaikyō tenchikai" (Society of Heaven and Earth), 175–79, 181, 187; "Kaizō ni shita nakiya" (Walrus Has No Tongue), 176; "Kanzen hanzai" (Perfect Crime), 136–39, 171, 177; "Kokushikan satsujin jiken" (Murders at the Black Death Mansion), 171; "Nanpō kūri" (Tamil Coolie), 179–81; nationalism of, 151, 173–82, 183; *Shupio* magazine and, 148–49; "Yūbijin" (Tailed Tribe), 171
Ōhashi Shin'ichi, 153
Ōi Hirosuke, 187, 193
Ōishi Masahiko, 138
Oka Kyūjirō. *See* Unno Jūza
Osanai Ken, 84
Oshikawa Shunrō, 195
Ōshima Nagisa, 101
Ōshita Udaru, 155, 158

panopticon, 43
Phillpotts, Eden, 214
photography: of criminals, 51–54, 52f, 53f
Poe, Edgar Allan, 20, 21, 23; "Man of the Crowd," 48; *Murders in the Rue Morgue*, 141, 142
pornography, 72, 86
post-traumatic stress, 205–6, 214
private investigators, 35–36, 229n18
propaganda, 147–48. *See also* censorship
psychoanalysis, 43. *See also* unconscious

Queen, Ellery, 156, 194–95, 223, 224

Ranpo. *See* Edogawa Ranpo
Ricoeur, Paul, 150
Rin Shukumi, 197
Robertson, Jennifer, 80, 137
Rodin, Auguste, 233n29
Rogues Gallery, 50–54, 51f–53f
Russell, Bertrand, 121
Russo-Japanese War (1904–5), 4, 34

sadomasochism, 65, 91, 104–6
Sakaguchi Ango, 187–88, 192–94, 217–18; "Darakuron" (On Decadence), 18, 189, 197–200, 218; "Fukuin satsujin jiken" (Demobilized Soldier Murder Case), 199; "Furenzoku satsujin jiken" (Nonconsecutive Murder Case), 188, 189, 194–97, 199–200; "Shōgo no satsujin" (Murder at Midday), 199; "Tōshu satsujin jiken" (Pitcher Murder Case), 194; "Zoku darakuron" (On Decadence Continued), 197
Sakai, Cécile, 151, 152
Sakaki Yasuzaburō, 123–24, 130
Sanger, Margaret, 121

Sas, Miryam, 227n38
Satō Haruo, 62, 133, 229n17; "Roji no oku" (In the Alleyway), 63–64; "Shimon" (Fingerprints), 115
Sayers, Dorothy E., 65
Scarlett, Roger, 26, 192–93
science fiction, 17, 66, 113–14, 141, 144–45, 149, 159, 237n4
scientism: attitudes toward, 114–24; definition of, 112; ethics and, 117–19, 120f, 125–28, 145–46, 150, 163; eugenics and, 112–13, 137–39, 240n62; genius and, 119–23; Marxism and, 112, 237n2; promotion of, 114–15. *See also* mad scientists
Screech, Timon, 32
Seaman, Amanda, 7–8
Shelley, Mary, 241n75
shell shock. *See* post-traumatic stress
Shikanogi Masanobu, 122–23
Shinseinen (magazine), 152–56, 157f, 185, 195; circulation of, 233n33; and detective fiction, 20, 82, 113, 136; prize competitions sponsored by, 195; as pro-militarist publication, 174–75, 191, 242n20
Shupio (magazine), 17–18, 148–50, 154, 159, 241n4
Siebold, Philip Franz von, 117
Silver, Mark H., 151–52
Simmel, George, 41
Sino-Japanese War: of 1894, 4, 34; of 1937, 169–70, 205–6
skull measurements, 53f
smallpox, 117–19, 125
stalking, 32, 54, 82, 231n55
Starrett, Vincent, 224
Stendhal syndrome, 131

Stevenson, Robert Louis, 66
subjectivation, 186, 189, 198, 218
Sun Liaohong, 24
surveillance, 50–51; Foucault on, 31, 43; tailing someone as, 29–32

tailing *(bikō)*, 29–68; in department store, 45–46, 47f, 54; as fun, 39–44; "physical," 38–39; stalking versus, 32, 54; types of, 36; voyeurism and, 63–64
Tajima Tomio, 155
Takada Giichirō, 86
Takada Tadayoshi, 84
Takahashi Oden, 76, 88; Abe Sada and, 103–5, 107; autopsy of, 83–85
Takamure Itsue, 2
Takeda Takehiko, 191
Takeuchi Kintarō, 105–6
Tamamura Kōun, 117–18, 119f
Tamanoi dismemberment case, 70, 108–10, 109f
Tanizaki Jun'ichirō, 16, 63, 133; "Himitsu" (Secret), 40, 41, 230n28
Terada Seiichi, 85, 91
Thomas, Ronald R., 226n22
Tipton, Elise K., 4
Treat, John W., 80

Uchida Ryūzō, 30–31
unconscious, 5, 30, 43, 58
Unit 731 (Harbin, China), 146
Unno Jūza, 17–18, 55, 121, 184, 220; blacklisting of, 191; "Fushū" (Possessed), 139–40; "Hae otoko" (Fly Man), 112–13, 140–44; "Kaitō-ō" (King of the Mysterious Tower), 18, 149–50, 159–63; nationalism of, 170, 171, 174, 183;

"Ningen kai" (Human Ashes), 140; *Shupio* magazine and, 148–49; Yokomizo and, 185
Uno Kōji, 228n7
urbanization, 31–32, 67–68; city as maze and, 34–39; ennui and, 39–42, 59, 61; studies of, 49–50

Van Dine, S. S., 66, 96–100, 193–94, 224
vivisection, 145–46
Voltaire, 31
voyeurism, 82, 161; legality of, 54, 231n55; tailing someone as, 63–64

Wallace, Edgar, 242n21
Washburn, Dennis, 6–7
Watanabe Keisuke, 65
Wells, H. G., 17; *Invisible Man*, 113; *Island of Doctor Moreau*, 113, 128–29
Wiene, Richard, 132
World War I, 4, 114, 162, 214
World War II, 138, 147, 190–94; censorship during, 148–59, 169–70, 182–85, 246n17; detective fiction after, 186–90; human experimentation during, 145–46; injured veterans of, 15, 190, 207–8, 214–15; posttraumatic stress and, 205–6

Yamamoto Seikichi, 33
Yamamura Masao, 191
Yanagita Kunio, 2

Yokomizo Seishi, 18, 148, 186–90, 192–93, 200–205; Ango and, 217–18; "Chōchō satsujin jiken" (Butterfly Murder Case), 25; English translations of, 224; genre conventions and, 25–27, 220; "Gokumontō" (Gokumon Island), 26, 202–5, 224; "Honjin satsujin jiken" (Murders at the Main Manor), 25–27, 200–202, 207–8, 214–16; "Inugamike no ichizoku" (Inaugami Clan), 210–14, 211f, 216–17, 224; "Jinmensō" (Face-Shaped Scar), 224; "Kuruma ido wa naze kiru" (Why Does the Well Kill?), 208; "Meirōsō no sangeki" (Murders at Meiro Manor), 224; nationalism of, 153, 158, 171; "Sarusuberi no shita nite" (Underneath the Indian Lilac Tree), 206–9; Unno and, 185
Yoshida Kenkichi, 44, 49, 58; "Ren'ai kōgengaku" (Modernology of Love), 55–56, 56f
Yoshimi Shun'ya, 6, 22
Yuasa Ken, 146
Yumeno Kyūsaku, 1–2, 7–8, 17, 112–14, 220; *Dogura magura*, 130–36, 138, 139, 145

Zerstreuung (distraction), 77–78
Žižek, Slavoj, 94, 95
Zola, Émile, 177

Sari Kawana is assistant professor of Japanese at the University of Massachusetts Boston.

www.ingramcontent.com/pod-product-compliance
Lightning Source LLC
Chambersburg PA
CBHW022003160426
43197CB00007B/249